William C. Roach

# DEFENDING EVANGELICALISM

## The Apologetics of Norman L. Geisler

William C. Roach

Christian Publishing House
Cambridge, Ohio

Copyright © 2020 William C. Roach

All rights reserved. Except for brief quotations in articles, other publications, book reviews, and blogs, no part of this book may be reproduced in any manner without prior written permission from the publishers. For information, write, support@christianpublishers.org

Unless otherwise stated, Scripture quotations are from New American Standard Bible (NASB) Copyright © 1960, 1962, 1963, 1968, 1971, 1972, 1973, 1975, 1977, 1995 2020 by The Lockman Foundation

*DEFENDING EVANGELICALISM: The Apologetics of Norman L. Geisler* by William C. Roach

ISBN-13: **978-1-949586-19-0**

ISBN-10: **1-949586-19-7**

# William C. Roach

## Table of Contents

CHAPTER ONE The Present-Day Conditions of Belief ................... 13

CHAPTER TWO Defending Classical Realism ............................... 45

CHAPTER THREE Defending Classical Apologetics and Theism...... 77

CHAPTER FOUR Defending the Classic Doctrine of Inerrancy ....... 111

CHAPTER FIVE Defending Classic Evangelicalism ........................ 149

APPENDIX A Norman Geisler: Professional Ministry.................... 178

APPENDIX B Norman Geisler: Publications................................. 182

APPENDIX C Norman Geisler: Debates ....................................... 190

APPENDIX D Tribute to Norman Geisler ..................................... 193

Bibliography .......................................................................... 197

William C. Roach

## Book Dedication

This book is dedicated to the students, faculty, and staff at *Southern Evangelical Seminary* and *Veritas International University*.

Remember those who led you, who spoke the word of God to you; and consider the result of their way of life, imitate their faith.--**Hebrews 13:7**

— May we all remember Dr. Norman L. Geisler and the legacy he gave to his family, students, and the Church of Jesus Christ.

———————————

Special thanks must be given to those who read and offered feedback to this manuscript. In particular, Toby Logsdon and Molly Roach.

## Book Endorsements

For 20 years my seminar students have asked me why my pastor didn't teach me of the impact of those like Hume and Kant and I didn't know what to tell them. Now we have at least one book that not only explains what happened, but also shows the unique contribution one man made to the evangelical church in the 20th and early 21st century to counteract their damage. I highly recommend Dr. Bill Roaches book...I know my dad would be very proud!—**David Geisler**, President and Co-founder, *Norm Geisler International Ministries.*

*Defending Evangelicalism* is a truly excellent book. Dr. William Roach, the book's author, has mastered and distilled for the reader what could have been difficult subject matter. Albert Einstein is reported to have said, "If you can't explain something simply, you don't understand it well enough." If that be the case, William Roach understands his subject and the issues very well, and when you finish his book, you will too!—**Richard Land**, President, Southern Evangelical Seminary.

Over the next decade there will certainly be many books describing the life and beliefs of the greatest and most prolific apologist of the twentieth-century, Norman Geisler. *Defending Evangelicalism: The Apologetics of Norman L. Geisler* is a fascinating look behind the scenes of a gifted man who defied the odds to educate an entire generation of believers. This book is a must read!—**Joseph Holden**, President, Veritas International University.

The main title of Roach's book—*Defending Evangelicalism*—is very significant. So many of us doing apologetics today were nurtured at the feet of Norman Geisler. And what always impressed me about his apologetic writings and talks was their thoroughly Evangelical focus. Geisler covered the waterfront in his work and took on many topics that most Christian philosophers ignore. What we have needed for years is a book that brings together the various threads of Geisler's thought into one resource. We no longer have that need. William Roach's book is a scholarly, readable, integrative presentation of Geisler's overall apologetic and we are indebted to him for doing so.—**J. P. Moreland**, Distinguished Professor of Philosophy, Talbot School of Theology, Biola University and author of *Scientism and Secularism.*

What moves me as a Catholic to plug this book by Bill Roach about an Evangelical apologist and philosopher? First is the fact that I was a Thomist like Norman Geisler for years before I became a Catholic--it is just excellent, common-sense philosophy. Good reasoning is not denominationally dependent. Second, there is a great need for classical, traditional common-sense realism among today's philosophers, including Christian philosophers. Many theological errors have philosophical roots. Third, for the sake of philosophy itself. Geisler, like MacIntyre, Adler, and many others, helps heal our confused and conflicted philosophical climate.—**Peter Kreeft**, Professor of Philosophy, Boston College, and author of *Summa of the Summa*, *Summa Philosophica*, and *The Platonic Tradition*.

As one privileged to know Bill and Dr. Geisler, I perceive both to be cut from the same aspirational cloth. I have witnessed their commitment and drive contending for the faith in the seminary classroom, during home studies at Norm's, and more significantly, while just hanging out together as brothers in Christ. We both can attest, "We've learned just as much from Dr. Geisler outside the classroom than inside!"

In Geisler-like fashion, Bill not only picked up Norm's zeal for grounding himself in the philosophical foundations of the Christian faith, but he also recognizes the significance of its application in academia, evangelicalism, and now more than ever, cultural discourse. In this work, Bill captures the essence of Dr. Geisler's apologetic approach to defending evangelicalism. This book is needed, well thought out, and in the style of Dr. Geisler himself, "It ties all the strings!" I hope this book will pass on Dr. Geisler's classic, historical approach for generations to come.—**Mike E. Jackson**, MAA, MAPC, LPCMH, NBCC, and former ministry assistant to Dr. Norman Geisler.

I was blessed to have studied under Dr. Geisler, written books with him, and spoken at countless conferences with him. Through the decades, his apologetics — expressed in over 100 books — profoundly shaped my thinking and work of ministry. Because of Geisler's impact on me, I am enthused to recommend William Roach's new book, *Defending Evangelicalism: The Apologetics of Norman L. Geisler*. This concise and readable book effectively introduces the reader to Geisler's defense of the nature of truth, God, and the inerrancy of the Bible — three battleground issues of our day. This book receives two enthusiastic thumbs up.—**Ron Rhodes**, President, Reasoning from the Scriptures Ministries

Never was there a more prolific apologist than Norm Geisler, who authored or co-authored well over a hundred books. A downside to that productivity is that some people fail to appreciate the systematic breadth and depth of his contribution to Evangelical theology because they only encounter it in bits and pieces. Bill Roach has done us a great service in *Defending Evangelicalism: The Apologetics of Norman L. Geisler*. He has synthesized Geisler's approach in one handy volume, clearly written and faithful in both substance and spirit to the thought of its subject. Roach will send you back to Geisler with enhanced understanding and renewed appetite—and that will serve well both Geisler's memory and the Kingdom in which he labored.—**Donald Williams**, Professor Emeritus, Toccoa Falls College, and author of *Mere Humanity: G. K. Chesterton, C. S. Lewis, and J. R. R. Tolkien*, and *Deeper Magic: The Theology Behind the Writings of C. S. Lewis.*

The annals of Christianity provide the rise of only a few men over 2000 plus years whose contribution to the Church can only be reckoned in superlative strains. Such were Augustine, Spurgeon, Luther, and a few others. Among those of this generation, Norman Geisler penned books in proliferation, was faithful in his home church, was devoted to his family, and assisted a host of young men to achieve their academic heart's desires. That is why I rejoice Dr. Bill Roach, life-long assistant to Dr. Geisler, has opted to write *Defending Evangelicalism: The Apologetics of Norman L. Geisler.* One of the essential volumes for the scholar's bookcase and challenging reading for all believers, this monograph by Dr. Roach will be irreplaceable.—**Paige Patterson**, President, Sandy Creek Foundation, Parker, Texas.

Dr. William Roach has inscribed a stunningly powerful expose of the thought and life of Norman Leo Geisler, the greatest Scriptural apologist of the 20th and early 21st century. Being a young Timothy to Dr. Geisler, Roach is eminently qualified to delineate the tremendous contributions that Dr. Geisler made in defense of the inerrant words of Scripture. Dr. Geisler was known affectionately as "Stormin' Norman" because of his unswerving defense of inerrancy, as well as his clear, logical thinking. Ironically, Geisler often received great opposition, not from liberals, but from the evangelical critical scholars who professed belief in the same Scripture. The old worn aviator adage that one knows that the plane is precisely over the target by the amount of flack received is true in Dr. Geisler's case because of his vigilant apologetics that affirmed Scriptural trustworthiness. Geisler's thought and logic were the Kevlar vest against onslaughts thrown by both liberal and evangelical critical scholars who, or played hermeneutical games, with the trustworthiness of the plain, normal sense of God's Word. Dr. Roach has delineated the prime aspects of Geisler's theology in a very formidable work. I encourage all readers to carefully read through this work to gain inspiration and understanding of the life and work of Geisler.—**F. David Farnell**, Co-editor at Defending Inerrancy, and co-author of *The Jesus Crises* and *The Jesus Quest.*

I was honored to not only meet and work with Norman Geisler nearly 30 years ago but was blessed to be able to call him friend ever since that day. I can attest to Bill Roach's statement, "Norman Geisler was one evangelical figure who worked his entire life to demonstrate the fact that God is *there,* and he is *not silent.*" This commitment influenced everything Dr. Geisler did from academics to evangelism and discipleship. Bill Roach has done an admirable job of describing how Norm Geisler thought and why he believed certain issues were the main plain elements of the faith. Fudging on those not only compromises evangelicalism but abandons the faith delivered "once for all delivered to the saints." (Jude 4).—**L. L. (Don) Veinot Jr.**, President, Midwest Christian Outreach, Inc and Evangelical Ministries to New Religions. Co-author of *A Matter of Basic Principles: Bill Gothard and the Christian Life* and *Richard Rohr and the Enneagram Secret.*

Bill Roach has provided a concise and readable defense of Norman Geisler's commitment to classical realism, classical theism, classic evangelicalism, and inerrancy. This book will contribute to Geisler's legacy which shaped thousands of his students like myself who, in the trenches of pastoral ministry and preaching, continue to declare that God's Word is truth and therefore without error. This book will help to keep fresh these fundamental issues and provide a source for a new generation seeking to defend the faith in today's world.—**John Munro**, Pastor of Calvary Church, Charlotte, NC.

Evangelicals owe an enormous spiritual debt to the late Dr. Norman Geisler, whose stalwart commitment to the inerrant Word of God and obedience in defending it against modernity's lies forged his lasting apologetics legacy. As the Church today faces increasing pressure to abandon classical evangelicalism, Dr. Bill Roach skillfully and effectively reminds us why his mentor's approach to defending the faith was so fruitful and why evangelicals today must emulate Geisler's mind and heart in courageously standing for the gospel and biblical truth.—**Janet Mefferd**, nationally syndicated host of *Janet Mefferd Today.*

My experience with Dr. Norman Geisler is probably different from many others who are endorsing *Defending Evangelicalism*. I first met him in print as I edited his book on *The Roots of Evil.* Sadly, I never took a class from him. For many decades we joined together speaking in classrooms and doing a number of debates together. We even wrote a book together. This book by William Roach reminds us all of the debt of gratitude we owe to Dr. Geisler as he ably defended the Bible with thoughtful apologetics.—**Kerby Anderson**, Host, *Point of View* radio talk show.

## Preface

For most of my life, I have diligently trained in traditional martial arts. I grew up wrestling in Iowa. I have obtained three black belts: one in Okinawan Karate, Kobudo (i.e., traditional Karate weapons), and Tae Kwon Do. I currently train in Brazilian Jiu Jitsu and teach Okinawan Karate. I have always loved to see a calculated and methodological defense and offense against any strong opponent. There is nothing more exciting than to see a person in a martial arts match, whether it be Vale Tudo or a high school grappling match, technically and methodically control and eventually submit their opponent. You can see who has invested the time and effort into physical training and technical development. The mats do not lie. You can either handle your opponent or you cannot. World-famous Olympic wrestling champion and historic coach of the Iowa Hawkeye wrestling team, Dan Gable, used to say, "*The 1$^{st}$ period is won by the best technician. The 2$^{nd}$ period is won by the kid in the best shape. The 3$^{rd}$ period is won by the kid with the biggest heart.*" All the locker room talk and spewing forth of hot air in the world will not save you after the referee has blown the whistle. You better be prepared to fight, or you will lose the match.

Dan Gable also used to say, "*Gold medals aren't really made of gold. They're made of sweat, determination, and a hard-to-find alloy called guts.*" Norman Geisler represents the heart of an evangelical made from that special alloy called guts. Geisler worked like a master grappler and martial artist who dedicated his life as a technician who got in the best shape to win the match. But what separates Geisler from so many other formidable evangelical apologists, and the reason he was able to endure so much pressure and criticism was because he had the heart to defend the truth of the gospel. Several wrestlers are willing to study technique and get in shape. Those things can be taught to you by a skilled and motivated coach. But you cannot teach heart. Either the wrestler has it, or he do not. You can immediately see the difference between the two types of wrestlers.

The one with heart seems to just never give up. You slam him to the ground; he gets up. You control him with endless pressure; he keeps moving. You attempt to submit him; he keeps fighting. Geisler faced sizeable opponents both inside and outside of evangelicalism. He could have given up. He could have tapped. He could have laid down and accepted the pin. But he did not. Why? Geisler had the heart and determination to stand for the axioms of classic evangelicalism. This dedication was a gift given to Geisler from above, and God used it to preserve the truth of the gospel in our age.

This book is aptly titled *Defending Evangelicalism*. That title precisely captures the life of Dr. Norman Geisler. Geisler spent his entire ministry before God attempting to ward off aberrant beliefs from eroding the tenets of Christianity and evangelical belief. The effects of modernity are upon us, and we must size up our philosophical opponent. Evangelicalism has historically been a resistance movement to secular humanism and modernity. The three most pressing issues facing evangelicalism regard the nature of truth, God, and the Bible. This book will focus upon those three areas because they are essential to any evangelical apologetic. Geisler knew we were in a war for the truth. He stormed the beaches, fighting the battle for truth, the battle for God, and the battle for the Bible. These three battles summarize the key matches Geisler faced throughout the twentieth and early twenty-first centuries.

In the final analysis, we must remember modernity seems never to sleep. Opponents to Christianity seem to keep coming, and new objections pounce upon us when we least expect it. We cannot grow lazy in our defense of truth. We may start to lose heart and get tired. When we do, we need to remember these famous words from Dan Gable, who said, "*When I'd get tired and want to stop, I'd wonder what my next opponent was doing. I'd wonder if he was still working out. I'd try to visualize him. When I could see him working, I'd start pushing myself. When I could see him in the shower, I'd push myself harder.*" As evangelicals, we need to keep in mind that our opponent, Satan himself, and false ideologies do not sleep, nor do they stop training. I hope this book will motivate a new generation of Christians to keep working hard, start pushing themselves, and pray to God and ask him to provide them with a heart for the gospel and guts to defend it. In many respects, I pray each of us can look to the lion-like heart of Norman Geisler, who served as a mighty figure raised up for such a time as this.

William C. Roach, PhD
President, *International Society of Christian Apologetics*

# CHAPTER ONE

# The Present-Day Conditions of Belief

## Introduction

The apologetic situation of present-day evangelicalism is located within the broader sphere of modernity's epistemological crisis. We are now living in the wake of the breakdown of philosophical and theological cohesion in Western society. The truths of historic Protestantism are no more welcome in the arena of ideas than they are within the broader culture. The chasm between the pre-modern era and modernity has been brought about almost entirely by a change in the concept of truth. Wherever you look today, the new concept of truth or anti-truth holds in every arena of society. The agreement about this denial of the concept of truth is nearly ubiquitous, whether you hear it on the news, see it in politics, or experience it in society. The new methodology of modernity—namely, the total disregard for any concept of truth or the surety of divine revelation—has left modern man in complete despair and is the crucial problem facing Christianity.

We live in an age marked by great hostility towards the concept of truth, especially the truth of Christianity. Not only do we exist this side of Eden and the Fall, but we also live on this side of what Francis Schaeffer declared to be the great "Line of Despair."[1] Each arena of life from philosophy, art, music, general culture, and theology has been affected by the demise of truth. Christianity is a supernatural religion that makes specific truth claims about the God who has revealed himself and provided objective truth through Scripture, whereby sinners may be saved. David Wells warns:

> Those in the evangelical church today who are being lured by the siren calls of postmodern relativism, who are increasingly uncertain that truth can be known, or that it matters all that much

---

[1] Francis Schaeffer, *The Complete Works of Francis Schaeffer* (Wheaton: Crossway, 1982), 1:8.

anyway, would do well to ponder the fact that this uncertainty goes to the very heart of what Christianity is all about.[2]

Wells also claims in his book, *Courage to be Protestant*, it takes no courage to be Protestant in a generalized sense. History indicates to us that millions of people have embraced Protestantism, and they are in no peril. "To live by the truths of historic Protestantism, however," Wells says, "is an entirely different matter. That takes courage in today's context."[3] The same argument could be made about present-day evangelicalism. It does not take much courage to be an evangelical in a generalized sense, but given the crisis of truth in our age, it takes great courage to live by the truths of historic evangelicalism.

Enter Stormin' Norman. Norman L. Geisler (July 21, 1932—July 1, 2019), was a man who was courageous enough to live by the truths of historic evangelicalism. During the eulogy for Dr. Geisler at his funeral, Ravi Zacharias said, "We have come to bury a giant. A man who stood tall above so many in the determination to be a warrior for the Word of God."[4] Zacharias reminded everyone that Geisler's middle name was "Leo," which means lion, and how Norman Geisler was a lion for the Christian worldview. Geisler was unique because, like David's mighty men, he had an understanding of the times, to know what Israel ought to do (1Chron 12:32). God gave Dr. Geisler the gift of discernment to understand the prevailing ideas of our age and the condition of our culture. When God commissioned Dr. Geisler, he gave him the mind of a skillful surgeon of ideas with the tender heart of a shepherd and the zeal of an evangelist. Francis Schaeffer prophetically summoned the evangelical movement to recognize we live in unstable days. What is needed is a mind for God's truth and a heart for genuine Christian spirituality. One of the men God raised up to fulfill this vision was Dr. Norman Geisler. This book will argue that Geisler's unique synthesis of theology and apologetics are representative of twentieth-century (and early twenty-first century) evangelical identity, and that his convictions are valuable for present-day evangelical theologians and apologists. Many of the applications will be offered in each chapter as they relate to truth, God, and the Bible. Then, in the final chapter, we will return to a broader discussion of modernity and discuss several key aspects of Geisler's method and their relevance for evangelicalism. Finally, we will

---

[2] David F. Wells, *The Courage to Be Protestant: Truth-lovers, Marketers, and Emergents in the Postmodern World* (Grand Rapids: Eerdmans, 2008), 77.

[3] Ibid., 1.

[4] I attended this funeral and heard this message in person. *Southern Evangelical Seminary* recorded this message and these quotes can be found here: https://www.youtube.com/watch?v=57RJ6pkDoAs They were accessed on 10/8/2019.

apply Geisler's method to the issue of hermeneutics, subjectivity, and critical theory to serve as an example of the *way* his method could be applied to new topics, or a paradigm for Geisler studies going forward.

No introduction would be complete without discussing my personal indebtedness to Dr. Geisler. I was a young man who had serious questions about Christianity and needed a role model and a father figure in the faith. God used Dr. Geisler to provide for those great needs. He was full of knowledge and unafraid to defend the Christian faith against all opponents. He was full of love and willing to disciple me during a pivotal point in my life. In no small way, my own calling as a theologian and an apologist can be traced back to Dr. Norman Geisler's influence. I was inspired by Dr. Geisler's intellectual engagement and deeply motivated by his vision to defend the historic Christian faith. Dr. Geisler seemed to be there at every significant event in my adult life. Dr. Geisler was there the day I graduated from college and seminary; he was the first one to call and congratulate me when I finished my Ph.D. and consoled me in the weeks following my father's death. He officiated my wedding and offered some of the best marriage advice minutes leading up to the ceremony. Geisler was numbered among the elders who laid hands on me at my ordination. Lastly, Dr. Geisler was influential in helping me become an author, speaker, professor, and President of the *International Society of Christian Apologetics*. Truly, the stamp of Dr. Norman Geisler is over so much of my adult life, and for that, I am eternally thankful.[5]

With these personal accolades in place, let us start drawing the intellectual road map to understand twentieth-century evangelicalism's apologetic situation and intellectual climate. In due course, this historical overview and the influence of philosophical modernity upon twentieth-century thought will serve as a paradigm to understand the significance of Dr. Geisler's apologetic for evangelicalism.

## Modernity: The Search for a New Type of Belief

Ideas not only have consequences; they have origins too. Peter Kreeft writes, "When a patient is sick, a medical analysis is in order, and nearly all thoughtful observers agree that Western civilization is sick. We need, therefore, a medical analysis of Western civilization."[6] The analysis required

---

[5] For a much longer explanation of Geisler's influence in my life, please consult my written eulogy: https://williamroach.org/2019/07/01/i-am-put-here-for-the-defense-of-the-gospel-the-legacy-of-dr-norman-l-geisler/

[6] Peter Kreeft, *Back to Virtue* (San Francisco: Ignatius, 1986), 37.

is not a material analysis, such as the poverty levels or death rates of individuals, but an analysis of Western society's spiritual status and intellectual ideas. How did we get to this point in history? More importantly, what can we do to overcome the sickness?

Academic theorists claim history can be told from different viewpoints. Religious history will provide one point of view, secular history books will tell it from another vantage point, science textbooks will tell it from a theoretical perspective, and philosophy books from a more abstract position. No one perspective is ever exhaustive or seen from God's point of view, but we can seek reality and approach it, rather than completely ignore it, or reduce it to personal subjectivity.

This section will attempt to explain the present-day situation according to three key ideas:

1. Charles Taylor's Three Types of Beliefs
2. Philosophical Precursors to an Age of Unbelief
3. Responses to the Age of Unbelief

Step three will be understood according to two rivers emerging from the Age of Unbelief: 1) The stream of religious accommodation; and 2) The stream of religious resistance. This paradigm of thought will help to recognize classic evangelicalism as a religious resistance movement because it did not accommodate unto philosophical modernity.

### Charles Taylor's Three Types of Belief

Charles Taylor's book, *A Secular Age*, asks the question: What does it mean to live in a secular age?[7] The place of religion in our society has changed greatly, and it has left a profound influence upon religion in general and evangelicalism in particular. Taylor takes up the question of what it means for a society to move from the position in which it is virtually "impossible not to believe in God" (i.e., people find belief in God so strong that to deny theistic belief seems intellectually impossible), to a transition in which, even for the most devout Christian, belief in God becomes only one viable possibility among a host of other answers (i.e., Christianity or belief in God is not seen as the sole explanation, but one of a variety of options). Taylor's book masterfully describes how this transition did not occur because of one single fact or event in history, but a series of new departures and events which dissolved and destabilized the forms of religious belief that marked pre-modernity from modernity and postmodernity. Taylor's purpose in writing his book was not to understand

---

[7] Charles Taylor, *A Secular Age* (Cambridge: Harvard University Press, 2007).

what changed in society or when society changed, but rather *how* society changed from a religious to a secular age. Namely, Taylor is concerned not just with *what* people believe but *how* people believe.

James K. A. Smith notes, "Taylor is concerned with the 'conditions of belief'—a shift in the plausibility that make something believable or unbelievable."[8] Note, Taylor beckons his readers to focus not only *on what the person believes but also* on what is *believable* and *how* someone holds that particular belief. Taylor explains this concept, claiming:

> In fact, we have to understand the differences between these options not just in terms of creeds, but also in terms of differences in experience and sensibility. And on this latter level, we have to take account of two important differences: first, there is a massive change in the whole background of belief or unbelief, that is, the passing of the earlier 'naïve' framework, and the rise of our 'reflective' one. And secondly, we have to be aware of how believers and unbelievers can experience their world very differently.[9]

Taylor contributes to an evangelical assessment of our present-day situation by providing a psychology of the conditions of belief. Taylor's point is that religion and religious belief ought to do more than chart *what* a group believes or the history of ideas and the network of beliefs; rather they ought to consider the very *mode* of holding a particular belief. He insists it would have been virtually impossible for a person not to believe in God prior to the rise of modernity in Western society, while the current landscape in Occidental society finds itself in the predicament where it is not only easy to "not believe in God," but virtually *impossible* for many to believe in God.[10] To better understand the distinctions between "impossible not to believe", "possible not to believe," and "impossible to believe," Smith notes how Taylor nuances his position by offering a threefold taxonomy of "secular" belief.[11] Taylor and Smith categorize belief according to three definitions of "secular," claiming:[12]

1. Classical or medieval accounts of "secular" or *secular(1):* "A more 'classical' definition of the secular, as distinguished from the

---

[8] James K. A. Smith, *How (Not) To Be Secular: Reading Charles Taylor* (Grand Rapids: Eerdmans, 2014), 18.

[9] Taylor, *A Secular Age*, 14.

[10] Ibid., 14, 25.

[11] Smith, *How (Not) To Be Secular*, 20.

[12] Ibid., 20-21; 142.

sacred—*the earthly plane of domestic life. Priests tend the sacred; butchers, bakers, and candlestick makers carry out 'secular' work.*

2. Modernity, particular in the wake of the Enlightenment or *secular(2)*: *A more 'modern' definition of secular as areligious—neutral, unbiased, 'objective'—as in a 'secular' public square.*

3. Contested Religious Belief or *secular(3)*: *Taylor's notion of the secular as an age of contested belief, where religious belief is no longer axiomatic. It is possible to imagine not believing in God.*

In other words, secularism comes in a variety of ways and can be applied to society in a multifaceted fashion. Secularism in one sense, could be understood as a proper separation between the Church and State. The American experiment might be an example of a secular society whereby the State does not dictate a particular religion or denomination. What makes Taylor's contribution unique is not only his qualification of different ways to understand the term "secular", but the taxonomy of the psychology of belief throughout each definition of "secular." Not only does modern man reject the concept of God in society, but he also psychologically finds it nearly impossible to believe in the mere concept of God.

Twenty-first century evangelicalism cannot dismiss the insights provided by Taylor and other sociologists of religion. We find ourselves in an era of contested religious belief and in a society where the intellectually dominant mood is that of exclusive secularism. Belief in God is no longer considered axiomatic for people in Western society. The intellectual horizon no longer presents anything beyond the material age, and the notions of God and transcendent truths have been eclipsed because the conditions of belief no longer allow for such a belief. Evangelicals must continue to ask the question: *How do we communicate the Christian faith in an age of skepticism?*[13]

Timothy Keller attempts to answer these types of questions in his book, titled, *Preaching: Communicating Faith in a Secular Age.* Keller argues that preaching in today's environment requires the minister to diagnose his patients in ways ministers in previous generations did not have to. The hidden web of secularity and its conditions of belief present the preacher with a new challenge of communicating the Christian worldview, for our age no longer believes God is required to explain the world, nor are they open to the idea of God being a necessary precondition to explain our

---

[13] Timothy Keller, *Preaching: Communicating Faith in an Age of Skepticism* (New York: Penguin Random House, 2015).

world. Keller explains the psychological effects of secularism and diagnoses its effects, claiming:

> The late-modern mind presents itself as something like this. We have come to realize that we don't need God to explain the world we see—science does that job for us. We don't need God or religion to be moral, to love and work for a better world, or to have meaning and fulfillment in life. What we need is to be free to live life as we see fit and to work together to make the world a better and more just place to live. Religion gets in the way of all this—it constrains our freedom to live as we wish and divides us so we can't work together.[14]

Modernity is on a quest to explain the world apart from belief in God. In the modern understanding of reality, we cannot ground truth (if it exists) or morality (which is not objective) in anything outside of ourselves—such as God, metaphysical virtue, or ideals. This leaves modern man in a predicament: *How can late-modernity ground its ideals?* The standard upon which modern society seeks to ground its ideals are found within itself. However, this thesis has proven to be found lacking because unstable foundations cannot offer any fixed or binding sense of moral motivation, obligation, or lasting truth value. The apologetic situation facing modern secularism can be summarized in this dilemma: They cry there is injustice and error in the streets, but they cannot account for there being such a thing as justice or truth within their worldview. They fault the Christian for holding to intolerant and dogmatic positions; all the while, they cannot account for such a criticism or the concept of criticism itself. Unfortunately, by their very own standards, modern secularists offer no good reasons or grounds to live according to their ideals and ethics. G. K. Chesterton captures the secularist predicament well, observing:

> But the new rebel is a sceptic [sic], and will not entirely trust anything. He has no loyalty; therefore he can never be really a revolutionist. And the fact that he doubts everything gets in his way when he wants to denounce anything. For all denunciation implies a moral doctrine of some kind; and the modern revolutionist doubts not only the institution he denounces, but the doctrine by which he denounces it. Thus he writes one book complaining that imperial oppression insults the purity of women, and then he writes another book (about the sex problem) in which he insults it himself. He curses the Sultan

---

[14] Ibid., 124.

because Christian girls lose their virginity, and then curses Mrs. Grundy because they keep it. As a politician, he will cry out that war is a waste of life, and then, as a philosopher, that all life is a waste of time. A Russian pessimist will denounce a policeman for killing a peasant, and then prove by the highest philosophical principles that the peasant ought to have killed himself. A man denounces marriage as a lie, and then denounces aristocratic profligates for treating it as a lie. He calls a flag a bauble, and then blames the oppressors of Poland or Ireland because they take away that bauble. The man of this school goes first to a political meeting, where he complains that savages are treated as if they were beasts; then he takes his hat and umbrella and goes on to a scientific meeting, where he proves that they practically are beasts. In short, the modern revolutionist, being an infinite sceptic [sic], is always engaged in undermining his own mines. In his book on politics he attacks men for trampling on morality; in his book on ethics he attacks morality for trampling on men. Therefore the modern man in revolt has become practically useless for all purposes of revolt. By rebelling against everything he has lost the right to rebel against anything.[15]

Chesterton would remind the Christian preacher and apologist we serve in a unique place in history because we face generations of people infected with the side-effects of what C. S. Lewis warned about in his book, *The Abolition of Man*, when society jettisons the concept of objective metaphysical reality.[16] Namely, the inability to ground any truth claims, morals, or value judgments.

The modern belief that science offers the best explanation of reality, and that technology can solve nearly every problem is naïve at best and nihilistic at its core. We can engage this cultural narrative of *sola reason* (based upon modern psychology, sociology, and technology) and *sola materialism* by showing the worldview of the secularist cannot account for the very tenets of its own worldview (including its moral denunciations or basic epistemological claims). Francis Schaeffer declared this act to be "Taking the Roof Off" of a person's worldview. Having the roof ripped off your worldview is a dangerous position to find oneself in. The entire web of a person's beliefs is now exposed as a fraud and a failure without any grounds to justify not only their beliefs, but any beliefs, or the concept of

---

[15] G. K. Chesterton, *Orthodoxy* (San Francisco: Ignatius, 1908), 46-47.
[16] C. S. Lewis, *The Abolition of Man* (New York: Harper One, 1974).

belief itself. It is at this very point the Christian must engage, lovingly engage, but engage, nonetheless.

Norman Geisler was an expert in this type of engagement. If you survey any of Geisler's apologetic books, you will find he tried to situate each belief historically. Ideas flow like the streams of a river coming from a particular place to its final destination.[17] There are both origins and consequences of each idea. Geisler understood it was essential to diagnose a patient correctly and not just treat the symptoms of the disease. Unless a Christian apologist can surgically refute the aberrant idea of a person's network of beliefs and destroy each vain argument raised against the knowledge of Christ, they are merely left treating the symptoms of faulty worldviews. The conditions of secular unbelief define the apologetic situation before twenty-first century evangelicalism. Taylor reminds us we cannot just dismiss or disregard the belief structures of our audience. Geisler would also remind us that to properly treat our patient, we must not only understand the conditions of their belief, but we must also understand the philosophical precursors and origins of this Age of Unbelief. To properly engage in the twenty-first century, we must engage both the *origin* and *validity* of each belief, and *how* beliefs are held.

## Philosophical Precursors to an Age of Unbelief

The best way to understand contemporary unbelief is against the backdrop of key figures and their philosophical claims. The modern world is marked by skepticism, agnosticism, scientism, relativism, and atheism. It is not uncommon for a person to hold to one or many of these positions, or to move from a weaker agnostic position to a strong atheist position. Therefore, the best way to understand *why* some people found it "possible not to believe" is to see *how* modernity unfolded through a rigorous study of the history of philosophy, not just a set of analytical propositions.[18] Without going into an extensive survey, since time does not permit such a venture, we can illustrate the point by focusing on three key philosophical movements—skepticism, agnosticism, and postmodernism—to understand the preconditions of the psychology of unbelief. Each movement is different

---

[17] Richard M. Weaver, *Ideas Have Consequences: Expanded Edition* (Chicago: University of Chicago Press, 2013).

[18] Frederick Copleston's *A History of Philosophy* still remains probably the best history of philosophy in print. For a much fuller and complete understanding of the grand narrative of philosophy please consult Copleston.

and holds key distinctives, but all exemplify the notion that belief(s) (or unbelief) can be held in a variety of *ways*.

### The Skepticism of David Hume (1711-1776)

David Hume is considered the famous Scottish skeptic. The basis of Hume's position can be summarized by the prominent line from his book *Enquiry Concerning Human Understanding:* "If we take in our hands any volume; of divinity or school metaphysics, for instance; let us ask: *Does it contain any abstract reasoning concerning quantity of number?* No. *Does it contain any experimental reasoning concerning matter of fact and existence?* No. Commit it then to the flames: for it can contain nothing but sophistry and illusion."[19] In short, unless an idea is definitional, mathematical, or empirical, they are meaningless. Of course, all statements concerning God do not meet these two-criterion; therefore, our knowledge of God becomes meaningless, if not impossible.

For Hume, there are only two valid forms of reasoning: (1) Relations of Ideas and (2) Matters of Fact. Relations of ideas are equivalent to definitional and mathematical statements. To deny them would be a contradiction. We know 1 + 1 = 2 not by observation or scientific experiment but by analyzing the relationship between the symbols and ideas. Matters of fact operate quite differently. Hume illustrates this latter type of reasoning by discussing the rising of the sun each day. Hume notes it is highly probable the sun will rise tomorrow, even though it is not logically contradictory to claim the sun will *not* rise tomorrow. All matters of experience imply a possible contrary state of affairs. For, logically speaking, anything we experience could be one way or another. There is a chance the sun may rise tomorrow, or it may not rise tomorrow; we cannot know which is true by way of a relationship of ideas but through customary conjunction (i.e., it has always been this way, so we project it will always be the same going forward).

Hume continues this thought experiment by questioning the traditional understanding of causality. For Hume, all reasoning that concerns matters of fact resemble *cause* and *effect* reasoning. This knowledge does not arise from *a priori* preconditions but from *a posteriori* experience. Causality is merely one event following another event, and there is no real logical, or causal, connection between the two events. Hume uses the sun again to illustrate his point. For example, it is true the sun regularly rises after certain events in the morning (e.g., rooster crowing,

---

[19] David Hume, *An Inquiry Concerning Human Understandings*, ed. C. W. Hendel (1748; repr., New York: Bobbs-Merrill, 1955).

the alarm clock going off). But one would not want to claim they know the rooster crowing or the alarm clock is the *cause* of the sun rising. Instead, the reason we believe the sun will rise after the alarm clock is by customary conjunction and because of that, we posit a connection between them.[20]

Hume demands we ask about the necessary connection between different events. There is certainly a difference between rationally understanding the nature of a triangle and cause and effect events. Unlike geometric figures, we could imagine a world in which the relationships between physical events were different. There could be a world in which ice cream will burn your tongue, not cool it. This is why scientists have laboratories and mathematicians do not. Ideas, in this sense, are merely joined and never truly connected. Consequently, Hume has shown that all our judgments concerning scientific knowledge are without a rational basis. Therefore, we must remain skeptical about cause and effect reasoning, including any divine cause and effect reasoning.[21] Hume also used this type of reasoning to disregard the concept of a miracle completely. He viewed miracles as something irrational because they could not be repeated or tested by science. Miracles were believed by naïve men at best, and modern men who believe in miracles down deep know they are false and maintain that belief solely based upon personal religious reasons, not rational reasons.

### *The Agnosticism of Immanuel Kant (1724-1804)*

David Hume affected Kant's rationalism significantly. Kant was initially trained in the tradition of Leibniz's rationalism. In particular, he embraced a version of it advocated by Christian Wolff (1679-1754). Although immersed in this form of philosophy, Kant admits that after reading Hume's empiricist philosophy, it awakened him from his "dogmatic slumber."[22] Kant grew disillusioned with his predecessors' dogmatic rationalism because it was overly committed to the role of human reason, even to the neglect of empirical investigations. Kant spent the remainder of his career attempting to synthesize rationalism and empiricism into his version of the "transcendental method" or "synthetic a priori" method. In doing so, however, Kant so limited humanity's knowledge of metaphysics that one could no longer affirm a positive knowledge of God, the self, or any aspect

---

[20] Frederick Copleston, *A History of Philosophy: Modern Philosophy: The British Philosophers from Hobbes to Hume*, vol. 5 (New York: Doubleday, 1994), 258-292.

[21] Ibid., 271-288.

[22] Immanuel Kant, *Prolegomena to Any Future Metaphysics*, trans. Paul Carus, revised by James W. Ellington (Indianapolis: Hackett, 1977),

of the real world. Consequently, Kant's philosophy ushered in what has traditionally come to be known as agnosticism.

Kant's philosophy has been declared a "Copernican Revolution" in the history of philosophy.[23] Similar to the Copernican revolution, where Copernicus claimed that the earth revolved around the sun, rather than the sun revolving around the earth; Kant claimed it is no longer true the mind conforms to reality, rather, reality conforms unto the mind. For Kant, he claims it is true that knowledge begins in experience; however, it would be incorrect to claim all knowledge arises from the senses. Kant referred to this approach as "critical philosophy." His most important work in this regard was the *Critique of Pure Reason*.[24] By labeling his philosophy as a critical philosophy, Kant did not advocate for a negative or cranky approach to philosophy. Instead, deriving the term from the Greek word "to sort," Kant attempted to sort out or set out true, proper, and legitimate claims of reason and disregard groundless and illegitimate claims to reason.[25]

Kant's view claims humanity cannot know the metaphysical realm, including God, because the content of such knowledge is above human reasoning. Historically, there have been two types of judgments: analytic and synthetic. Analytic judgments are those in which the predicate is contained in the subject (e.g., All bachelors are unmarried men). Synthetic judgments are those in which the predicate is not rationally contained in the subject (e.g., All bachelors are unmarried men who wear red shirts). In the latter illustration, there is nothing in the rational definition of bachelors/unmarried men that requires them to wear red shirts. They could wear any colored shirt. The point being synthetic judgments offer new information about reality. In addition to two types of judgments, Kant recognizes there are two kinds of knowledge: *a priori* (knowledge obtained prior to and independent of experience) and *a posteriori* (knowledge obtained from experience). The following chart summarizes this point:

---

[23] Peter Kreeft, *Socrates Meets Kant: The Father of Philosophy Meets His Most Influential Child* (San Francisco: Ignatius Press, 2009), 78-108.

[24] Immanuel Kant, *Critique of Pure Reason* (New York: Cambridge University Press, 1998).

[25] S. Korner, *Kant* (London: Penguin Books, 1990), 13-32.

|  | | |
|---|---|---|
| Derivation of Knowledge: | **A priori:** not verified by sense experience, universal. | **A posteriori:** based on or verified by sense experience, contingent, may be universal in form but are not strictly or really universal |
| Content of Knowledge: | **Analytic:** the predicate is part of the meaning of the subject. So these propositions are a priori (or necessary and universal) because of the meaning of the terms. | **Synthetic:** the predicate is not part of the meaning of the subject. |

With both judgments and types of knowledge in place, we can now understand Kant's claims to knowledge:

1. **Analytic *a priori*:** the law of non-contradiction is the basis for this type of knowledge. By analyzing the terms we can know the truth of the judgments (e.g., All bachelors are unmarried men). By understanding the terms "bachelor" and "unmarried" men we understand the truth of the judgement.

2. **Analytic *a posteriori*:** This form of knowledge is considered contradictory. If knowledge were analytic it could not be *a posteriori*.

3. **Synthetic *a posteriori*:** the basis for this type of knowledge is experience. This is a form of empirical knowledge, for our knowledge comes from ordinary experience, which adds to the content of our knowledge (e.g., the quarterback threw the ball). These types of claims can be tested by the scientific method.

4. **Synthetic *a priori*:** the basis for this type of knowledge is something that is *synthetic*, meaning it tells us something about the real world. But it is also *a priori*, meaning it does not require experience to confirm them.

From these four types of judgments, we can understand the genius of Kant's revolution. Kant and Hume part ways because of the fourth category of knowledge. Up to this point in history, rationalists and empiricists debated the validity of analytic *a priori* and synthetic *a posteriori* forms of knowledge. However, Kant claims there is a different type of judgment or approach to knowledge. He grants the mind collects information based upon particular experiences; however, as Hume demonstrated this would lead to skepticism and could undermine any surety undergirding traditional science. Therefore, to assure us of true knowledge for *all* events Kant claimed there must be an *a priori* aspect to knowledge. Hence, he claims there is a type of knowledge that gives us knowledge about the real world (i.e., synthetic) that does not require knowledge of the real world (i.e., *a priori*).[26]

The effects of Kant's approach to knowledge result in the impossibility of knowing reality. The content of knowledge comes *via* the senses, but the structure of knowledge is derived from the mind. This is the key synthesis between rationalism and empiricism. However, the consequence of Kant's agnosticism is that if someone cannot know anything until it is structured by the *a priori* forms of sense perception (e.g., time and space) and categories of understanding (e.g., quantity, quality, relation, and modality),[27] then there is no way to genuinely know reality prior to it being structured, because one only knows reality according to the way the mind structures reality, not reality in and of itself. In Kant's words, we can have knowledge of the *phenomena* but not the *noumena*. There is an impassible gulf fixed between reality and the way we can know it. Moreover, whenever humanity attempts to reason about transcendent metaphysics, their thinking ends in antinomies, because metaphysical reasoning goes beyond the proper limits of knowledge. Theoretical knowledge is limited to the realm of experience, and to believe pure reason can go beyond experience results in paradoxes and illusions. Hence, because God is a concept beyond our experience and beyond the categories of legitimate understanding and pure reason, humanity cannot know God through reason, natural theology, or the traditional proofs for God's existence.[28]

In the wake of Kant's revolution, several of his successors attempted to overcome Kantian dualism and subjectivity. The primary movements resulting from agnosticism were German idealism, dialecticism, romanticism, positivism, utilitarianism, historical materialism, and existentialism. The tension many of Kant's successors attempted to overcome was a contradiction in Kant's system. On the one hand, Kant

---

[26] Howard Caygill, *A Kant Dictionary* (Cambridge: Blackwell Publishers, 1995), 384-85.

[27] Kant, *Critique of Pure Reason*, 122 (B93).

[28] Frederick Copleston, *A History of Philosophy: Modern Philosophy: From The French Enlightenment to Kant*, vol. 6 (New York: Doubleday, 1994), 277-307.

limited all knowledge to the spatial-temporal material world (i.e., the phenomenal realm). On the other hand, Kant could not deny or overcome his belief in the reality of the noumenal realm. Hence, Kant's critics quickly noted it was contradictory for him to claim we can only know the phenomenal realm and claim to know there is a reality which transcends human experience. A second criticism they had against Kant's system is if all claims to knowledge require the categories to know reality, then how did Kant come to a knowledge of the categories? It seems viciously circular to posit someone comes to a knowledge of the categories through the categories.[29]

The heirs of Kantian philosophy were known as the German idealists. This view advocates that all of reality must be understood as intrinsically dependent on some sort of mental or spiritual reality.[30] Idealists charged Kant with limiting the range of experience too severely to the neglect of moral and aesthetic experience. From this posture, individuals such as Johann Gottlieb Fichte (1762-1814) argued that reality is known through moral experience. Another German idealist, Friedrich Wilhelm Joseph von Schelling (1775-1854) argued from the other angle, claiming reality is known through aesthetic experience. Together, both figures had a significant impact upon the Romantic movement, and most importantly, G. W. G. Hegel, who argued reality is not static but evolving *via* his dialectic (e.g., thesis, antithesis, and synthesis).

Moreover, Hegel also adopted the idea that reality is a continuously unfolding spiritual force, and we must have a broader definition of reason, one that includes moral and aesthetic intuitions as modes of knowledge. Finally, each of these German idealists attempted to revive the concept of metaphysics again. However, in doing so, they opened the door for an ever-evolving and changing view of reality. These figures were also unable to overcome the negative effects of personal and radical subjectivity.[31] Following this philosophical trajectory, came the great existentialists who had a disdain for the pretensions of philosophical reason and philosophical certainty. However, they did adopt the Enlightenment "ideal of progress"

---

[29] Carl F. H. Henry, *God, Revelation and Authority*, 6 vols (Waco: Word Books), 1: 344-363.

[30] Frederick Beisner, *German Idealism: The Struggle Against Subjectivism* 1781-1801 (Cambridge: Harvard University Press, 2002).

[31] Ibid., 217-334.

thesis, and called for a new understanding of human existence and knowing.³²

*Postmodernism and the Denial of Truth*³³

Postmodernism is a diverse group of thinkers united around the belief that modernity is dead, and we that should reject its ideals. They have not completely done way with each ideal from modern philosophy. For instance, postmodernisms still maintain Hume's skepticism about knowing material reality, Kant's agnosticism about knowing metaphysical reality, and they embrace the evolving and changing view of reality held by German idealists. Granted, they hold each of these beliefs for different reasons and may hold them based upon different arguments; nonetheless, following in the spirit of modern philosophy, postmodernism has been committed to limiting humanity's knowledge. Unlike Kant, who claimed humanity has the same general categories of knowledge and that we can all generally appropriate knowledge in the same way, postmodernists claim that humanity does not have the same general categories of knowledge; hence, humanity does not have a similar type of knowledge of reality. In addition, like Kant, postmodernists affirm an idealistic method. Unlike Kant, postmodernists have gone even farther and embraced an existential metaphysic and a dialectical method.

Beyond these observations, postmodernists can be understood as a group of thinkers united on the front of what they stand *against*. Individuals such as Michel Foucault (1926-1984), Jacques Derrida (1930--), and Richard Rorty (1931--) are united in their battle on the destruction of truth, death of the metanarrative, demise of any text (including the biblical text), the disregard for all authority, the elevation of feelings over fact, the radical perspectivalism of feminist and race theories to offer different standpoint epistemologies of reality, and the displacement of any traditional morality. William F. Lawhead, goes even farther to note postmodernists are united in their attack against modernism, claiming.

> Postmodernists are a loose-knit group of thinkers united around the belief that they are the pallbearers of the modern tradition that originated in the Enlightenment. The tradition of modernism they reject includes the following beliefs: (1) there is one true

---

³² More will be said about this later under the consequences of the Age of Unbelief.

³³ Like it was said above, time does not permit an exhaustive explanation of each turn in modern and contemporary philosophy. It goes without saying that one must include the effects of nineteenth century empiricism, pragmatism, process philosophy, analytic philosophy, the linguistic turn, phenomenology, and existentialism. Hume, Kant, and Postmodernism were chosen because they best illustrate *how* a belief is held and the consequence of ideas.

picture of reality, (2) it is possible to obtain universal, objective knowledge, (3) science is a superior form of knowledge, (4) the history of modern thought has been a cumulative progression of increasingly better theories of reality, and (5) the autonomous, knowing subject is the source of all ideas.[34]

Norman Geisler understood the significance this shift in thinking had upon the evangelical church. Throughout his career, Dr. Geisler helped evangelicals recognize the faulty thinking of postmodernism and how to respond to its contradictory worldview. For example, in his book, *Christian Apologetics*, Geisler offers the following chart and series of deduced propositions to help his readers understand and evaluate modernism and postmodernism. Geisler claims, "Postmodernism can be seen as a reaction to modernism in the following way:

| Modernism | Postmodernism |
| --- | --- |
| Unity of thought | Diversity of thought |
| Rational | Social and psychological |
| Conceptual | Visual and poetical |
| Truth is absolute | Truth is relative |
| Exclusivism | Pluralism |
| Foundationalism | Antifoundationalism |
| Epistemology | Hermeneutics |
| Certainty | Uncertainty |
| Author's meaning | Reader's meaning |
| Structure of the text | Deconstructing the text |
| The goal of knowing | The journey of knowing |

---

[34] William F. Lawhead, *The Voyage of Discovery*, 2nd edition (Belmont: Wadsworth, 2002), 559.

*The Result of Postmodernism.* Postmodernism is an outworking of Nietzschean atheism. If there is no Absolute Mind (God), then there is

1. No absolute (objective) truth (epistemological relativism),
2. No absolute meaning (semantic relativism),
3. No absolute history (reconstructionism).

And if there is no Absolute Author, then there is

4. No absolute writing (textual relativism),
5. No absolute interpretation (hermeneutical relativism).

And if there is no Absolute Thinker, then

6. There is no absolute thought (philosophical relativism),
7. There are no absolute laws of thought (antifoundationalism),

If there is no Absolute Purposer, then there is

8. No absolute purpose (teleological relativism).

If there is no Absolute Good, then there is

9. No absolute right or wrong (moral relativism).

In brief, postmodernism is a form of relativism and subjectivism. At its base, it is a form of antifoundationalism."[35]

Geisler was masterfully skilled in his ability to understand properly both the source and shift in ideas. Moreover, Geisler was able to pinpoint the rational conclusions of postmodernism's reaction to modernism. Postmodernists recognize the consequences of their beliefs, especially Christian postmodernists such as Stanley Grenz and Robert E. Webber.[36] However, instead of rejecting those consequences, they celebrate them as something to be embraced. Grenz and Webber are examples of evangelicals who believe Christians ought to adopt postmodernism. They also recognize the effects it has upon evangelical apologetics. Grenz and Webber are calling for evangelicals to move away from what they consider reason-based and evidentially supported forms of apologetics. In its place, the Church ought to embrace an incarnational method that focuses upon the community of its recipients and the notion of truth as embodied versus

---

[35] Norman L. Geisler, *Christian Apologetics* 2nd edition (Grand Rapids: Baker, 2013), 10-11.

[36] See: Stanley J. Grenz, *A Primer on Postmodernism* (Grand Rapids: Eerdmans, 1996); Robert E. Webber, *The Younger Evangelicals: Facing the Challenges of the New World* (Grand Rapids: Baker, 2002).

truth as rational and propositional.[37] Geisler would reject such thinking and consider it a form of methodological unorthodoxy because the net result will undermine the truthfulness of Christianity.

This short excurses ought to illustrate *how* modernity and postmodernity disregard objective truth and undermine humanity's ability to know reality or justify truth claims about reality. Modern thought played a dominant role in the academy and society to help bring about the Age of Unbelief. Secular thought, in the sense of non-Christian thought, as well as the Church, had to respond to the new intellectual objections presented by modernity.

## Responses to the Age of Unbelief

*Secular Responses*

There are significant consequences to embracing the worldview found in the Age of Unbelief. There are a myriad of ways to embrace unbelief. Not every individual holds to each tenet of modernity in the same way or to the same degree. Nonetheless, Taylor reminds us we are children of modernity and now, postmodernity. Probably the most significant impact the Age of Unbelief had upon the world was the rise of atheism. During the 1800s, the "God is Dead" movement was on the rise. In 1859 Charles Darwin released his famous book, *On the Origin of Species*, which postulated that all animals evolved from primate ancestors through purposeless ancestorial mutations over millions of years. Twelve years later, Darwin released *The Descent of Man*, in which he asserted that humans arose from the same common species as well.

When Darwin unveiled his theory of common descent, which included a process he called "Natural Selection," evolution gained academic and scientific legitimacy. Specifically, natural selection was used by Darwin as a means to do away with God. He writes, "I speak of Natural selection as an active power or deity; but who objects to another author speaking of the attraction of gravity as ruling the movement of the plants? ... It is difficult to avoid personifying nature."[38] Karl Marx, the famed atheist, rejoiced to see that day because he believed evolution had buried our concept of God. Marx proudly proclaimed, "But nowadays, in our evolutionary concept of

---

[37] Webber, *The Younger Evangelicals*, 105-106.
[38] Cited in Bennette, *The Index of Leading Cultural Indicators*, 25.

the universe, there is absolutely no room for either a Creator of a ruler."[39] Marx's writings are foundational to both atheism and communism. He is a reminder that ideas have consequences.

Scientists and philosophers drew the implication that evolution had replaced the need for God. Friedrich Nietzsche went one step further and concluded that without God, neither were there absolute foundations for morality. He declared, "God is dead. God remains dead. And we have killed Him. How shall we, the murders of all murderers, comfort ourselves?" Nietzsche replied, "Must we ourselves become gods simply to seem worthy of it?"[40] Unfortunately, when man killed belief in God in the 1800s, he also killed man in the 1900s. Darwin's theory of Natural Selection was used by atheists to justify the mass-murder of millions of people. In 1924 Adolf Hitler, in his book *Mein Kampf*, explicitly made it clear that Darwin's theory was the basis for his belief in Arian superiority and that he had used it as his moral justification for the mass-murder of the Jews. He wrote:

> If nature does not wish that weaker individuals should mate with the stronger, she wishes even less that a superior race should intermingle with an inferior one; because in such cases all her efforts, throughout hundreds of thousands of years, to establish an evolutionary higher stage of being, may thus be rendered futile. But such a preservation goes hand-in-hand with the inexorable law that it is the strongest and the best who must triumph and that they have the right to endure. He who would live must fight. He who does not wish to fight in this world, where permanent struggle is the law of life, has not the right to exist.[41]

This worldview became the basis for Hitler's execution camps. It was also used to justify Benito Mussolini and Joseph Stalin to justify their atheistic quests for domination and power. The consequences of the Age of Unbelief brought a change in philosophy and ethics as well. Consequentially, it changed the lives of millions of people by sending them to an early grave.[42]

---

[39] See: Karl Marx, *Marx and Engels on Religion*, Introduction by Reinhold Niebuhr (New York: Schoken Books, Inc., 1964), 337.

[40] Friedrich Nietzsche, *Gay Science*, in Walter Kaufmann, *The Portable Nietzsche* (New York: The Viking Press, 1968), 95-96.

[41] Adolf Hitler, *Mein Kampf* (London: Hurst and Blackett Ltd., Publishers, 4th printing, 1939), 239-240; 242.

[42] Norman L. Geisler, *Is Man the Measure? An Evaluation of Contemporary Humanism* (Eugene: Wipf and Stock, 1983).

But at its core, the Age of Unbelief affected Western society in an even greater way. We know atheism and evolution have been used to justify the mass-murder of people in both concentration camps and abortion mills. And as unfortunate and tragic as the deaths of millions of innocent people have been, and as severe the consequences they brought upon society and families, the most significant effect modernity brought was a change in the *way* people hold their beliefs. In his book, *The Real Face of Atheism*, noted evangelist and apologist Ravi Zacharias charts the true consequences of atheism.[43] Throughout his career, Zacharias has been privileged with the opportunity of speaking before audiences in the post-Soviet world. Zacharias is famous for his open question and answer formats. During one Q&A forum, after Zacharias spent an hour explaining the intellectual, moral, and societal consequences of atheism, a student came up to the microphone to ask a question. The student asked, "What do you mean by the word God?" Think of the true condition of that man. He grew up under the strict confines of a Communist country where the concept of God was not only dismissed academically but was banned politically. The consequences of such a belief are profound for our day and age, for that man serves as a paradigm to understand our secular age: *We live in an age where the conditions of belief have not only made it impossible for people to believe in God, but to have any rational understanding of what we mean by the very term "God."*[44]

There have been severe secular consequences for Western society as it has embraced the philosophical tenets of skepticism, agnosticism, atheism, and postmodernism. However, there have also been religious responses to the Age of Unbelief.

*Religious Responses*

When modernity burst on the scene, it did not diffuse equally or at the same rate. One would be academically irresponsible to claim that secularism has affected small-town Iowa in the same way it has affected New York City or the University of North Carolina at Chapel Hill. There have been two broad responses to modernism: accommodation and resistance. Accommodation to modernity is found in two forms: secular and religious accommodation. Secular accommodation finds its identity in a variety of schools of thought including skepticism, agnosticism, existentialism, and atheism. Religious accommodation is unique in that,

---

[43] Ravi Zacharias, *The Real Face of Atheism* (Grand Rapids: Baker Books, 2004).
[44] Ibid., 20.

unlike secular accommodations, religious figures wanted to merge or synthesize Christianity to fit with the accepted academic philosophies of the academy. They were unwilling to completely disregard Christianity altogether; instead, they wanted to make it more palatable with academic elites and their vision for society at large. Religious resistance, on the other hand, was unwilling both to embrace the tenets of modernity and its vision for society. Resistance figures believed the philosophical presuppositions of modernity undermined the core tenets of the Christian faith. If there is no way to know if God exists, then any meaningful concept of the doctrine of God or divine revelation are futile. If miracles are impossible, then belief in any of the biblical miracles are irrational and mythical. Therefore, religious resistance figures rejected modernity's agnosticism, skepticism, and an anti-supernatural worldview in favor of the Christian worldview.

The differences can best be understood against the backdrop of history. The father of modern-day theological Liberalism is Friedrich Schleiermacher (1768-1834).[45] During Schleiermacher's time, Kant's agnosticism was the prevailing philosophy. Kant had already published his famous *Critique of Pure Reason*; however, he also published a lesser-known work titled, *Religion within the Boundaries of Mere Reason*.[46] The purpose behind Kant's book was to synthesize religion with agnosticism. If it is true that reason has limits and that humanity is unable to have any true or sure knowledge of transcendental metaphysics, then all knowledge of God is left wanting. Kant, therefore, attempts to delineate a view of religion, which includes Christianity, based solely upon reason, not revelation. No longer can theologians come to theological conclusions *via* natural theology or special revelation. Schleiermacher agreed with Kant and attempted to take his theses even further by applying them to Christianity. For that reason, Schleiermacher is considered the father of modern-day theological Liberalism.[47]

In his work, *Christian Faith*, Schleiermacher attempts to synthesize the modern Kantian worldview in order to make it palatable to what he considers the "Cultured Despisers of Religion."[48] In this work, Schleiermacher attempts to argue that God is known by feeling or of a sense

---

[45] John Frame, *A History of Western Philosophy* (Phillipsburg: R&R Publishing, 2015), 293.

[46] Immanuel Kant, *Religion within the Boundaries of Mere Reason*, edited by Allen Wood and George di Giovanni (Cambridge: Cambridge University Press, 1998).

[47] C. W. Christian, *Friedrich Schleiermacher: Makers of the Modern Theological Mind* (Peabody: Hendrickson Publishers, 1979).

[48] Friedrich Schleiermacher, *Christian Faith: A New Translation and Critical Edition* (Louisville: Westminster John Knox Press, 2016); *On Religion: Speeches to its Cultured Despisers*, edited by Richard Crouter (Cambridge: Cambridge University Press, 1996).

of "absolute dependence." He critiqued individuals like Kant, who viewed religion primarily as a way of living or doing (i.e., as a type of morality and character). For Schleiermacher, true religion is found in feeling. He writes, "Look especially at those extraordinary moments when a person's spirit is so caught up in the highest reaches of piety that all other activities known to you are restrained, almost supplanted by it—moments in which one's feeling is wholly absorbed in an immediate sense of the infinite and eternal and of its fellowship with the soul."[49] In addition, divine revelation must be understood as non-cognitive and non-propositional. John Frame argues that a "Principle of Radical Autonomy" is prevalent in Schleiermacher's work, claiming:

> Schleiermacher's work does not contain the adulation of reason characteristic of Kant and Hegel. He prefers to speak of autonomous feeling rather than of autonomous reasoning. But in the end, there is not much difference between these. And of course, Schleiermacher's writings are not merely expressions of feeling. They are rational analyses of feeling. And because of Schleiermacher's understanding of revelation, these analyses are immune to the authority of divine revelation.[50]

The consequence of this view of radical autonomy of human reason is revelation no longer communicates meaningful content in propositional form. Schleiermacher's view reduces to the position "God is unknowable to the human intellect." Instead of looking for God in nature or special revelation, we must look within. God is known through a special kind of feeling, that feeling of absolute dependence.

Schleiermacher went on to reinterpret most of the major doctrines of the Christian faith in terms of ultimate dependence, which he subjectively considered the essence of the Christian faith. Throughout his works, Schleiermacher viewed God as absolutely transcendent, so much so that Jesus Christ is essentially an "archetype of religious feeling."[51] Frame also claims Schleiermacher attempted to escape Lessing's ditch by redefining the nature of redemption. He writes:

> Schleiermacher describes redemption not as an accomplishment of divine acts in history, but as (a) a universal process through which all people are raised to their highest potential of religious

---

[49] Friedrich Schleiermacher, *On Religion: Addresses in Response to Its Cultured Critics* (Richmond: John Knox Press, 1969), 55.
[50] Frame, *A History of Philosophy*, 299-300.
[51] Ibid., 300.

consciousness, and (b) a subjective, individual process wherein that religious consciousness progresses to perfection in each individual. So the history of redemption becomes a mere metaphor for the development of man's religious sensibility. And the grace of God becomes synonymous with man's best efforts.[52]

Religious accommodationists from the nineteenth-century such as Friedrich Schleiermacher, Albrecht Ritschl, Wilhelm Herrmann, Adolf von Harnack, Soren Kierkegaard; and from the twentieth-century such as Karl Barth, Emil Brunner, Rudolf Bultmann, or Paul Tillich were to some degree willing to accommodate Christianity to the intellectual *milieu* of their day. It would be unfair to claim each person went as far as Schleiermacher and completely redefined the traditional notion of the Christian faith. Some, such as Karl Barth, attempted to take a mediating position by synthesizing it with existentialism and the dialectical method, creating present-day neo-orthodoxy. Soren Kierkegaard did not completely disregard historical Christianity; instead, he attempted to synthesize Christianity with existentialism to create a subjective form of Christianity. Unfortunately, whether we are talking about Schleiermacher or Ritschl, Kierkegaard or Barth, each one in their own way undermines some tenet of historic and orthodox Christianity.[53]

In response to this trajectory towards liberalism and neo-orthodoxy there were several orthodox religious figures who resisted modernity. Many Christian apologists and pastors, such as Jonathan Edwards and Charles Spurgeon, were considered resistance type figures. Edwards resisted liberalism and its attack on confessional Christianity by penning several books responding to the academic elites at schools such at Harvard and Yale; Charles Spurgeon stood for biblical truth during the Downgrade Controversy publishing several defenses of Christianity; and the Princetonian theologians, Hodge and Warfield, tirelessly worked to defend historic Christianity. Each of these figures, in their own way, recognized that divine revelation (whether it be natural or special revelation) is the grounds to resist the modern worldview. However, for our purposes, one figure stands out above the rest not because he published more works or because he was the most influential figure; rather it is because he resisted to the point of founding a new seminary and denomination. That figure is J. Gresham Machen.

---

[52] Ibid., 300-301.

[53] Geisler spent ample time throughout his career critiquing neo-orthodox theology and Higher Criticism.

During the height of the Modernist controversy, which sought to reconcile Christianity with modernity, Princeton Theological Seminary was locked in a battle for biblical truth. The American battle was initiated by the Warfield/Briggs debate when Charles Briggs, a professor at Union Seminary in New York, denied biblical inspiration. B.B. Warfield and A.A. Hodge responded strongly with both with books and articles. Hodge and Warfield wrote *Inspiration* (1881). Their views formed what has come to be known as the Old Princeton view, which taught that the Bible *is* the very Word of God. It does not *contain* or *become* the Word of God; rather, it is the Word of God. Debates over the total truthfulness of the Word of God dominated the fundamentalist-modernist controversy in the 1920s and 1930s. It was centered in the Presbyterian Church in the USA over the Auburn affirmation and was expressed by some withdrawing from Princeton Theological Seminary in 1929. That year a group of students followed Machen, including Robert Dick Wilson, Oswald T. Allis, Cornelius Van Till, and Ned Stonehouse to form Westminster Theological Seminary.[54]

Machen's most influential and well-known book discussing the controversy between liberalism and Christianity is titled *Christianity and Liberalism*.[55] Commenting in the foreword of the book, Carl Trueman notes:

> The context of *Christianity and Liberalism* (the so-called modernist-fundamentalist battles of the early twentieth century) and its central thesis (that liberalism is not a legitimate form of historic Christianity but rather a different religion entirely) meant that, from the moment of its publication, it was seen as a piece of religious fundamentalism, albeit well written and originating from the pen of an academic whose intellectual and scholarly credentials could not be questioned. . . . It is no wonder, then, that liberalism is totally different from Christianity, for the foundation is different. Christianity is founded upon the Bible. It bases upon the Bible both its thinking and its life. Liberalism on the other hand is founded upon the shifting emotions of sinful men.[56]

Throughout the book, Machen proceeds to compare Christianity with modern theological liberalism. He argued that modernity's worldview

---

[54] Norman L. Geisler and William C. Roach, *Defending Inerrancy: Affirming the Accuracy of Scripture for a New Generation* (Grand Rapids: Baker, 2011), 19.

[55] J. Gresham Machen, *Christianity & Liberalism*, New Edition (Grand Rapids: Eerdmans, 2009).

[56] Ibid., ix-x, xv.

demands its adherents be hostile to "doctrine" traditionally defined. Historically, doctrine was viewed as the effect of divine revelation, which is forbidden within the modern worldview. Christianity must also be based upon real historical events, not myth or religious sentiment. Machen writes, "It is conceivable that Christianity may now have to be abandoned, and another religion substituted for it; but at any rate the question what Christianity is can be determined only by an examination of the beginnings of Christianity."[57] Machen argued that we can neither do away with the teachings and life of Jesus, nor the doctrines of Paul. He contended that Jesus was not the founder of a non-doctrinal, non-historical religion.[58] Rather, he asserted that Christianity is founded upon real historical events and the surety of divine revelation. In short, for Christianity to be *Christianity* it must resist and reject modernity.

Following this time period there arose a host of younger evangelicals, who were committed to historic Protestant doctrine, but had to engage in an ever-changing era.[59] These figures included men such as Carl F. H. Henry, Gleason Archer, Harold Ockenga, Billy Graham, John Gerstner, Gordon Clark, Cornelius Van Til, Roger Nicole, and the like. Each of them were highly skilled and university-trained theologians and philosophers. Their goal was to make an impact upon American and Western society at large through either mass evangelism, publications, or by founding robust academic institutions.[60] For our purposes, however, we will not attempt to retrace the history of early evangelicalism. Rather, what must be understood about this period is that its key figures rightly understood that evangelicalism was situated within the broader context of modernity. For evangelicals to engage with the gospel, they had to resist modernity's children (e.g., skepticism, agnosticism, relativism, atheism, etc.).

Ideas have consequences, and the origin of modernity's ideas left Western society reaping the ill effects of skepticism, agnosticism, atheism, and theological liberalism. The spiritual consequences of modernity are of eternal significance. We have gone from a time when the goal was that every plowboy knew the New Testament to an age in which entire countries no longer seem to understand what we mean by the very term "God." Western civilization is sick, and Christianity is the answer. The twentieth-century required an apologetic engagement. Not only were

---

[57] Ibid., 18.

[58] Ibid, 26.

[59] George M. Marsden, *Understanding Fundamentalism and Evangelicalism* (Grand Rapids: Eerdmans, 1991).

[60] George M. Marsden, *Reforming Fundamentalism: Fuller Seminary And The New Evangelicalism* (Grand Rapids: Eerdmans, 1987).

Christians required to deal with the content of modernity's ideas, but the conditions of belief upon which those beliefs are held. In brief, twentieth-century evangelicals had to prepare for an apologetics battle, and twenty-first century Christians had better learn from their forefathers in the faith *how* to engage apologetically in an Age of Unbelief.

## Evangelical Resistance to the Age of Unbelief

The prophetic voice for evangelical apologetic engagement during the twentieth-century was the late Francis Schaeffer. Schaeffer penned several famous books calling for Christians to engage the culture in the arena of ideas and beckoning them to rational and moral consistency. Of course, Schaeffer did not believe the non-Christian worldview was consistent, or could the non-Christian could live according to the axioms of that false worldview. The breakdown of the non-Christian worldview provided the opportunity for the evangelical to demonstrate the comprehensive cohesion of the Christian worldview. Christians are not to merely engage within their intellectual and social ghettos; rather, we are to engage in God's world and demonstrate both the foolishness of unbelief and the wisdom of God manifest in the Christian worldview.

There was a trailblazer in many ways in the person of Francis Schaeffer. Several individuals took up Schaeffer's call for evangelical engagement. These figures include apologists who came from Reformed and non-Reformed camps, presuppositionalists and evidentialists, academically trained and non-academically trained. They engaged through a variety of means, whether that be through the academy and publishing like Carl F. H. Henry, or in the arena of the academy and debating like Greg Bahnsen. Some, such as D. James Kennedy and John MacArthur, served in both academic and pastoral roles; others such as R. C. Sproul founded *Ligonier Ministries* and developed a large media outlet to train Christians to defend the historic Christian faith. Christians such as Kenneth Kanzter worked to solidify theological institutions to create platforms for evangelicals to engage academically and train future pastors and theologians. The point being the figures from this era are each unique in their approach and influence; however, each one in their own way and in their own context attempted to fulfill Schaeffer's vision to let the world know that God *exists* and he is *not* silent. Who took up that challenge to let the world know that God really exists and is not silent, and that the Scriptures are still relevant? Who let evangelicals know they must not escape from reason? This book will argue that Dr. Norman Geisler is one man who took on that challenge to bring intellectual credibility to the presentation of the gospel. This book will argue that Geisler ought to be considered an indispensable figure for twentieth-century evangelicalism, and in many ways, evangelicalism would not be as evangelical in its theology today if it were not for the person and work of Norman Geisler.

*Thumbnail Sketch of Norman Geisler*

To those who ask, "Who is Norman Geisler?", some have said, "If you can imagine a cross between Thomas Aquinas and Billy Graham, you're not too far off." Dr. Geisler was known for his brilliant mind and evangelistic heart. Geisler lived during a time in which evangelicalism was growing and thousands—if not millions—of people were embracing Jesus Christ as their Lord and Savior. On the other hand, evangelicalism was also facing several battles outside of the Church from secularists who opposed the Christian message, as well as from mediating evangelicals who were willing to compromise evangelical convictions for a place at the table.[61] One could truly say, throughout this time period, that it was both the best of times and the worst of times for evangelicalism.

However, to understand the impact of Norman Geisler, one must recognize the tremendous obstacles he had to overcome in life. Dr. Geisler was born into a working-class family in Warren, Michigan, on July 21, 1932. Many of Geisler's readers are unaware of the fact that he did not come from a Christian family, nor was he raised in an educated family. At the age of nine, Norm was invited by a little boy down the street to attend Vacation Bible School. After VBS was over, Mr. Costie or Mr. Keel, and his family faithfully picked Geisler up every Sunday to go to church. At the age of seventeen, as a senior in high school, Norman Geisler came home one Sunday and knelt by his bed and accepted Jesus Christ as his Lord and Savior. Dr. Geisler used to like to tell this story and joke about how he was saved because of a local church "bus ministry." In the grand scheme of things and God's providence, those bus drivers were used to help launch the ministry of one of America's greatest Christian theologians and apologists.[62]

During his senior year of high school, someone brought up the idea of Dr. Geisler going to college. "It never even crossed my mind to go to college" Geisler would say on numerous occasions. As was said, Geisler was

---

[61] John A. D'Elia, *A Place at the Table: George Eldon Ladd and the Rehabilitation of Evangelical Scholarship in America* (New York: Oxford University Press, 2008).

[62] This information is well known about Geisler's life. However, the print version of this story is taken from Geisler's obituary published at his funeral on July 1, 2019 at Calvary Church in Charlotte, NC 28226.

born into a working-class family where no one in his family and most people from his community did not attend college. In addition, Geisler had to overcome one more significant obstacle before he entered college—namely, by his own admission, Geisler graduated high school virtually illiterate. When asked, "How did you get through high school without knowing how to read?" He would reply, "I just listened to the lectures and somehow figured out how to pass the tests." Not only was Geisler illiterate, he also suffered from a typical teenage attitude. For example, in school one time a teacher asked him, "How did the *Tale of Two Cities* end?' and Geisler replied, "With a period!" As funny as his answer may have been, Geisler told several of us that that answer granted him a one-way ticket to the principal's office. The point being Geisler was completely unqualified by all worldly standards to attend college. This is a significant point that marks Norman Geisler's life. It is a testimony to God's grace who took this man from being a snarky illiterate high school kid to one of the most prolific authors in the evangelical world.

It took Dr. Geisler eight years to complete college. He originally attended Emmaus Bible School, earning a diploma in 1950. He also attended William Tyndale College from 1950-55, earning another diploma, and the University of Detroit from 1956-57. It was not until 1958 Geisler completed his B.A. in philosophy from Wheaton College. During this time, he also married Barbara Jean Cate on June 24, 1955, and they started their family. Barbara was a graduate of Fort Wayne Bible College, where she pursued a degree in music. Norm and Barbara were married for sixty-four years and had six children. Norm went on to complete a M.A. in theology from Wheaton in 1960 and a Th.B. from William Tyndale College in 1964. For several years, Geisler studied philosophy at Wayne State University (1964), Northwestern University (1968), and eventually Loyola University in Chicago, where he earned a Ph.D. in 1970.[63]

Throughout this period, Dr. Geisler also served on staff at several churches and institutions. He worked as a graduate assistant at Wheaton College and a part-time and full-time professor at Detroit Bible College from 1959-1966. During this same period, he worked as the Director of the Northeast Suburban Youth for Christ, near Detroit, from 1952-1954. He also served as a pastor at Dayton Center Church in Silverwood, MI, from 1955-1957. Geisler was ordained in 1956 at Dayton Center Church. He also served as an assistant pastor of River Grove Church in River Grove, IL from 1958-59. Other ministry experience throughout his career, beyond his well-

---

[63] This information can be found on Dr. Geisler's website: http://normangeisler.com/about/ Accessed on 10/11/2019.

known speaking ministry included: Pastor of Memorial Baptist Church, Warren, MI 1960-1963; interim pastorates in Michigan, Illinois, and Texas; "Quest for Truth" radio ministry from 1981-1991, and the senior pastor of Southern Evangelical Church, Charlotte, NC 2003-2007. Dr. Geisler was most famous for his teaching ministry. His most notable institutions include: *Trinity Evangelical Divinity School* 1970-1979, where he served as the chairman of the philosophy of religion program. *Dallas Theological Seminary* from 1979-1988, where he served as professor of Systematic Theology. He was the dean of the Liberty Center for Research and Scholarship at Lynchburg, VA from 1989-1991. Geisler also co-founded *Southern Evangelical Seminary* in 1992, serving as a dean from 1992-1999 and president from 1999-2006. He also co-founded *Veritas Evangelical Seminary in 2007*, which is currently named *Veritas International University*. Geisler was influential in co-founding the *Evangelical Philosophical Society* and the *International Society of Christian Apologetics*. He served as the president of the *Evangelical Theological Society*, *Evangelical Philosophical Society*, and *International Society of Christian Apologetics*. Geisler also was a co-founder of the *International Council on Biblical Inerrancy* and on the draft committee of the *Chicago Statement on Biblical Inerrancy*. Finally, Dr. Geisler was a prolific author and debater, holding debates with several top thinkers and co-authoring over one hundred and twenty books and hundreds of articles.

God clearly gifted Dr. Geisler with a great sense of calling and self-discipline. He was given the ability to serve the evangelical church through the power of the pen and the pulpit. There is no other explanation on this side of heaven, other than the grace of God, for why Dr. Geisler overcame such difficulties. Throughout biblical history, we see God using people whom the world deems to be unqualified. By a great demonstration of his power and wisdom, God takes these types of individuals and molds them into key figures to be used for his kingdom. One anonymous writer penned a poem that captures this sentiment well, titled: *When God Wants to Drill a Man*. The poem reads:

> When God wants to drill a man,
> And thrill a man,
> And skill a man
> When God wants to mold a man
> To play the noblest part;
>
> When He yearns with all His heart
> To create so great and bold a man
> That all the world shall be amazed,
> Watch His methods, watch His ways!

> How He ruthlessly perfects
> Whom He royally elects!
> How He hammers him and hurts him,
> And with mighty blows converts him
>
> Into trial shapes of clay which
> Only God understands;
> While his tortured heart is crying
> And he lifts beseeching hands!
>
> How He bends but never breaks
> When his good He undertakes;
> How He uses whom He chooses,
> And which every purpose fuses him;
> By every act induces him
> To try His splendor out-
> God knows what He's about.
>
> – Anonymous

The life and ministry of Dr. Geisler capture the sentiments of this poet's writing well. When God set out to mold the man of Norman Geisler, when he yearned with all his heart to create so great and bold a man, that all the world shall be amazed—watch his methods, watch his ways. For all of those who knew Dr. Geisler personally, they will tell you he was a very bold man for Christ. He was unwilling to back down from any formidable opponent who revolted against the knowledge of Christ. Geisler was wholeheartedly committed to defending evangelicalism in an age that voiced strong opposition to evangelical convictions.

## Approach to This Volume

The approach to this volume is not merely to restate Dr. Geisler's arguments, but rather to summarize some of the essential arguments as they relate to classical realism, classical apologetics, and the classic doctrine of inerrancy. The approach will attempt to situate the person and work of Norman Geisler within the twentieth and twenty-first century context and explain the significance of his apologetic method. Geisler's views represent the core convictions of historic evangelicalism, many of which are not in vogue or held by several present-day evangelical theologians.[64] It will be

---

[64] In order to understand many of the different ways a person can define and apply the definition in our day, please consult: Andrew David Nasalli and Collin Hansen, *Four Views*

demonstrated that Geisler's unique blend of biblical truth, theological insight, robust knowledge of philosophy, and ability to engage with conviction, zeal, and love are valuable for present-day theologians and apologists. Throughout Geisler's career, he sought to defend historic Christianity, which means he sought to defend classic evangelicalism. Geisler never minced words; therefore, he clearly defined what he meant by the term "evangelicalism" and the scope of issues he sought to defend. In his *Systematic Theology*, Geisler defines evangelical theology in the following terms:

> *Evangelical* theology is defined here as a discourse about God that maintains there are certain essential Christian beliefs. These include, but are not necessary limited to, the infallibility and inerrancy of the Bible alone, the tri-unity of God, the virgin birth of Christ, the deity of Christ, the all-sufficiency of Christ's atoning sacrifice for sin, the physical and miraculous resurrection of Christ, the necessity of salvation by faith alone through God's grace alone based on the work of Christ alone, the physical bodily return of Christ to earth, the eternal conscious bliss of the saved, and the eternal conscious punishment of the unsaved.[65]

The title of this volume is *Defending Evangelicalism*. In many ways, Dr. Geisler spent his career defending the essential Christian beliefs of classic evangelicalism. His life's work and career were dedicated to defending the legitimacy of philosophical realism and its role in Christian prolegomena, the core tenets of classical theism, classical apologetics, and the inspiration and inerrancy of the Bible. The following chapters will draw from many of Geisler's published and posthumously published works to unapologetically present Geisler's approach against the backdrop of modernity and engage the conditions of belief presented by present-day secularism.

---

on *The Spectrums of Evangelicalism* (Grand Rapids: Zondervan, 2011). I would contend that Norman Geisler fits the "Confessional Evangelicalism" model advocated by Dr. R. Albert Mohler.

[65] Norman L. Geisler, *Systematic Theology: Introduction and Bible* (Minneapolis: Bethany House, 2002), 15.

# CHAPTER TWO

# Defending Classical Realism

## Introduction

In the previous chapter, it was claimed Norman Geisler's theological approach appeared in the context of classic evangelicalism.[66] This world contained noted figures such as Kenneth Kantzer, Carl F. H. Henry, J. I. Packer, R. C. Sproul, John Gerstner, Greg Bahnsen, D. James Kennedy, and many more. One common theme amongst this group was a philosophical orientation to their theological enterprise and apologetic methodology. When Norman Geisler took up his post as one of evangelicalism's foremost apologists, the apologetic situation presented by theological and philosophical modernity required a robust defense of the nature of truth before the watching world. Classic evangelical figures from the twentieth-century, Geisler included, devoted their thinking to demonstrate a consistent Protestant worldview and evangelical theology. They were committed both to the inerrancy of the Bible and a worldview able to engage the broader world of philosophical ideas and secular theses.

This chapter will establish the fact Norman Geisler operated within the context of a traditional evangelical apologetic, which argued that reality is knowable and that the nature of apologetics is to defend the Christian faith rationally. Second, it will explain the significance of Geisler's Thomistic approach to philosophical prolegomena and apologetics. Third, it will explain the nature of first principles, objectivity in interpretation, and the objective nature of cognitive-propositional language. Finally, it will discuss several key factors that make Geisler's approach unique amongst evangelical apologists.

---

[66] See: Andrew Davis Naselli and Collin Hansen, eds, *Four Views on The Spectrum of Evangelicalism* (Grand Rapids: Zondervan, 2011).

William C. Roach

# Evangelicals and The Question of Truth

Robert E. Weber wrote a book titled, *The Younger Evangelicals*.[67] Throughout his book, Weber attempts to introduce his readers to many of the leaders who shaped the evangelical movement. Specifically, Weber's book attempts to explain *how* these leaders tried to "Face the challenges of the new world." By the "new world", Weber means the new world of philosophical and theological modernity and postmodernity.[68] Anyone familiar with Weber's work knows he attempts to embrace much of theological and philosophical modernity and postmodernity. Weber believes the best way to engage a post-truth age is to embrace that philosophical axiom as an operant part of theological and apologetic methodology. While classic evangelicals ought to reject Weber's embrace of postmodernism, we might want to welcome the analysis of his idea evangelicals ought to reflect upon many of the challenges we face in the new world, specifically as they affect the categories of biblical worldview, evangelical apologetics, and systematic theology.

*The way* we answer the question, "How ought evangelicals face the new world?" will determine much of our philosophical views and apologetic methodology. Weber provides his readers a helpful way to understand the differences between what he labels as: Traditional, Pragmatic, and Younger Evangelicals. He claims:[69]

|  | Traditional Evangelicals | Pragmatic Evangelicals | Younger Evangelicals |
|---|---|---|---|
| Place of Reason in Faith | The evidence demands a verdict | Rational<br><br>Experiential | Mystery, but Christianity is intelligible |
| Worldview | Truth can be separated from experience so that a worldview can stand on its own | Truth and experience go hand in hand | Truth must be embodied<br><br>Truth is known only by those who live it |

---

[67] Robert E. Weber, *The Younger Evangelicals: Facing the Challenges of the New World* (Grand Rapids, Baker, 2002).

[68] Ibid., 44-54.

[69] Ibid., 105-106.

| Type of Apologetic | Rational apologetics. It stands the test of reason | Success apologetics<br><br>It works | Incarnational apologetics<br><br>The community lives it |
|---|---|---|---|
| Revelation | An inerrant Bible is the foundation upon which truth is based | The Bible is the foundation of our knowledge<br><br>Christianity starts with an authoritative Bible.<br><br>Inerrancy held, but not an issue | Knowledge is incarnate in the person of Jesus Christ<br><br>The Bible infallibly takes us to Jesus, the living embodiment of truth |
| Christian Theory and the Social Sciences | Social sciences are used to support Christianity | The social sciences are points of contact | Theology is the queen of sciences<br><br>Sciences are interpreted by theology, not the other way around |
| Christianity and Philosophy | Philosophy is used to support a Christian worldview | Attention is given to Christianity as a philosophy of meaning | Philosophy returns to a way of life: wisdom and guidance |
| Christianity and World Religions | Christianity is right; world religions are wrong | Little attention is paid to other religions | New interest in comparing Christianity with Islam |

For evangelicals of all varieties, the challenge presented was the nature of truth in a post-truth, post-foundationalist, and post-propositional age. More importantly, evangelicals had to deal with the fact that they claim to have an absolute, objective, inspired, infallible, and inerrant Bible, which maintains that facts are true for everyone, whether they are in America, Asia, or Africa, and that people can know those truths. For classic evangelicals, reason is the same everywhere and brings all people, regardless of their circumstances or cultural situation, to the same objective knowledge.[70] Many pragmatic evangelicals responded by suggesting there are many subjective factors in the appropriation of truth. They claim that truth must be understood in its proper cultural setting (i.e., we must contextualize truth unto the particular people group we are trying to reach).[71] Weber insists:

> This view created confusion among evangelicals over the use of the word *inerrant*. With the admission that scriptural interpretation is in some measure a personal and subjective enterprise, *inerrant* lost its meaning and has never recovered. Furthermore, the rise of contextual interpretation made a crack in the strict propositionalism of the evangelical who had demanded uniformity of interpretation. Now a clear allowance for the different cultural interpretations of Scripture was fully accepted. Because contextualism made the defense of Scripture through reason more difficult to maintain, more general approaches to Scripture were presented, such as "Scripture is inerrant in all that it *intends*," or "Scripture is inerrant in matters of faith and practice but not in matters of history and science."[72]

This transition within evangelicalism gave way to a new understanding of truth, and a new trajectory for evangelical hermeneutics and apologetic methodology. Most of the posturing by this new group of evangelicals was a conscious effort to distance themselves from classic evangelicals and their apologetic methodologies.

In his book, *Reforming Fundamentalism: Fuller Seminary and the New Evangelicalism*, George Marsden illustrates this battle between the spectrums of evangelical belief at Fuller Theological Seminary. Fuller Seminary was established as a bulwark for evangelical theology. Many of its key founders, including Carl F. H. Henry and several influential faculty, such as Harold Lindsell, embraced the core tenets of classic evangelical prolegomena and theology. However, as time progressed and there continued to be a changing of the guard, Fuller Theological Seminary had to respond to the questions of modernity both before the watching world and before the gazing mirror. There was a clear crisis and turning point at the seminary over the very nature of truth and the Bible as God's inerrant Word. Marsden claims, "The tensions over the struggles for control and the parallel tensions over differing views of Scripture suddenly erupted in a scene that left everyone shaken. After 'Black Saturday,' as the incident came

---

[70] Ibid., 98.
[71] Ibid.
[72] Ibid.

to be called, little hope remained for reconciliation."[73] The faculty were divided over issues related to Mosaic authorship of the Pentateuch, the historicity of Adam and Eve, the erosion of the classic doctrine of inerrancy, reservations about the doctrinal statement (in particular, as it speaks to the doctrine of inerrancy), and the nature of theological method.[74] Inerrancy was the watershed issue that divided the faculty. Many of the "new guard" were trying to escape from the classic definition of inerrancy under the guise of "hermeneutics" and a revised definition of "truth" and "error."[75] As history marched forward, Fuller Seminary proved to undo its evangelical identity and consistency because they jettisoned a clear commitment to both the inerrancy of Scripture and the objective nature of truth. Harold Lindsell proved to be correct when he claimed, "Down the road, whether it takes five or fifty years, any institution that departs from belief in an inerrant Scripture will likewise depart from other fundamentals of the faith and at lease cease to be evangelical in the historical meaning of the term."[76] In short, many pragmatic evangelicals faced the new world of modernity by accommodating unto it. The net result was the erosion of its philosophical and theological foundations.

The rise of the new evangelical left was marked by a post-foundational, post-conservative, and in many ways a post-liberal approach to philosophy and theology. Post-foundational theologians jettisoned the objective nature of truth in favor of postmodernism. For postmodernists, the belief in grounding or knowing metaphysical reality is over. They happily embraced metaphysical idealism and gave up on the so-called "modernist" pursuit of one true picture of reality, objective knowledge, and the knowing subject as a source of knowledge.[77] Stanley Grenz in his *Primer for Postmodernism*, claims:

> Meaning is not inherent in the text itself, they [deconstructionists] argue, but emerge only as the interpreter enters into dialogue with the text. And because the meaning of a text is dependent on the perspective of the one who enters into the dialogue with it, it has as many meanings as it has readers (or readings).[78]

---

[73] George M. Marsden, *Reforming Fundamentalism: Fuller Seminary and the New Evangelicalism* (Grand Rapids: Eerdmans, 1987), 208.

[74] Ibid., 208-215.

[75] Ibid., 216.

[76] Harold Lindsell, *The Battle for the Bible* (Grand Rapids: Zondervan, 1976), 120-121.

[77] William F. Lawhead, *The Voyage of Discovery: A Historical Introduction to Philosophy* 2nd ed (Belmont: Wadsworth, 2002), 559.

[78] Stanley J. Grenz, *A Primer on Postmodernism* (Grand Rapids: Eerdmans, 1996), 6.

Stanley Grenz, John Franke, Brian McLaren, and Robert Weber each illustrate postmodern approaches to truth and evangelical theology. Weber claims, "Postfoundationalism asserts that Christianity can stand on its own; it needs no rational defense."[79] Since reality cannot be known directly, there is no need to rationally defend the Christian faith. Apologetics reduces unto lived experiences and incarnational appropriations, not the objective defense of the Christian faith.

Post-liberalism and post-conservative approaches to the nature of truth are dominant in many evangelical circles. Many are not willing or brave enough to embrace a fully orbed postmodernism, so they rest their uneasy consciences by embracing what they deem as a nuanced or moderate approach to the nature of truth, hermeneutics, and evangelical apologetics. This predominant "Third-Way" approach attempts to embrace many subjective elements of Pragmatic and Younger evangelicalism, while trying to maintain some sense that humanity can form knowledge about reality. The key figure representing this approach to Scripture and theology is George Lindbeck. Lindbeck encourages Christians to have the biblical text's framework determine the cultural-linguistic lenses through which we attempt to view everything else. For Lindbeck, theological exegesis is something that takes place by the community and in the community. Theology is something that is the practice and participation in what has been labeled as a "sociology of knowledge" approach. Lindbeck rejects the conservative tendency to label doctrine as some type of cognitive-propositionalism and the liberal tendency to identify doctrine as nothing more than symbolic expressions of personal experience. For Lindbeck, the truth of theology is not found in its proper exegesis or systematic formulation. Rather, exegesis is to be something practical, with the purpose of edifying the cultural-linguistic community of the local church.[80] Moreover, apologetics is something that is supposed to be a community engagement. We are to move beyond the pursuit of reason and truth. Apologetics is reduced unto the embodiment of truth, not the rational defense of the truth of the Christian faith.[81]

So far, we have seen there are three predominant ways evangelicals answer the question: How *ought* evangelicals face the new world? The answers range from outright rejections to complete accommodation unto

---

[79] Weber, *The Younger Evangelicals*, 99.

[80] William C. Roach, "Modern and Contemporary Hermeneutics" in *Hermeneutics as Epistemology: A Critical Assessment of Carl F. H. Henry's Epistemological Approach to Hermeneutics* (Eugene: Wipf and Stock, 2015), 32.

[81] See: James W. Sire, *Apologetics Beyond Reason: Why Seeing Reality is Believing* (Westmont: Intervarsity Press, 2014).

modernity, with a plethora of approaches somewhere in the middle. The following section is going to answer the question: How did Norman Geisler face the new world? Moreover, we live in a time when many evangelicals are claiming traditional approaches to truth (such as Geisler's) ought to be forgotten. Many say yes, but this author says no!

## Methodical Realism and Question of Truth

For several years, I served as the personal assistant to Norman Geisler. One of my position's benefits included meeting top evangelical scholars at various conferences, schools, and events. I remember one time before Dr. Geisler gave a lecture at a large evangelical seminary, several of us went out to eat at a local restaurant. The current dean of the seminary at the time, who in many ways was an up and coming intellectual within broader evangelicalism, asked Geisler, "How did you come to your personal theological and apologetic views?" I believe the man asking the question was looking for a much more elaborate answer, mainly because this individual was favorable to many trends within the TIS (Theological Interpretation of Scripture) approach to theology and hermeneutics. The TIS approach is hesitant to embrace the objective nature of truth, objectivity in interpretation, and the consistency of cognitive-propositional approaches to truth and language. Geisler said, "I embraced the idea from Augustine, Aquinas, the Reformers, and the Princetonians that truth about reality was knowable." I could tell the dean was taken back: Was it really that simple? Does so much of our theological method really boil down to whether truth exists and truth is knowable?

Norman Geisler was trained within the broader Platonic tradition in philosophy. By claiming Geisler was committed to the "Platonic tradition" one should not interpret it to mean he was a Platonist. The use of the term "The Platonic tradition" is used to mean he was committed to both ontological and epistemological realism. Peter Kreeft claims, "The Platonic tradition in Western philosophy is not just one of many [equal] traditions. It is so much *the* central one that the very existence and survival of Western civilization depends on it."[82] Plato was committed to a stable reality of forms that can be known by reason. Several key figures throughout Western philosophy embraced this tradition, including Aristotle, Plotinus, Augustine, Anselm, and Aquinas. The main difference between these thinkers is not that each one denied the forms, but rather that they gave the forms a new

---

[82] Peter Kreeft, *The Platonic Tradition* (South Bend: St. Augustine's Press, 2018), 3.

metaphysical address.[83] Moreover, much of modernity can be understood as abandoning the Platonic tradition, starting with Ockham's Nominalism, which gave rise to all sorts of philosophical errors resulting in the Empiricism of Locke and Hume, Kant's Copernican Revolution in philosophy—resulting in Agnosticism, and the so-called "analytic philosophy" which dominates English and American philosophy departments.[84] In brief, what separates Norman Geisler's approach from many predominant evangelical approaches is his robust commitment to philosophical realism or the Platonic tradition of metaphysical and epistemological realism.

Not only was Norman Geisler committed to the broader Platonic tradition; he was, in particular, committed to the philosophical views of Thomas Aquinas.[85] Geisler used to say in many of his classes, "There is Thomism . . . and False" and "Don't throw out the philosophical baby—Aquinas with the Roman Catholic—bath water."[86] Geisler was a committed Thomist because of the way it brought systematic and methodological unity between philosophy and theology.[87] Due to Geisler's training in the history of philosophy, he was able to see many of the trends and trajectories (whether good or bad) throughout the history of ideas. In order to understand the various experiments in philosophy, Geisler used to recommend his students read Etienne Gilson's book, *The Unity of Philosophy Experience.*[88] Gilson, who was also a committed Thomist, recognized that Christian philosophy was marked by various philosophical tests or experiments. Gilson noted that there was the Medieval, Cartesian, and Modern experiments. The Medieval experiment claimed that reality exists and humanity could know it. The Cartesian and Modern experiments started to question the knowability of reality by jettisoning a commitment to metaphysical realism in favor of philosophical idealism. For example, Gilson claims that Cartesian and modern idealism can be understood as affirming the notion, "all that can be clearly and distinctly known as belonging to the idea of a thing can be said of the thing itself. As a matter of fact, it is the thing."[89] In other words, man does not know reality directly,

---

[83] Ibid.

[84] Ibid.

[85] Norman Geisler, *Thomas Aquinas: An Evangelical Appraisal* (Eugene: Wipf and Stock, 1991).

[86] https://normangeisler.com/twelve-things-from-doctor-g-for-his-students/

[87] See: Norman L. Geisler, ed. Paul A. Compton, *The Collected Essays of Norman L. Geisler, vol. 3: 1986-1994* (Matthews: Bastion Books, 2019), 218-223.

[88] Etienne Gilson, *The Unity of Philosophical Experience* (San Francisco: Ignatius Press, 1964).

[89] Ibid., 122.

but only their idea or the representational realism of the idea of the thing in reality; hence, idealism.

For Geisler and other committed Thomistic realists, the way to answer the questions of modernity is to reject the method of modernity at its very core. One of the key and distinct aspects of Geisler's philosophy is his commitment to discard the modern experiment. The way forward in philosophy is not found through accommodating and embracing Cartesian Idealism, Kant's Critical Philosophy, Representational Realism, Common Sense Realism, or Critical Realism. Rather, to have a proper methodical realism, one must embrace a specific understanding about nature and the philosophical order of being in reality (i.e., Scholastic Realism).[90] Quoting A. N. Whitehead, Gilson claims:

> 'When you find your theory of knowledge won't work, it's because there is something wrong with your metaphysics.' To this I [Gilson] would add, for my part, a further remark: in idealism nothing works. One ought not therefore to look for the remedy to idealism along the idealist path. The only conceivable remedy is to change one's metaphysics. No one can overcome idealism by opposing it from inside, because one cannot oppose it in such a way without surrendering to it. Idealism can only be overcome by dispensing with its very existence.[91]

Geisler and Gilson both recognized a variety of "realisms" existed throughout Western philosophy. The bold and unique claim by Thomistic realists is that many forms of realism erroneously embrace some type of idealistic or critical metaphysic or method. When describing the Thomistic method, Gilson quotes Spinoza, claiming, "'The scholastics,' said Spinoza, 'start from things; Descartes from thought; I start from God.'"[92] For Thomists, God is a transcendent Being, and there is a metaphysical fissure separating God as a necessary Being and creatures as contingent beings.[93] The world is seen as the free creation of God; hence, creation is not the rational or ontological deduction of God (i.e., Spinoza's Pantheism). Gilson claims:

> In fact, it is the opposite that is true—which shows how impossible the thing is. Not only can one not deduce the existence of the world from the existence of God, but equally,

---
[90] Etienne Gilson, *Methodological Realism* (Front Royal: Christendom Press, 1990).
[91] Ibid., 36.
[92] Ibid., 72.
[93] Ibid.

because we are ourselves part of the world, our knowledge comes up against the same metaphysical breach as our being. The human mind cannot have God as its natural and proper object. As a creature, it is directly proportioned only to created being, so much so that instead of being able to deduce the existence of things from God, it must, on the contrary, of necessity rest on things in order to ascend to God. So the smallest trace of Spinozism would be enough to ruin Thomist Epistemology.[94]

What this means is the human that mind has created reality as its proper object. We do not start with God or the presupposition of God as our proper starting point. Since human beings are part of the created world we are also restricted by the metaphysical limitations of the world. This means the infinite, eternal, immutable God of all creation is not the proper object of knowledge for finite, temporal, and changing beings. Aquinas, Geisler, and Gilson should not be interpreted at this point to be affirming some type of agnosticism pertaining to our knowledge of God. Rather, they recognize that a finite being can only have a finite knowledge of an infinite Being. Moreover, since humanity is made to know directly the essence of created things, and because God is not a created thing, the essence of God is not something we are able to know directly, but indirectly.[95] Finally, even the presupposition of the belief in God is still a finite mode of knowledge about an infinite Being, and because it is a finite idea, it bears a resemblance to a created essence; hence, it still is not direct knowledge of the very essence of God.

"No such radical break opposes Thomism to Cartestianism;" claims Gilson. "Far from it, for the two metaphysics are in agreement on more than one point. But their methods, at least, are irreducibly opposed."[96] "The opposition," Gilson says, "between these two methods rests on the opposition between two theories of knowledge. While Descartes finds being in thought, St. Thomas finds thought in being. What is at issue is not a paradox, but what for St. Thomas is an unshakable truth. The thought In question is our thought. But our thought, left to its own resources, is strictly incapable of passing from the virtual knowledge it has of itself to actual knowledge."[97] For Thomism, human beings know reality and then derive thoughts about reality. For idealism or critical approaches to knowledge, one starts with the mind and searches for reality. The difference between

---

[94] Ibid.

[95] See: Garrigou LaGrange, *God, His Existence and Nature: A Thomistic Solution to Certain Agnostic Antinomies* (New York: Herder Books, 1934).

[96] Gilson, *Methodical Realism*, 73.

[97] Ibid.

the two methods is that for idealism, the object of thought is thought; and for Thomism the object of thought is reality. The ability to start with reality and to know reality directly is one of the key and distinguishing marks of Thomistic realism.[98]

In Geisler's book, *Thomas Aquinas*, he writes, "Aquinas believes that all knowledge is based on basic undeniable principles that provide the foundation for sure knowledge. Without these first principles there can be no true knowledge."[99] For Aquinas, knowledge must be based upon first principles in order to avoid skepticism. Geisler claims, "There are two basic differences between a cause and a principle. First, a cause is not part of the effect, whereas a principle can be part of that which proceeds from it. Second, a principle is merely that from which something follows; a cause is that from which something follows in dependence."[100] Geisler goes on to state:

> A principle by its very nature, is the first in its order, since all else within that order follows from it. 'A first principle is, therefore, a first among firsts.' It may be first in the order of knowing, being, or becoming. That is, each of the various orders of knowledge or reality have their points of beginning; these are known as first principles if they have that irreducible premise upon which all else depends in that order. There may be other principles under this first principle, but the first principle is that from which conclusions may be drawn. Of course, a first principle 'does not signify priority [in time], but origin.' It is logically (but not necessarily chronologically) prior to its sequent. It is the ultimate starting point from which all conclusions may be drawn in a given area of knowledge or reality. First principles are necessary constituents of all knowledge, but they do not supply any content of knowledge.[101]

For Geisler, reality is based upon basic ontological principles. These principles must be understood as a pre-critical form of realism. Pre-critical forms of realism are not asking, "How do I know that I know?" Rather, they are giving an ontological explanation about reality as the properly

---

[98] Joseph Owens, *Cognition* (Houston: Center For Thomistic Studies, 1992); Peter Kreeft, *Socratic Logic: A Logic Text Using Socratic Method, Platonic Questions, and Aristotelian Principles* (South Bend: St. Augustine's Press, 2014); Henry Veatch, *Two Logics: The Conflict Between Classical and Neo-Analytic Philosophy* (Editiones Scholasticae, 2019).

[99] Geisler, *Thomas Aquinas*, 71.

[100] Ibid., 72.

[101] Ibid.

known object in the act of cognition. Geisler's view has also been understood as bypassing many of the criticisms labeled against narrow foundationalism.[102] He observes, "Foundationalists argue that no knowledge, not even about ideas that cohere, would be possible unless there were first principles such as the law of noncontradiction. These principles make it possible to know if ideas are consistent and noncontradictory."[103] Geisler also claims, "It is unreasonable to try and get behind them [self-evident principles]. Hence, one cannot have an 'open mind' about whether they are true. One cannot even have a mind without them."[104] Geisler also distinguishes between ontological and epistemological foundationalism. He claims that ontological foundationalism differs from the more narrow epistemological deductive foundational approach because the former tests the truthfulness of something by *reducing* the claim against reality, not by *deducing* the justification of claims from reality.[105] In that sense, Geisler could be understood as an ontological foundationalist, since within a Thomistic framework, metaphysics is the foundation of all epistemological justification.[106] This view is also known as classic Aristotelian-Thomistic realism. Geisler states:

> Realists also believe that there is a correspondence between thought and thing, between mind and reality. For classical realists, such as Aristotle and Thomas Aquinas, this correspondence is made possible by means of first principles.

---

[102] Ronald Nash claims there are narrow and broad definitions of foundationalism. Nash writes, "*Narrow foundationalism* insists that only beliefs that satisfy two or three specific criteria are properly basic, that is, belong properly in the foundation of a rational noetic structure. *Broad foundationalism* agrees with the distinction between basic and nonbasic beliefs and with the claim that the rationality of nonbasic beliefs depend on the extent to which they are supported by properly basic beliefs." For Nash, broad foundationalism breaks with narrow foundationalism over the limitation of properly basic belief's ability to satisfy two or three criteria. Broad foundationalists are willing to allow many different kinds of beliefs to function as properly basic. See: Ronald H. Nash, *Faith and Reason: Searching for a Rational Faith* (Grand Rapids: Zondervan, 1988), 81

[103] Norman L. Geisler, *Baker Encyclopedia of Christian Apologetics* (Grand Rapids: Baker, 1999), 259.

[104] Ibid., 259-260.

[105] In many ways this aspect corresponds with Geisler's notion of a "Retroductive Method." This idea consists of the notion that, "The biblical teaching is fleshed out in view of the facts known from general revelation and the data (phenomena) of Scripture." See: Norman L. Geisler, *Systematic Theology: Introduction and Bible* (Grand Rapids: Bethany House, 2002), 222-223. In other words, the hypotheses we develop can and must be reduced to things which are known (i.e., reality).

[106] It must be admitted that Dr. Geisler defended some forms of foundationalism, see: Norman L. Geisler and Paul D. Feinberg, *Introduction to Philosophy: A Christian Perspective* (Grand Rapids: Baker, 1980), 152-161.

Since Immanuel Kant it has been customary to distinguish between critical realism from classical realism. The former begins with the premise that we know the real world, and the latter senses an obligation to prove we do. To state it differently, the post-Kantian realist sees a need to address Kant's agnosticism, since the Kantians do not believe we can know reality.[107]

Geisler also states, "Classical realists believe first principles are self-evident. That is, once the terms are known, it is clear to a rational mind that they are true. . . . However, for classical realists such as Aquinas, self-evident does not necessarily mean *a priori* or independent of experience. For realists, first principles are known because the mind knows reality. In fact, these epistemological principles have an ontological basis in reality."[108] Realism then is something that is unavoidable. The fact people are sometimes mistaken about reality or deceived about reality does not negate knowledge of reality. A partial understanding of truth does not equal a false understanding of truth. Going through a process to understand truth does not entail error. In fact, reality is required for any knowledge at all. For we could not know if we were wrong or had false knowledge unless it was seen against the backdrop of reality, and we could compare the two positions against one another and reality.

Geisler claimed that the primary objection to this realist approach comes from Kantian agnosticism. Kant claims, "we cannot know things [i.e., reality] in-themselves." There are multiple forms of this objection. Geisler dealt with these types of objections showing the internal inconsistency of each position. Kant's theory objects to the belief that we can actually tell the real relation between knowledge and being. Kant is insistent upon the belief that our experience necessarily limits our knowledge, and the subjective aspects of the individual make it impossible for any absolute, unconditioned, non-perspectival point of view. Geisler's approach to the question is unique because he recognized that evangelicals cannot move forward by playing modernity's philosophical games according to modernity's rules. Rather, we must reject modernity's categories. In this debate, the two positions are clear: either we can know the real relation between knowledge and being, or we cannot.

For example, Geisler believes it is self-defeating to claim we cannot know the real relation between knowledge and being. First, for Kant and others to claim the ability to draw out the limits concerning knowledge

---

[107] Geisler, *Baker Encyclopedia of Christian Apologetics*, 634.
[108] Ibid.

(appearances and things-in-themselves), they must be able to think both sides of the limit. It is self-defeating for Kant to claim we cannot know things-in-themselves (i.e., objective facts or reality independent of our mind), and then say we cannot know the real relationship between knowledge and being. For, in that very act itself, the Kantian is claiming to offer a robust theory that tells us about the real relation between knowledge and being. According to their own standards, this is precisely what human beings are not able to know. The issue is this: For Kant to state his very theory he must presuppose the opposite theory, namely, epistemological realism. In fact, no theory, even the communication of one's own theory, can be stated without presupposing Aristotle's and Aquinas's common-sense theory of truth.[109]

In sum, Geisler claims that reality can be known in-and-of-itself. There is a rational correspondence between the way things actually exist in reality and the way they appear unto the human mind. Because all of reality can be known directly according to its mode of being, humans can have knowledge of reality. This is based upon fundamental features of being, first principles, and forms that order reality and allow for reality to be known. Geisler's response to modernity is that one must reject philosophical idealism and the critical turn. According to modern Thomists, Geisler included, Christians must return unto a robust philosophy based upon the Platonic tradition. Throughout his life-time, Geisler was unique amongst twentieth and twenty-first century Protestant apologists for championing a return to pre-critical philosophy.[110] In that sense, Geisler was *re-blazing* a trail that was already established throughout the broader "Catholic" (not necessarily Roman Catholic) tradition by figures such as Augustine, Anselm, Aquinas, Calvin, Edwards, the Princetonians, and others who were willing to embrace the idea of "common notions" upon which the mind can know reality and develop a rational, biblical apologetic.[111]

In the following sections of this chapter, we will explore the notion of objectivity and interpretation, the function of first principles, the nature of cognitive-propositionalism's ability to ensure an objective communication of reality, and offer a response to subjectivist and conventionalist objections

---

[109] Ibid., 10-15.

[110] Another key work in this regard by Protestants has been the book *Classical Apologetics* by R. C. Sproul, John Gerstner, and Arthur Lindsley. See: R. C. Sproul, John Gerstner, and Arthur Lindsley, *Classical Apologetics: A Rational Defense of the Christian Faith and a Critique of Presuppositional Apologetics* (Grand Rapids: Zondervan, 1984).

[111] See: J. V. Fesko, *Reforming Apologetics: Reviving the Classic Reformed Approach to Defending the Faith* (Grand Rapids: Baker, 2019).

brought against Geisler's view (and consequently the Classical Realist position).

## The Objective Interpretation of Reality

For Geisler, Thomism establishes the objective nature of truth. Truth is a fundamental principle of reality, and to deny a fundamental principle of reality is self-defeating. For Geisler, there are as many first principles as there are orders of knowledge and reality. Since Geisler is a philosophical realist, the *mode* of knowing is grounded in the *realm of being*. For that reason, first principles have both an ontological and philosophical dimension. First principles, due to their ontological nature, provide the order upon which everything else in reality follows; hence, first principles of knowledge are those basic premises from which all else follows within the realm of knowing reality.

*First Principles*

For Geisler, the first principles (also sometimes known as laws) of knowledge are:

*The Principle of Identity*. In the order of being, there are many ways to describe this principle: (1) A is A; (2) being is being; (3) everything is what it is; (4) being and one are convertible; (5) there is a fundamental unity of things. When rightly applied to epistemology, the principle of identity entails that being is intelligible and being can be known. To deny this fundamental principle leads to logical and practical absurdities, and the absolute inability to conceive of anything concerning anything, since it would render all thought unintelligible.[112]

*The Principle of Noncontradiction*. Like the principle of identity, this principle rests upon the metaphysical notion that "being cannot be nonbeing." The law of non-contradiction recognizes that it is impossible for being to be nonbeing. Epistemologically, and in the realm of truth, this principle expresses the notion that it is impossible for A and non-A to be both true and not true at the same time and the same sense. It also implies that if A is true, then non-A is necessarily false. Based upon the principle of identity, we know that being is intelligible; hence, non-being would be unintelligible. However, whenever someone denies the principle of noncontradiction they are making an intelligible sentence; therefore, it is

---

[112] Geisler, *Introduction and Bible*, 81-82.

self-refuting to make an intelligible statement concerning the unintelligibility of reality. Without the law of noncontradiction we could make God into the devil, the devil into Jesus, or any person into God.[113]

*The Principle of Excluded Middle.* Ontologically, something either exists, or it does not exist. Something must either be or not be. It cannot both be and not be, exist and not exist, at the same time and in the same sense. The principle of excluded middle gives us the either/or nature of rational thought since a being cannot both exist and not exist; it either exists or does not exist, but not both. This entails a proposition is either true or false. A sentence cannot be both true and false simultaneously and in the same sense. Much of life would reduce unto absurdities if our language, actions, and morals were a simultaneous yes and no about the same things concerning the same aspect.[114]

*Principle of Causality.* Classical Realists recognize the is a difference between necessary and contingent being. Properly speaking, this principle applies to finite and contingent beings. This principle entails that whatever has the possibility of existing or not existing (i.e., contingent being) has a cause, and that cause must be outside of itself. Something cannot cause itself. Nonbeing does not give way to being. Everything that is contingent is caused. Everything in which it is possible for it to not be, is therefore dependent and caused. From a Thomistic perspective, Geisler and others recognize this process cannot go on to infinity. Therefore, they posit an Uncaused Cause, whom we deem as God. Epistemologically, this principle recognizes that any proposition which is not self-evident depends upon the source of another for its truthfulness and existence. Unless something is true by necessity, its truthfulness is dependent on some other truth. Ontologically and epistemologically, this process could not go on to infinity; hence, there must be some first, self-evident, first principles that are necessary and self-evident.[115]

For Geisler and other Classical Realists, first principles are by nature considered certain and true infallibly. These truths are necessary and indemonstrable. They are considered self-evident in-and-of-themselves. For Geisler, "First principles are necessary and indemonstrable because an infinite regress of knowledge is impossible."[116] Also, "Since we in our present state of knowledge must think discursively, it would be impossible for us to

---

[113] Ibid.
[114] Ibid.
[115] Ibid.
[116] Geisler, *Aquinas*, 77.

know anything if there were an infinite regress of terms in our syllogisms."[117] Geisler continues, "Since first principles are self-evident, there is a sense in which it is absurd to attempt a direct proof or demonstration of them. Since some people deny their validity, however, there is an indirect sense in which some attempt to prove them. This is done by showing that first principles cannot actually be denied without absurdity."[118] Geisler points to Aristotle, who lists several arguments for an indirect way to demonstrate (or properly recognize) the first principle of contradiction:

1. To deny it would deprive words of their fixed meaning and render speech useless.
2. Reality of essences must be abandoned. There would be becoming without anything that becomes, flying without a bird, accidents without substance.
3. There would be no distinction between things. All would be one.
4. It would mean the destruction of truth, for truth and falsity would be the same.
5. It would destroy all thought, even opinion, for its affirmation would be its negation.
6. Desire and preference would be useless, for there would be no difference between good and evil.
7. Everything would be equally true and false at the same time. No opinion would be more wrong than any other, even in degree.
8. It would make impossible all becoming, change, or motion, for all this implies a transition from one state to another, but all states would be the same, if contradiction is not true.[119]

First principles are objectively certain and intelligible, regardless of the subjective certitude we may have about them. They are indemonstrable because they are required to make any demonstration. Rather, they are undeniable. Whenever someone attempts to deny any first principle or law of logic, they must use them in order to deny them. In short, since first

---

[117] Ibid.
[118] Ibid., 78.
[119] Ibid., 78-79.

principles are knowable, any denial of knowledge, whether it be skepticism, agnosticism, or any other "ism", is self-defeating and refutable.

*Objectivity and Hermeneutics*

The basis of an objective hermeneutic is grounded firmly in its undeniable nature. Like an objective truth or first principle, one cannot deny an objective hermeneutic without affirming it. To deny objectivity in interpretation and hermeneutics is to imply that there is an objective way to understand the very denial of that claim. Indeed, to know that an interpretation is not and cannot be objective, one must first be in possession of an objective interpretation of the claim, "There is an objective interpretation of reality." Throughout modern universities and several evangelical seminaries many forms of subjectivism in hermeneutics exist. Each one of them fails. Geisler claims, "Since all involve self-defeating statements, and any attempt to deny an objective interpretation implies that one is possible, namely, the one by which the subjectivist's view is expected to be understood. That is, every subjectivist expects that readers can and should come to an objective understanding of his subjectivistic views."[120] In other words, what is sauce for the goose is sauce for the gander. The subjectivist cannot deny objectivity and latter complain someone misread or wrongly interpreted their view.

For classic evangelicals who affirm classical theism and classical realism, subjectivism fails not only because of its self-defeating nature, but because good arguments can be made for objectivity in biblical interpretation. There is a clear belief and affirmation that there is only one correct interpretation of the Bible. They do not deny a plethora of applications of one verse, but they insist one must maintain that there is only one correct interpretation. My interpretation or your interpretation may not be right, but if they are different, they cannot both be right. To deny objectivity is to embrace a form of relativism. Whenever someone says, "That's your interpretation," we ought to respond, "Let's try and get at the objective meaning of the text and beyond our personal prejudices."

Geisler provides in several places the ontological and epistemological basis for objectivity. These include:

1. The existence of an absolute Mind (God);
2. The absolute nature of meaning;

---

[120] Geisler, *Introduction and Bible*, 171.

3. The analogy between infinite understanding and finite understanding; and
4. The ability of finite minds (made in God's image) to understand truths revealed by God.[121]

### The Existence of an Absolute Mind

In the next chapter, we will demonstrate the existence and attributes of God. For the sake of this chapter, it must be noted that the existence of an absolute Mind is axiomatic given a classical view of God. A rational defense of this Mind goes something like this:

(1) At least one finite mind exists (me,) for I cannot deny that I am a thinker without thinking. And I am limited in my thought, or I would not doubt or discover new thoughts, which I do.

(2) But the principle of causality demands that every finite thing needs a cause.

(3) Hence, it follows that there must be an infinite Mind that caused my finite mind.

There are several reasons to affirm this conclusion. First, according to the doctrine of analogy, a cause cannot give what it does not have. Two, effects cannot be greater than their cause. So, if the effect is intelligent, then the Cause must be intelligent. Hence, an infinite Mind must exist. Since this absolute Mind exists, and this absolute Mind is a Necessary Being, then it necessarily entails there is an absolute Mind as the ground for absolute meaning.[122]

If God were not an infinite, perfect, eternal, immutable, and simple Being, then one could argue that there is not an absolute ground for absolute meaning. If God happened to be finite, imperfect, temporal, mutable, and composed (in all or just one respect), then there are defeaters to affirm absolute meaning has rational grounds. If God were able to change, then the grounds for claiming the standard of all truth (God) is in flux; hence, all truth or meaning could be in flux. The classic doctrine of God and classic ontological realism are interconnected. As the existence of the classical attributes of God are jettisoned, then it opens the doors for the classic view of meaning, truth, and objectivity to go along with it. For that

---

[121] Ibid.

[122] Norman L. Geisler and William C. Roach, *Defending Inerrancy: Affirming the Accuracy of Scripture for a New Generation* (Grand Rapids: Baker, 2011), 289-290.

reason, Geisler argued for the necessity of affirming both classical realism and classical theism as the necessary preconditions for classic evangelicalism.

### Absolute Meaning

If there is an absolute Mind, then there can be absolute meaning. The objective basis for meaning is found in the Mind of God. Whatever an infinite Mind means by something is what it means objectively and absolutely. Hence, the existence of objective and absolute meaning is grounded in the existence of an absolute Meaner (God).[123]

Since God is an infinite, eternal, immutable, simple Being, it offers an absolute perspective. Without this absolute Being, all truth would reduce unto mere perspectivalism. There would be no ontological factors that serve as universal validating norms between different perspectives, whether they arise from culture, ethnicity, gender, or any other factor. The issue evangelicals face is, "Why should we prefer one perspective over another?" If there is no absolute truth, then it would reduce unto a matter of personal preference. The claim, "All truth is perspectival", however, offers a nonperspectival truth claim; otherwise, it could be relegated to the category of another relative perspective. Hence, we are back to the possibility of nonperspectival truth claims. But such claims are only possible if there is an absolute Mind.

### Analogy of Meaning

Classical theism and classical realism recognize that different beings exist; moreover, that different *kinds* of beings exist. There are necessary and contingent beings. God by definition is a necessary Being. God is the Creator, not the creation. God is the cause of all things, who has no cause in his Being. God is all-powerful, all-knowing, and all-wise; hence, he has the power, knowledge, and wisdom to communicate with/to finite and fallen human beings. As an infinitely powerful and infinitely knowing Being; God can do whatever is logically not contradictory. And it is not logically contradictory for an infinite Mind to convey meaning to finite creatures, since there is a common ground between them in both the undeniable laws of thought and in the similarity that both have being (analogously) between the Creator and the creature.[124]

How we talk about God has been debated amongst theologians. There are three views: equivocal, univocal, and analogous. Plotinus and other medieval mystics claimed we can only speak of God through the use of negative terms. Since God is so transcendent and beyond our categories,

---

[123] Ibid., 290.
[124] Ibid.

we only have the ability to say what God is *not*. We lack the ability to positively claim what God is. God is wholly other than anything we experience. Hence, any positive attributions concerning the nature of God will not really be the way God is in his essence but merely what we attribute to him because he causes this characteristic in his creatures. Historic Christianity has rejected this view because it believes both general revelation and special revelation entail God has communicated both his nature and his will in meaningful propositions to humanity. It would be incorrect to claim we have no knowledge of God. The central objection to *via negativa* approaches as a sole sufficient way to know God is that a person cannot know "not that' unless he knows "that." All negative knowledge presupposes some positive knowledge. Hence, completely equivocal knowledge is no knowledge at all and is contrary to both reason and revelation.[125]

Univocal God-talk is the belief that our understanding of God must be in terms that have the same meaning when applied to God as they do when applied to creatures. Scotus's argument can be summarized as claiming that we are left in skepticism unless there is a correspondence between our concept of God and the words we use to communicate those concepts. Unless words have the same meaning for us as they have for God, we are left with inadequate (or false) knowledge. We know from reason and revelation that humanity has knowledge of God. It would be self-defeating to claim that we have no knowledge of God, for in the very claim, we are affirming some truth about God.[126]

Thomas Aquinas rejected both purely univocal and equivocal God-talk. Each view has an element of truth. Equivocal God-talk is correct that our words do not exhaustively depict the nature of God. Univocal God-talk is correct in that our words do positively say something of God. Aquinas was correct to affirm analogical God-talk. God is an infinite Being, and all our terms are finite, and there is necessarily an infinite difference between an infinite and a finite. The reasoning goes as follows. One can say, "Simon is good" and "God is good." One cannot, however, apply the term "good" in entirely the same (univocal) way. After all, the term "good" is applied to God infinitely and Simon finitely. This is because by nature God is an infinite Being, and Simon is a finite being.[127]

---

[125] Ibid., 256-257.
[126] Ibid., 257.
[127] Ibid.

Aquinas's doctrine of analogy answers the challenge of a univocal definition of meaning because it understands terms according to their mode of *being*. Truth is that which corresponds unto *its* reality. This does not mean that truth is relative, nor that there are there different realities. It recognizes there is a great chain of being between the Creator and the creation. Whenever we read a proposition concerning the nature of God, we recognize that term is applied to an infinite, eternal, and immutable Being. Whenever we read a proposition concerning the nature of man, we recognize that term is applied to a finite, temporal, mutable being. The point is that each term used must be understood in the same *sense* or definition of the term, but the *application* of each term will be different. In short, Scotus was right that terms must be understood univocally, whereas Aquinas was correct about the predication of terms analogically.[128]

So, how can finite terms have any meaning whatsoever when applied to an infinite Being? "Infinite" means "not finite." How can a finite term retain any meaning when applied to an infinite God? Isn't there an infinite distance between a finite and an infinite? Thomas's response was that although there is an infinite distance between God and creatures, there is nonetheless not a total lack of similarity. Both God and finite beings have being. There is also a relationship between an efficient Cause and its effect. The principle of causality entails that God cannot give what he does not have. He cannot produce what he does not possess. God cannot share being if he does not have being to share, just like a teacher cannot share knowledge unless he has knowledge to share. In short, there is an intrinsic relationship between an efficient cause and its effect. There must be both a similarity between the Creator and the creature. There must be a similarity because they are both "being"; they both exist. There is also a difference because one is an infinite Being, and creatures are finite. God *is* Being, and creatures *have* being. But what is similar yet different is analogous.[129] Hence, the analogy of being is based on the intrinsic relation of the Creator and his creature, who must be both similar (because he has being) and different (because he is a different kind of being).[130]

According to both Aquinas and Geisler, finite terms apply to an infinite Creator without losing all of their meaning because there is a similarity based on a causal connection and because all limitations are removed from the term (*via negativa*) before it can be appropriately applied to God. There is still meaningful content left after the *via negativa* because the term is really an attribute of God and not just a metaphor. Human language can

---

[128] Ibid., 258.
[129] Ibid.
[130] See: Geisler, *Introduction and Bible*, 24-26.

be used to convey objective truth about the infinite God, but only analogously. And this analogy is based on the real causal relationship between the Creator and the creature. Whatever the effect has, it was received from the Cause. Unlike an instrumental cause, an efficient cause always places its imprint on the effect, so there is some similarity between them.[131]

### *The Imago Dei in Human Beings*

Since it is not impossible for an infinite Mind to communicate with a finite mind, and because there is an analogous ground between them, it is possible for absolute meaning to be communicated to a finite mind. The objective disclosure of meaning is possible between an infinite Mind and a finite mind.

Within the context of the Christian worldview and Thomistic realism, it is possible for a finite mind to discover objective truth because truth is disclosed and revealed. Not only can an author's thoughts be communicated in an objective way (i.e., a book), but it is also possible for a reader to discover and understand what the author has revealed. First of all, we know it is possible to know what God has revealed, since all the necessary preconditions for knowing the objective meaning expressed by God have been met, as discussed above. Second, whether one will actually know the objective meaning will depend on having an objective hermeneutic, a means of understanding this objective meaning. Because God has fashioned humanity in his very image, we bear rational principles to know the world he created. The image of God links humanity to have knowledge of both God and God's creation. Third, as has already been established, God has fashioned humanity to know reality directly. For Geisler and other Classical Realists, part of the *sine qua non* of their approach is that humanity can know reality in a direct and real sense. Therefore, since there is an absolute meaning and because God has fashioned human beings in his image to know reality, that it is possible for humanity to have an objective knowledge of reality. Finally, for Geisler and many other classic evangelicals, they insisted upon the use of a historical-grammatical interpretation of Scripture as the only consistent approach to understanding Scripture in an objective sense.[132]

Many people today question whether or not certain knowledge about reality is possible. They object to the concept of certainty because many of the theoretical arguments about probability and certainty show that we

---
[131] Geisler and Roach, *Defending Inerrancy*, 259.
[132] Ibid., 291-305.

know truth only with probability, not with certainty. They claim that probability is sufficient to guarantee our knowledge for all practical purposes, and that it helps to prevent people from growing dogmatic or narrow-minded, which seem to be more serious than doubt. They also insist that much harm has been done by Descartes and his follows who insist upon philosophical certainty. Descartes set the bar too high and many of his theses can be doubted, and not all claims to knowledge must be known with certainty.

While it is true that many people have been led down odd and twisted paths over the pursuit of certainty, that does not mean we ought to jettison the notion of philosophical certainty. First, with our use of daily language we make several key distinctions between certain knowledge and opinion. We use words such as, "I know" and "it seems." We even have the very words "certain" and "probable." If the first set of expressions correspond to nothing real, it would mean there is a breakdown between our knowledge, language, and their correspondence to reality. However, as has been demonstrated above, such a thesis is self-defeating. Self-evident principles are known with certainty and indubitability. Therefore, some aspects of reality can be known with certainty. Second, epistemological probabilists, much like semi or quasi skepticism, seem to hold this belief in probabilism with some very certain and almost dogmatic closed-mindedness, almost like a gnostic insight into reality known only to those really in the "know." Finally, just because Cartesian philosophers over emphasized and incorrectly made a judgment about the absolute certain knowledge of all of reality does not entail that we ought to forego any commitment to aspects of philosophical certainty. One ought to properly recognize that aspects of our knowledge are probabilistic, while other aspects of our knowledge can be certain. If we upheld this standard consistently, we would have to jettison any belief whenever someone made a false claim or judgment about it. According to this standard, hardly any philosophy would ever measure up to this test.

In his book, *Summa Philosophica*, Peter Kreeft, a fellow Thomistic scholar, responds to these types of objections, claiming:

> *I answer that* (1) Probabilism, like simple skepticism, is self-contradictory. For either it is certain or only probable that all human knowledge is only probable and not certain. If that is certain, we have an immediate self-contradiction. If it is only probable, then it *may* be false. As with simple skepticism, where the skeptic forgets to be skeptical about his skepticism, the probabilist forgets to be probabilistic about his probabilism. (2) In order to make the judgment that something is probable, one

needs to know the standards of probability and how to apply them. But this knowledge must be more than merely probable. Thus, when statistical probabilities are given, they are accompanied by ranges of possible error. But these ranges of error are not also subject to statistical probabilities. "Possible error" is meaningful only in contrast with "impossible error," and what is *impossible* is a kind of certainty.[133]

Therefore, it is clear that we can not only know reality, but in qualified respects, we can have certain knowledge about aspects of reality. The nature of objectivity requires direct knowledge of reality. Direct knowledge requires that we have more than a probable knowledge of reality, since probabilism can entail elements of skepticism, which necessarily undercuts our belief that we have direct knowledge of reality.

Now that the objective nature of reality has been demonstrated, we will see how Geisler's unique Thomistic approach allows for there to be objective communication through the means of cognitive-propositional language between God and man, and between man and man.

## The Objective Communication of Reality

Philosophical realism provides a stark alternative to many of the competing views affecting philosophy of language. Since the advent of the linguistic turn, which is a focus on the particular uses of language as they pertain to communication, logic, and argumentation, there has been a growing skepticism over the clarity and objectivity of language. The predominant view held by many present-day evangelical theologians is known as Conventionalism. This approach claims all meaning is relative. Since there is a correspondence between one's theory of meaning and one's theory of truth, consequently, Conventionalism necessarily implies that all truth is relative. But it has already been demonstrated that it is self-defeating to claim all truth is relative, hence, it will also be demonstrated that it is self-defeating to claim that meaning is relative.

The history of philosophy presents a debate between Platonic essentialism and Conventionalism. Plato (427—347 B.C.) defended an essentialist view of language in the *Cratylus*. St. Augustine (A.D. 354—430) also defended an essentialist approach to language in three of his famous works: *Principia Dialectiae*, *De Magistro*, and *De Trinitate*. There is a difference between Plato's and Augustine's views. Augustine did not defend

---

[133] Peter Kreeft, *Summa Philosophica* (South Bend: St Augustine's Press, 2012), 145-146.

a purely pictoral view of language and meaning. This approach claims language is a picture of reality, much like a picture or a photograph and an object. Ludwig Wittgenstein (A.D. 1889-1951) critiqued Platonic essentialism in his famous *Tractatus*. The central thesis defended by essentialism is the claim that there is a natural or essential relationship between statements and meaning. There is a one-to-one correspondence between language and meaning.[134]

Some of the primary critiques against Platonic essentialism in favor of a conventionalist theory of meaning arose from Ferdinand de Saussure, Gottlob Frege, and Ludwig Wittgenstein. More recent thinkers include Gilbert Ryle, John Austin, and several evangelical thinkers such as Grant Osborne, Kevin Vanhoozer, and Andreas Kostenberger. Wittgenstein challenged the belief that a proposition is a picture or model of reality as we imagine it. The notion of a language game is used to depict the plurality of ways of speaking. The argument states that just as there are a diversity of literal games, our multiple ways of speaking (which are equivalent to language-games) do not conform unto a singular model. Wittgenstein grants that some language games are pictorial in nature, but he denies the claim that all language games function in this manner. Some of our language depicts reality; however, other functions include telling jokes, translating, questioning, praying, suggesting, non-verbal modes of communication, and so forth. Each instance may all be language (a game) but the rules for each game function and operate differently. For him, this entails, there is no essential nature to language. It also serves as a way to claim context *and* use are the *only* proper means of understanding a proposition or any other form of communication.

For our purposes, the axiomatic aspect of Wittgenstein's approach is the fact that he not only grants a conventionalist theory of symbols, but of meaning. Someone can use different symbols to communicate the English word "man."[135] However, Wittgenstein goes beyond this to claim there is both a conventionalist theory of symbols and a conventionalist theory of meaning. For him, the meaning of a sentence can change, not just the symbols. In addition, there are specific limitations placed upon language since each function of language must operate according to its own rules. Because religious language and other non-religious forms of language address different topics, such as emotive elements (e.g., prayer, confession, praise) they are operating according to two different rules for their particular language game. Consequently, God-talk and religious language could be viewed as non-sense when interpreted according to normal and

---

[134] Lawhead, *The Voyage of Discovery*, 510-524.
[135] Ibid.

non-religious language. For Wittgenstein, whenever God-talk or religious language is used, it must operate according to an equivocal use, since religious talk must operate according to that particular family of use or set of rules.[136]

Geisler was aware of the effects of Conventionalism upon evangelical theology. First, Geisler claims, "This also means that since language games have an intrinsic (internal) criterion of meaning, and since religious language is a language game, religious language must be judged by its own standards and not by standards imposed upon it, which is a form of fideism."[137] Second, "Religious beliefs have commissive force; that is, they orient our lives. However, says Wittgenstein, they are not informative about reality. We are allegedly locked in a linguistic bubble, and while religious language is meaningful as a language, it tells us nothing about God or ultimate reality."[138] One of the ironic trends of twentieth-century evangelical theology has been the embrace of Conventionalism by so many theologians. If this approach to language is correct, then all of our exegesis of the Bible does not offer us real knowledge of God. Therefore, human language lacks the ability to offer real and meaningful statements about God, since all meaning is culturally and experientially relative. In brief, it seems like many evangelical scholars rightly understood that different languages may use different names for the same referent. Nonetheless, they failed to recognize symbols can be conventional while meaning remains the same.[139]

Geisler throughout his career demonstrated that a conventionalist approach to language is self-defeating at its very core.[140] For example, he claims, "Conventionalism is self-defeating. If the statement "All linguistic meaning is conventional" were true, then this statement itself would be relative, for it claims to be an objectively meaningful affirmation that there are no such objectively meaningful statements. It offers itself as a nonrelative statement affirming that the meaning of all statements is relative."[141] From what has already been discussed, it ought to be clear that the reason a conventionalist theory of meaning is self-defeating is because it contradicts the foundational laws of logic or first principles of reality. This approach to language is making a meaningful and accurate depiction of

---

[136] Geisler, *Introduction and Bible*, 101.
[137] Ibid.
[138] Ibid.
[139] Ibid.
[140] Ibid., 103-105.
[141] Ibid., 103.

reality (principle of identity), while claiming that no one language or language game is able to make an accurate depiction of reality. If the principle of non-contradiction is true, which it is; and if the principle of excluded middle is true, which it is; then this approach to language seems to be affirming both A and non-A at the same time and the same sense, which is non-sensical and contradictory.

Geisler also responds to a conventionalist theory of meaning by noting that there is a significant difference between Plato and Augustine's essentialist theory of meaning and Aristotle and Aquinas's realist theory of meaning. Geisler writes, "The conventionalist's view of meaning is clearly an overreaction against Platonic essentialism. There is a third alternative that avoids the rigidity of essentialism and the relativism of conventionalism: realism."[142] Now it is true that Plato held to a form of ontological realism. Plato clearly affirmed the existence of the forms and the mind's ability to understand reality. However, Aristotelian and Thomistic realism, also known as Moderate Realism, provides an alternative to Plato's view, also known as Extreme Realism. For Plato, it is correct so say that meaning is objective; however, for him, symbols must also be objective. For Aristotle and Aquinas, their approach allows for there to be a similarity of formal cause (i.e., objective meaning) and a difference of material cause (i.e., symbols). This means symbols can be culturally relative, while meaning remains objective.

In his book, *Thomist Realism and the Linguistic Turn*, John O'Callaghan situates Thomistic realism in the context of modern philosophy's embrace of the linguistic turn. One of the historical considerations he discusses is the notion that language is nothing more than a mental representation of reality.[143] He considers the epistemology of figures such as John Locke, George Berkeley, David Hume, Thomas Reid, and others to note each figure viewed mental thought as the ground of ideas, not being or reality itself. For a figure such as Berkeley, the mind can only know ideas, not real extra-mental reality. For Hume, the internal object of knowledge is still some form of an idea or a mental representation of reality. These representations do not actually represent external objects in a proper sense; hence, we are left with a form of skepticism. O'Callahan notes that there is a relationship between language and thought.[144] If our thoughts cannot accurately depict reality, how could we expect our language to properly and accurately depict reality? If we have nothing more

---

[142] Ibid., 105.

[143] John P. O'Callaghan, *Thomist Realism and the Linguistic Turn: Toward a More Perfect Form of Existence* (Notre Dame: University of Notre Dame Press, 2003), 79-112.

[144] Ibid., 113-133.

than a mental representation of reality, and not reality itself, how can we really claim to *know* or *speak* about reality? For Aquinas, thought and understanding are immanent acts. When the intellect grasps reality, it is actually abstracting the form of the object from reality. The form that exists in reality and once had a physical material cause is the same form that exists in the mind, except now it has a mental material cause. One of the significant downfalls of modern philosophy is its embrace of philosophical nominalism. Since there are no forms in reality to grasp, how can we actually say we know reality? If reality is not actually grasped, but only represented, how do we know our language properly depicts reality? The fact is our language about reality must be relative if our knowledge of reality is relative. But if our knowledge is grounded in an objective reality, then our thought and language can both depict and accurately communicate reality.

For Geisler and other committed Aristotelian-Thomists, when they respond to the claim, "Don't look for the meaning; look for the use", the central critique against the view is to point out that language does not control thought, rather thought controls language. The meaning of a word (i.e., its formal cause) controls the potential use of a word.[145] Geisler applies Aristotle's six causes to the meaning of a written text. He claims:

1. The writer is the *efficient* cause of the meaning of a text.
2. The writer's purpose is the *final* cause of its meaning.
3. The writing is the *formal* cause of its meaning.
4. The words are the *material* cause of its meaning.
5. The writer's ideas are the *exemplar* cause of its meaning.
6. The laws of thought are the *instrumental* cause of its meaning.[146]

Geisler rightly notes that there are different aspects or causes to any written work. In many ways, one of the errors of conventionalism is revealed in that its proponents confuse a writer's purpose with the formal cause of a writer's work. There is difference between understanding "that of which something comes to be" and "that for which something comes to be." Geisler claims:

---

[145] See: Mortimer Adler, *Ten Philosophical Mistakes* (New York: Simon & Schuster, 1985), 54-82.

[146] Geisler, *Introduction and Bible*, 105-106.

> The meaning (formal cause) of an intelligible expression, such as a writing, is not found in the "meaner"; he is the efficient cause of the meaning. The formal cause of meaning is in the *writing itself*. What is signified is found in the signs that signify it; verbal meaning is found in the very structure and grammar of the sentences, *in* the literary text itself (formal cause), not the purpose (final cause). Note that meaning is *not* found in the individual words (material cause).[147]

The Platonists err by claiming material signs only have one meaning, regardless of the context of the sentence. The Conventionalists err because they deny the existence of any forms, and hence, there is no real relationship between language, thought, and reality. Realism can overcome these errors by recognizing that words have potential meaning in the context of a proposition. Individual words are not solely bound to one immutable use. However, the formal aspect of a being is bound by its nature, which can be rightly used in a variety of ways. Geisler agrees with this sentiment, claiming, "Words in themselves have no actual meaning; they have only potential meaning. Words have usage in a sentence, which is the smallest unity of meaning."[148] In short, meaning is found in the text as a whole unit, not as a segmented part.

Forms are found in things, not behind, above, around, or beside things. Forms do not exist in an external Platonic world, nor do they exist as mere representations. Forms, on the other hand, exist in things, and that existence can be properly abstracted into the mind or placed into a verbal text or proposition. There is a formal correspondence between the object in reality, thought, and the proposition. For Geisler and his Thomistic system, since this is the case, a text's meaning is not found beyond the text (since forms are in things, not in a Platonic reality, or in this sense, possibly in the author's mind), nor is it beneath the text (since forms cannot exist apart from their object, such as the unexpressed intention of the author); rather meaning is found in the text (since forms correspond to their object, which in this case, is in the author's expressed meaning—i.e., his book, paper, or object of communication).[149]

Geisler's paradigm of meaning is found in the Aristotelian-Thomistic understanding of the ground of objective truth. If there is an absolute Mind, then there can be an absolute ground for truth; if there is an absolute ground for truth, there can be an absolute ground for thought; if there is

---

[147] Ibid., 106.
[148] Ibid.
[149] Ibid.

an absolute ground for thought, there can be an absolute ground for meaning; if there is an absolute ground for meaning, then meaning and language can be objective. The same objective meaning of any text can be expressed in a diversity of languages. Unlike essentialism, which insists upon a one-to-one correlation, and unlike conventionalism, which argues for a many-to-one correlation, realism affirms there is a one-to-many correlation. There can be one meaning expressed in many ways, even in the same language.[150]

# Conclusion

*The way* we answer the question, "How ought evangelicals face the new world?" will determine much of our apologetic methodology. We must remember Geisler once explained to the dean of a major evangelical institution the essence of his argument when he claimed, "I embraced the idea from Augustine, Aquinas, the Reformers, and the Princetonians that truth about reality was knowable." The core of Geisler's philosophical prolegomena is summarized by the claim: Truth about reality is knowable. If truth about reality is knowable, and reality consists of undeniable first principles, and reality is structured because an absolute Mind (God) formed and fashioned reality so it could be known, and he fashioned reality so it could be communicated, then we have a philosophical means to engage the philosophical contours of modern philosophy.

Geisler's unique approach to prolegomena was his embrace of the Aristotelian-Thomistic or Scholastic synthesis. Geisler's use of this synthesis is not novel within historic Protestantism. It has been embraced by historical figures such as Francis Turretin and contemporary figures such as R. C. Sproul. In fact, there is a good argument to be made for claiming that the embrace of common notions and common ground, as expressed by Classical Realists and Classical Apologists, is the central and historic Catholic and Protestant tradition. While we do not base our views solely upon tradition, we must recognize the influence of modernity upon the philosophical and apologetic methodologies of post-Enlightenment apologists.[151]

The forthcoming chapters will continue to explain Geisler's unique synthesis of theology and apologetics. The next chapter will explain Geisler's Thomistic approach to classical apologetics and classical theism.

---

[150] Ibid., 107.
[151] See: Fesko, *Reforming Apologetics*.

Special attention will be given to explain the difference between the Thomistic model versus other prevalent models of classical apologetics. Chapter four will explain Geisler's approach to defending the classic doctrine of inerrancy as expressed in the Chicago Statement on Biblical Inerrancy. The final chapter will lay out the specific significance of Geisler's approach for present-day evangelical apologists and offer a way to continue applying his method.

# CHAPTER THREE

# Defending Classical Apologetics and Theism

## Introduction

We live on this side of modernity. The issues of the knowability of reality and the existence of God are two matters we cannot avoid. The vast amount of literature throughout the twentieth-century, and now into the twenty-first century, has had to deal with the fact that the vast majority of people engage the question of God from the vantage point of skepticism, agnosticism, and atheism. Evangelical literature has even tried to capture this sentiment. For example, the late Francis Schaeffer penned two key books, *The God Who is There* and *He is There and He is Not Silent* to capture the modern *mood*. The God who is "There" and "He is There" are both phrases pertaining to the fact that the conditions of belief demonstrate the near impossibility for modern man to accept belief in the existence of God. Some people question whether God exists and others whether God can reveal himself. The diffusion of modernity, however, is not ubiquitous. There are certain regions of the world, due to God's providence and grace, which have not been affected by modernity to the same degree. Nonetheless, in a modern technological age, the number of those being infected by the pandemic of unbelief is going to rise.

Norman Geisler fulfilled Schaeffer's model of engagement by addressing the apologetic questions of his age. Geisler was not always able to answer the skeptic's questions. There was a time shortly after Geisler's conversion when he was out witnessing on the streets and he was confronted by a graduate of Moody Bible Institute. The drunken individual approached Geisler, opened his Bible, and pointed to a verse that said, "Go, and tell no one." Geisler was stumped and did not have an answer. "The Bible did clearly say, 'Go, and tell no one.'" Moreover, through these types of experiences, Geisler was stumped by Jehovah's Witnesses, Mormons, Skeptics, and other cults and world religions. Geisler knew he was in a predicament: He either had to quit sharing his faith, or he had to get answers. Since the former was not an option, Geisler chose the latter. Therefore, Geisler dedicated the remainder of his life to serve God as a

Christian apologist. He was committed to defending the gospel once for all given unto the saints.

To many people, the present-day apologetic situation seems daunting. They recognize the fact that Jesus Christ has called us to fulfill the Great Commission. We are to engage the unbeliever with the gospel of Jesus Christ. There is a scene in the Lord of the Rings before Frodo and the crew were about to leave the Shire to engage in the Fellowship of the Ring. After having the situation explained to him, Frodo grew very discouraged because of the daunting task. "I wish it need not have happened in my time," said Frodo. "So do I," said Gandalf, "and so do all who live to see such times. But that is not for them to decide. All we have to decide is what to do with the time that is given us." Tolkien's wise analysis of daunting situations is captured well by those words. As modern-day apologists, we may long for a simpler time. We may long for a time where the conditions of belief "made it easier." The reality set-down before us in Scripture is that since the Fall, we have always lived in a Romans chapter one kind of world. Sin has always manifested itself in the lives and minds of humanity. There has never been an "easier generation" to reach. One generation faced the paganism of the Roman Empire, another faced Medieval Roman Catholicism, and we face the Enlightenment and postmodernism in our Age of Unbelief. Each era presents its own challenges, but like Frodo and Gandalf, "All we have to decide is what to do with the time that is given us."

This chapter is going to address the unique *way* Norman Geisler addressed the existence and attributes of God. In the previous chapter, we saw that truth about reality is knowable. In this chapter, we are going to note that reality may be knowable, but reality does not all exist in the same way, nor is all of reality known in the same way. In other words, we are going to explain the significance of Geisler's Thomistic metaphysic and use of Aquinas's approach to argue for the existence of God. Moreover, Geisler's arguments for the existence of God not only tell us *that* a divine Being exists, they also tell us about the *nature* of God. The second half of this chapter will explain the significance that Thomistic realism has upon our understanding of the attributes of God and the importance that has for evangelical belief, and the *way* we engage the conditions of belief in an Enlightenment era.

## Evangelicals and the Existence of God

As was noted and explained in chapter one, David Hume and Immanuel Kant leveled severe charges against the existence of God. Present-day conditions of belief can be traced back to the work of a Scottish Skeptic and a German Agnostic. Historically, many prominent institutions and philosophers have taught that Hume and Kant exposed the invalidity of the theistic proofs.

Some evangelical philosophers who would label themselves as presuppositionalists, such as Gordon Clark and Greg Bahnsen, believe Hume and Kant were successful in their attempts to disprove the traditional arguments for the existence of God.[152] Bahnsen claims, "Historically, when David Hume and Immanuel Kant exposed the invalidity of the theistic proofs, apologists generally balked at returning to revelation as the basis for their certainty of God's existence."[153] Bahnsen also says, "They elected, rather, to maintain status in the blinded eyes of the 'worldly wise' by attempting to prove Christianity's credibility by means of arguments that hopefully *pointed* toward the *probability* of God's existence and Scripture's truth. They settled for a mere *presumption* (plus pragmatic assurance) in favor of a few salvaged items (i.e., "fundamentals") from the Christian system."[154] Carl F. H. Henry also discouraged the use of theistic proofs because the empirical and inductive method never rose above that of mere probability. Henry claims,

> My premise is the legitimacy of deductive theology and the invalidity of the evidentialist alternative. The so-called theistic proofs, I maintain, provide no conclusive demonstration of the existence of the self-revealing God of the Bible. To speak more modestly of 'evidences' instead of 'proofs' requires a fallback to probabilities. If evidentialist arguments 'establishes' the probability of any divine reality, it romances an un-Scriptural deity more than it reinforces Biblical theism."[155]

To be fair and balanced, not all presuppositionalists completely disavow the proofs for the existence of God. John Frame, for example, would not consider himself a purist when it comes to following Cornelius Van Til's method. This can be seen in his book, *Cornelius Van Til: An Analysis of His Thought*, where Frame discusses many of the strengths and weaknesses of

---

[152] Gordon H. Clark, *Religion, Reason, and Revelation* (Nutley: Craig, 1961).

[153] Greg L. Bahnsen, *Presuppositional Apologetics: Stated and Defended* (Nacogdoches: Covenant Media Press, 2011), 5. See also: K. Scott Oliphint, *Aquinas (Great Thinkers)* (Philipsburg: R&R Publishing, 2017).

[154] Ibid.

[155] Carl F. H. Henry, *Toward A Recover of Christian Belief* (Wheaton: Crossway Books, 1990), 40.

his mentor's approach.[156] Frame also incorporates the traditional proofs for the existence of God in his book titled, *Apologetics: A Justification of Christian Belief*.[157] Frame even offers an extended chart noting the similarities and differences between himself and Van Til.[158] Two significant differences are that, first, Frame does allow for a person to prove Christian theism through a series of steps; and secondly, he does not require epistemological certainty in all cases.[159] In other words, there is no one single definition of a presuppositionalist. There are a variety of different types of presuppositionalism. The essential difference is *how* committed they are to Van Til's method, specifically the absolute necessity and sole axiom of transcendental reasoning.[160]

There are many presuppositionalists, who in my opinion err in this assessment, wrongly claiming that there are only two types of methods: Presuppositional and Evidential. Granted, not all presuppositionalists would level this charge, for they recognize many significant contributions to the field of apologetics from figures such as Alvin Plantinga, who represents the Reformed Epistemology tradition. Nonetheless, one of the significant errors made by many is to confuse classical apologetics as a mere extension of evidentialism. R. C. Sproul responded to this type of claim during a Ligonier conference.[161] Sproul was quick to point out that he was not an evidentialist but a classical apologist.[162] One of the significant differences between an evidentialist and a classicalist is the ontological and epistemological necessity of demonstrating the existence of God prior to evaluating historical evidence for Christianity. Classical Apologists recognize that God provides the grounds of existence for all created beings, and the reality of God's existence is epistemologically necessary for the proper interpretation of events in the world, such as miracles.[163] In fact, point four of Geisler's historic twelve points is: If God exists, then miracles are possible;

---

[156] John M. Frame, *Cornelius Van Til: An Analysis of His thought* (Phillipsburg: R&R Publishing, 1995).

[157] John M. Frame, *Apologetics: A Justification of Christian Belief* (Phillipsburg: R&R Publishing, 2015).

[158] Ibid., 94.

[159] Ibid.

[160] Another figure who might represent the non-purest approach to Van Til would be James Anderson, professor at Reformed Theological Seminary. See: https://www.proginosko.com/

[161] https://www.ligonier.org/blog/2011-ligonier-national-conference-session-5-rc-sproul/

[162] See also: R. C. Sproul, John Gerstner, and Arthur Lindsley, *Classical Apologetics: A Rational Defense of the Christian Faith and a Critique of Presuppositional Apologetics* (Grand Rapids: Zondervan, 1984).

[163] See: Norman L. Geisler, *Miracles and the Modern Mind: A Defense of Biblical Miracles* (Eugene: Wipf and Stock, 1992).

and point five is: Miracles can be used to confirm a message from God (i.e., as acts of God to confirm a word from God).[164] For a figure such as Geisler, it would be incoherent to speak about an act of God, if there was not a God who can act. It is both rationally and methodologically necessary to establish the existence of God prior to discussing various miracles by God or evidences for Christianity, such as the resurrection. In that sense, classical apologetics is a two-step method. First, it seeks to establish the existence of God; Second, it evaluates the historical evidence for the truthfulness of Christianity. However, it must also be noted that Geisler's method is unique because it provides a step prior to the existence of God; namely, it establishes the fact truth about reality is knowable. For, just like it would be incoherent to discuss evidence for Christianity if there was not God, it would also be incoherent to discuss truths about God, if there were no such thing as truth.

Throughout the history of Western philosophy there have been profound disagreements over the issue of natural theology. The validity of natural theology has pit Aquinas against Scotus and Ockham. It has pit Karl Barth and Emil Brunner against the Princetonians. Natural theology was something Kuyper and Warfield disagreed over, and it pit Greg Bahnsen and Van Til against John Gerstner and R. C. Sproul. Each of these men disagreed over the matter, and as we have already seen: the law of non-contradiction entails they all cannot be right, nor can they all be wrong.[165] However, it does raise the question of the validity and proper place of natural theology in our epistemology and apologetic methodology. Historically, apologists down through the centuries have affirmed that truth about reality is knowable and based upon the light of nature and common notions or principles of reason found in all of humanity, we have legitimate common ground between humanity, and the ability to engage in both arguments for the existence of God and entertain the science of natural theology.

J. V. Fesko in his book, *Reforming Apologetics*, argues that the historic position of the Church is the *light of nature* and the concept of *common notions* entail the validity of natural theology. This idea of common notions or innate natural knowledge of God properly describes how human reason can function in a post-Fall world. Fesko argues that this type of realism,

---

[164] Norman L. Geisler and Frank Turek, *I Don't Have Enough Faith to Be an Atheist* (Wheaton: Crossway, 2004), 194.

[165] For more understanding on the matter, please consult: Diogenes Allen and Eric O. Springsted, *Philosophy for Understanding Theology*, 2nd ed (Louisville: Westminster John Knox Press, 2007), 103-112.

which in many ways is the manifestation of the Platonic tradition, finds its roots in Plato, Aristotle, Augustine, Boethius, Anselm, Aquinas, Calvin, and both the early and late Reformers.[166] According to Fesko, common notions and the light of nature are the Bible's depiction of common grace and the common ground found between the believer and the unbeliever.[167] He even sets these concepts over and against what he labels as "Historic Worldview Theory" because the latter is grounded in philosophical idealism, not metaphysical realism.[168] Fesko claims:

> The term *worldview* is quite common in evangelical and Reformed circles likely due to the popular and influential nature of Kuyper's 1898 Stone Lectures at Princeton Seminary, where he advocated the need for Christians to develop a holistic life and worldview. But seldom has anyone questioned the historical origin of the term and concept. Proponents of the worldview concept acknowledge that the term originated with nineteenth-century German philosophy and the term *Weltanschauung*, but few drill down below the surface and explore its specific philosophical content. Recent research has traced the first use of the term *Weltanschauung* to Immanuel Kant (1742—1804). In his *Critique of Judgment* (1790), Kant put forth the idea that people need to dig beneath the substrate underlying the world's appearance and our worldview: 'For only by means of this power and its idea do we, in a pure intellectual estimation of magnitude, comprehend the infinite world of sense *entirely under* a concept, even though in a mathematical estimation of magnitude *by means of numerical concepts* we can never think in its entirety.' Kant identifies worldview as a perch from which someone views the totality of the world and subsumes it under a concept, and organizing principle.[169]

Many Christians, such as James Orr in his published work, *The Christian View of God and the World*, and others such as Kuyper, Van Til, within the modern Reformed tradition, taught that worldviews offered a comprehensive view of reality.[170] These figures believed that Christian and non-Christian worldviews were incompatible and antithetical to one another. They also claimed that someone must necessarily deduce an entire

---

[166] Ibid., 11-48.
[167] Ibid., 97-134.
[168] Ibid., 101.
[169] Ibid., 100-101.

[170] James Orr, *The Christian View of God and the World as Centering in the Incarnation* (1893; Edinburg: Andrew Elliot, 1907).

system from a single concept. According to these figures, the proper single concept to deduce all of reality from was the historic biblical worldview. Namely, by presupposing the singular concept of the biblical worldview, and from that particular perch, we could provide an organizing principle to understand and subsume all of reality. This approach necessarily required the use of transcendental reasoning and the Transcendental Argument for the existence of God.

Based upon the content discussed in chapter two, it ought to be clear that Norman Geisler rejected the idealism prevalent throughout the so-called Historic Worldview Theory. He was committed to philosophical realism and the belief that reality is knowable directly, and that there are common notions manifest throughout humanity that allow for common ground between all people. Geisler was not only committed to common notions, but the light of nature and nature's God;[171] namely, he not only embraced natural theology but defended it. The following section will explain Geisler's approach to natural theology and the important contribution it made towards demonstrating an evangelical apologetic in a secular age.

## Natural Theology: A Posteriori Demonstration

Norman Geisler used to say, in most of his classes, that one issue prevalent throughout evangelicalism is that most Christians have a wrong view of God. The typical evangelical belief concerning the nature and attributes of God seems to never rise above a glorified Michael the Archangel. The primary reason for making this claim is because many evangelical views of God seem to give creaturely characteristics unto the Creator. False views of God could arise for a variety of reasons, which have led to the eclipse of the classical view of God. These include false philosophical notions concerning the nature of God,[172] or the vain idolatry from humanity's rebellion against the Creator,[173] or the prevalent

---

[171] It ought to be recognized that the use of "nature's God" ought not be used as a critique that the God of natural theology, especially as expressed by Christian theologians, is somehow an idol different from the Christian God. It will be demonstrated that God is an eternal, infinite, simple, and immutable being. It ought to be readily recognized the God of Trinitarian theism is nothing less than a being who possesses these divine attributes. Moreover, because these attributes are *divine*, they necessarily entail that only God could possess them, not some vain idol.

[172] See: Etienne Gilson, *God and Philosophy* 2nd ed (New Haven: Yale University Press, 1941).

[173] See: Romans 1.

negligence of catechizing our congregants in the historic confessions of the Christian faith. Whatever the reason may be, the existence of confusion and significant disagreement over *how* we know God and *what* we mean by the term "*God*" seems evident.

Historically, there was broad unity over the *way* Christians should answer these two questions. For example, the *Westminster Larger Catechism*, question 2, asks:

How doeth it appear that there is a God?

> **Answer:** The very light of nature in man, and the works of God, declare plainly that there is a God; but his word and Spirit only do sufficiently and effectually reveal him unto men for their salvation.

The catechism, question 7 asks: What is God?

> **Answer:** God is a Spirit, in and of himself infinite in being, glory, blessedness, and perfection; all-sufficient, eternal, unchangeable, incomprehensible, everywhere present, almighty, knowing all things, most wise, most holy, most just, most merciful and gracious, long-suffering, and abundant in goodness and truth.

Geisler took up the mantle of the historic Christian tradition to demonstrate that the light of nature in man and the works of God in creation, declare plainly there is a God. Much like the *Westminster* tradition, Geisler does not stop at natural theology. Rather, he goes on to teach who God is by way of special revelation both in his Word and by his Spirit. We must also notice that the historic position on God affirms the classical attributes of God. The full *Westminster Confession of Faith* goes on to state more classical attributes in Chapter 2, claiming: *God, who is infinite in being and perfection, a most pure spirit, invisible, without body, parts, or passions, immutable, immense, eternal, incomprehensible, almighty . . .* and so forth. Note the special emphasis upon the idea that God is without parts or passions. These two phrases indicate that God is a simple Being, meaning he is not composed of any parts; and God is an impassible Being, meaning he has no passive emotions (and depending upon the commentator, any emotions whatsoever, including active passions). The confession also states that God is eternal, or not in time. Just these few attributes indicate that Geisler's defense of the classical attributes of God is in keeping with mainstream Protestant orthodoxy.

More about this will be said later; however, for now, we must give attention to the way God is known. Can we know God *via* his effects? Is *a posteriori* reasoning about the nature of God possible? Can man have a comprehensible knowledge of God or is our knowledge of God only partial? Do we know God as he exists in and of himself or by means of analogy, perfection, and negation? These types of questions will be addressed throughout the rest of this chapter.

There are several characteristics of natural theology important to this discussion. Axiomatic throughout the realist tradition is a commitment to the belief that there is a present desire in man to know. Man will never cease to ask questions about himself and the universe. What is reality? Why do things exist? Why is there something rather than nothing? What does it mean to exist? Knowledge rests upon certain habits of the mind that inhere within man. Natural theology is a naturally acquired and operative habit by which man can acquire new types of knowledge. This special kind of knowledge gained through habit gives way to an understanding of the nature of metaphysics and natural theology. Metaphysical knowledge is deemed a type of scientific knowledge because it reasons about causes, or more specifically it provides knowledge through causes. To know a thing through its causes or principles is to draw a conclusion. Thus, scientific knowledge, and metaphysics as a type of scientific knowledge, is a type of knowledge gained by the habit of drawing conclusions from principles, which principles are the cause or reason why the mind draws the conclusion. These principles are readily found both in external reality and humanity. The causes of scientific knowledge are twofold. The first kind is one that is both ontological and logical. The second kind is one that is merely logical. In both cases scientific knowledge is knowledge gained through causes, which causes in the act of scientific knowledge, also known as premises. And since scientific knowledge is always something *concluded there unto*, it is inferred through other knowledge. This is also known as the act or process of reasoning from premises to a conclusion. The drawing of a conclusion is an act of reason.[174] Therefore, any act that proceeds *via* premises to a conclusion is reasoning, and this inferential search for causes is a type of science; hence, metaphysics is also considered a type of science.

Knowledge, however, even scientific knowledge, has different objects of knowledge, which are known according to their mode of being, and the mode of knowledge according to the knowing *being*. In other words, Classical Realists claim that each thing that exists is known in a particular way. Moreover, each thing that can know something must know according to their nature. The nature of knowledge must be according to the mode of existence of a being. Historically, this is affirmed based upon the claim to a grand hierarchy being (i.e., chain of being) and how beings come to

---

[174] Joseph Owens, *An Elementary Christian Metaphysic* (Notre Dame: University of Notre Dame Press, 1963), 17-130.

know things. Peter Kreeft charts this hierarchy with special emphasis upon both the nature of the being and kind of knowledge each being can have:[175]

| Name | Science | Matter & Form | Potency & Act | Kind of Knowledge |
|---|---|---|---|---|
| God | Theology | Pure form | Pure act | Knowledge = one with being |
| Angels | Angelology | Pure form | Essence (potency) & existence (act) | Intuitive |
| Men | Anthropology Psychology | Rational soul = form of body | Essence & existence and matter & form | Rational |
| Animals | Zoology | Sensitive soul | " | Sensory |
| Plants | Botany | Vegetative soul | " | None |
| Things | Physics | No soul; purely material forms | " | " |
| Chemical elements | Chemistry | First rudimentary forms (wet/dry, hot/cold) | " | " |
| Prime Matter | None | Formless matter | Pure potency | " |

---

[175] Peter Kreeft, *Summa of the Summa* (San Francisco: Ignatius Press, 1990), 135

From this chart, it is apparent that each thing or object of knowledge is known according to its own science, or knowledge by way of causes. There is a difference between intuitive, rational, and sensory forms of knowledge. These different forms of knowledge or modes of knowledge are what distinguish angels, men, and animals. God on the other hand, has knowledge of his own being. God may know what we know, but he does not know it in the same way or mode of knowledge that we know.

As the notion of forms or modes of knowledge apply to the subject of metaphysics, it must be remembered that there are two kinds of first principles the mind can know. There are first principles of *being*, things that cause or constitute being, such as essence, substance, accidents, and so forth. These first principles also exist in *reality*. Second, there are first principles that are not principles of being, but *first truths* about beings or statements about beings. And these principles exist only in the mind and are called logical or first principles of knowledge.[176] They are first truths about beings and considered indemonstrable first principles of knowledge. This latter type exists only in the mind but is caused by existing things; whereas first principles of being exist in reality.[177]

The formal object of metaphysics is the study of being as *being*. Through this science we are seeking to study the principles or causes of its subject, namely both incomplete and complete principles. The incomplete principles are things such as essence, act, potency, accident, and rightly deemed first philosophy, or a study of first principles. But in the study of metaphysics there is also a demonstration about complete principles of being as being, and the causality which extends to all beings. Complete principles are entirely perfect and entirely in Act, and are something different from incomplete being, and possess the characteristics of divine Being. And in this sense, insofar as metaphysics demonstrates the existence and nature of this first and complete principle of being, it is rightly and aptly declared to be a divine science or a natural theology. And because the subject matter or object is the same between metaphysics and natural theology, they are essentially one and the same science.[178] Finally, both metaphysically and theologically there is only one Being who fits into this type of category—God.

---

[176] Owens, *An Elementary Guide to Christian Metaphysics*, 213-310.

[177] Ibid., 43-56.

[178] Joseph Owens, *An Interpretation of Existence* (Houston: Center for Thomistic Studies, 1968), 14-43.

Whenever natural theology seeks to treat its object it is trying to explain the formal object of its scientific inquiry. Within special revelation or sacred theology, God reveals himself to us through the text of Scripture. But in a natural science, God cannot be the proper subject matter, since something that is directly given in nature or coming directly from nature, is to be investigated and known. And because God is not a being whose nature can be directly identified with nature, since God's nature is incompatible with the attributes or properties of created being, God is not directly offered to our intellect as an object of understanding about which we can make predicates, premises, and reason unto conclusions. Rather, given the natural order of being and our mode of existence, the term *God* is offered to our intellect as something that must be demonstrated through reason.[179] God's nature is not offered to our intellect directly, but indirectly; the term "God" is something given mediately, not immediately; not in and of himself, but through his creatures; God is not the principle subject, but only the principle cause of the subject. Natural theology attempts to treat God's existence and nature insofar as these can be known from an understanding of created being according to their mode of understanding.[180] In other words, natural theology proceeds to knowledge of God from effects to cause, or *a posteriori* reasoning, because knowledge of the sensible is prior to our knowledge of God, whose nature is suprasensible.[181]

The existence of an effect necessarily and immediately depends upon its proper cause. Therefore, given the existence of an effect; rationally, the existence of its proper cause necessarily and immediately follows. According to Aristotle and Aquinas, sensible or material things are immediately known to us and our knowledge of them is prior to our knowledge of God. Thus, if these material existent things can be shown to be effects, to be creatures, they can be legitimately used to demonstrate the existence of God. They have properties or characteristics of effects, of things that are produced, of things that receive their being. But because all effects pre-exist in their cause, these perfects must be found in a greater degree in the cause, and these beings must be necessarily and immediately dependent upon this Being as their proper cause.[182]

---

[179] Owens, *An Elementary Christian Metaphysics*, 353-364.
[180] Ibid., 276-292.
[181] Maurice R. Holloway, S.J., *An Introduction to Natural Theology* (New York: Appleton-Century, 1959), 60-79.
[182] For more information on the nature of *a posteriori* reasoning in Aquinas, see: Etienne Gilson, *The Christian Philosophy of St. Thomas Aquinas* (New York: Random House, 1956), 29-45; Etienne Gilson, *Being and Some Philosophers* (Toronto: Pontifical Institute of Mediaeval Studies, 1949), 154-189; Joseph Owens, "A Note on the Approach to Thomistic

With this background in mind concerning the nature of *a posteriori* reasoning and the historic understanding of natural theology, we will move to the existence and attributes of God. Since so many people are aware of Aquinas's explanation of the 5 Ways and because the proper focus of this chapter is Norman Geisler, we will not restate Aquinas's arguments. Rather, we will focus exclusively upon an extended argument developed by Geisler based upon Aquinas's 5 Ways. Geisler's form of the argument properly and accurately explains both his approach and specific contribution to theistic arguments and theology proper.

## Thomistic Arguments and Attributes of God

In the book, *Philosophy of Religion*, Norman Geisler and Winfried Corduan layout several arguments for the existence of God. Included in that list is Aquinas's 5 Ways.[183] Aquinas presents arguments from motion, efficient causality, the possibility and necessity of things, gradation (perfection) of things, and final causality.[184] Geisler and Corduan conclude, "Each argument begins in some characteristic of being (change, causality, contingency, and perfection respectively) and then argues to a first Cause:

1. Some dependent being exists.

2. All dependent beings must have a cause for their dependent existence.

3. An infinite regress of existentially dependent causes is impossible.

4. Therefore, there must be a first uncaused Cause of the existence of every dependent being.

5. This independent Being is identical with the I AM of Holy Scripture (the implication is that it is impossible to have more than one absolutely necessary and independent being upon which everything else exists for its being).[185]

The summation of this approach is the foundation for Geisler's extended Thomistic argument. Geisler grounds his arguments in self-

---

Metaphysics," *New Scholasticism*, 28 (1954), 454-476; Joseph Owens, "A Note on the Intelligibility of Being," *Gregorianum*, 36 (1955), 169-193.

[183] Norman Geisler and Winfried Corduan, *Philosophy of Religion* (Eugene: Wipf and Stock, 1988), 158-160.

[184] Ibid.,

[185] Ibid., 160.

evident, first principles of being, which he believes support a Christian worldview.[186] These include 1. Being is—the principle of existence; 2. Being is being—the principle of identity; 3. Being is not nonbeing—the principle of noncontradiction; 4. Either being or nonbeing—the principle of excluded middle; 5. Nonbeing cannot produce being—the principle of causality; 6. Being causes being similar to itself—the principle of analogy.[187]

From this overview of the principles of being, Geisler deduces what he considers "undeniable conclusions."[188] We will quote Geisler at length:[189]

7. A being can be either necessary or contingent but not both. This is based on the principle of excluded middle (#4).

8. A necessary Being cannot produce another necessary Being (#3). The opposite of this is reducible to a contradiction because (a) a necessary Being by its nature cannot come to be or cease to be, and (b) the being that is caused by a necessary Being comes to be (which is contradictory).

9. A contingent being cannot cause another contingent being (#3). This is because a contingent being is one that could not-be (i.e., could be nothing), and if it caused another being, then nonbeing would be producing being (which is contradictory).[190]

10. A necessary Being is Being of Pure Actuality, with no potentiality. This is so since a necessary Being has no potentiality to not exist. If a necessary Being exists, then it must exist necessarily, with no possibility not to exist.

11. A Being of Pure Actuality cannot produce another being with pure actuality. The being that is produced by a Being of Pure Actuality must have both actuality and potentiality, for this

---

[186] Note, the use of the term worldview differs from the HWT listed above. Geisler is not starting from a concept to explain reality. Rather, Geisler is starting in reality or first principles to build a worldview.

[187] Norman L. Geisler, *Christian Apologetics* 2nd ed (Grand Rapids: Baker, 2013), 266.

[188] Ibid.

[189] Ibid., 266-268. Note: I correct one editorial error in the original citation of premise 7. Geisler initially claimed it was based on the principle of excluded middle and cited (#3). However, in the chart the principle of excluded middle is (#4).

[190] It seems like Geisler is not clear at this point, or there is a bit of equivocation. When he says, "A contingent being cannot cause another contingent being," we can overcome the equivocation by stating "ultimately cause" or "ultimate originating cause." The point is not to do away with secondary causality, as is the case with parents "causing" a child. Rather, he is dealing with the topic of primary causality, or the ultimate cause of contingent being. I also believe Geisler could cite (#5) as justification for this point.

created being has the potentiality not to be, which Pure Actuality does not have.

12. Every being caused by a Being of Pure Actuality must be both like and unlike its Cause (#6). It must be like its Cause in its actuality, and it must be unlike its cause in its potentiality. And what is both like and unlike its cause is similar (or analogous) to it.

13. I am a contingent being. This is so since I undeniably exist (#2), and I am neither a necessary Being nor an impossible being. I am not an impossible being since I do exist. And I am not a necessary Being because I change or come to be (which a necessary Being cannot do). Hence, I am a contingent being. But only a necessary Being can cause a contingent being (#9). Even a pantheist, who claims to be identical to God, admits that he or she came to be in a state of "enlightenment," and thus was not always in it.

14. Therefore, a necessary Being (of Pure Actuality) exists that causes me to exist.

15. This necessary Being is a Being of Pure Actuality (with no potentiality) and has certain necessary attributes:

   a. It cannot change (= is *immutable*) since it has not potential for change.

   b. It cannot be temporal (= is *eternal*) since that involves change.

   c. It cannot be material (= is *immaterial*) since that involves change.

   d. It cannot be finite (= is *infinite*) since it has no potentiality to limit it.

   e. It cannot be divisible (= is *simple*) since it has no potential to be divided.

   f. It must be an *uncaused* being since it is a necessary Being, and a necessary Being cannot be caused to come to be. So, it can't be caused. Nor can it be self-caused, which is a contradiction. Hence, it must be an uncaused being.

   g. It must be only *One* being since there can't be two or more infinite Beings or two or more Beings of Pure Actuality;

> there is no way they could differ in their Being, for they are both the same kind of Being. And beings cannot differ in the very respect in which they are the same.
>
> h. It must be infinitely knowing (= *omniscient*) since I am a knowing being that it caused to exist, and a cause cannot give what it does not have to give (#6).
>
> i. It must be all-powerful (= *omnipotent*) since it is infinite, and it has the power to cause finite being to exist.
>
> j. It must be an absolutely *morally perfect* Being since it causes moral beings to exist, and it cannot share with it does not have to share (#6).
>
> k. It must be a *personal* Being since it made personal beings, and the effect is similar to its efficient cause (#6).

In keeping with his philosophical forefather—Aquinas—this infinite, eternal, morally perfect, omniscient, omnipotent, immutable, uncaused Being is the cause of all finite being(s) and it what we all mean by the term—God.

There are several things unique to Geisler's approach and the *way* he believes an apologist ought to engage an Age of Unbelief. These factors explain the significant contribution Geisler made to present-day natural theology and evangelical apologetics. Geisler's argument also uniquely addresses the conditions of belief in an Enlightenment era because he grounds them in a pre-Enlightenment metaphysic, which is the only metaphysic capable of addressing the errors of modernity. In other words, there has been significant talk amongst apologists to not allow the non-Christian, especially those steeped in modernist epistemology, set the terms and parameters of our epistemology. That claim in many respects is a central point in Alvin Plantinga's book, *Warranted Christian Belief*.[191] Plantinga requires that the parameters of Christian theism ground his epistemology. Why can't we do the same thing with our metaphysic? Geisler's career demonstrated that the best way to address modernity is to not buy into modernity's metaphysic. In rejecting modernity's metaphysic, one will not buy into modernity's epistemology. Moreover, one must recognize that there is such a thing as a uniquely Christian metaphysic. Figures such as Augustine and Aquinas did not merely "baptize" Plato and Aristotle. Rather, they saw elements of truth based upon first principles of reality coupled with the innovative aspects of Christian revelation and were

---

[191] Alvin Plantinga, *Warranted Christian Belief* (New York: Oxford University Press, 2000).

able to develop a unique understanding of being, essence, divine ideas, and many other specific ontological tenets grounded in the Christian faith.[192] In a similar sense, we can see that Geisler did the same thing in the following ways.

First, Geisler is not just arguing for a God who started the whole process at the beginning of time. Unlike the Kalam cosmological argument, which argues that God is required to explain the *origin* of the universe, Geisler's argument is made to discuss the *current* existence of the universe. This is the difference between the horizontal and vertical forms of the cosmological argument. Geisler states, "Both are causal arguments and both begin with an existing cosmos. However, the horizontal argument starts with a universe that had a *beginning* (long ago), and the second with a universe that has *being* (right now). The former stresses originating causality, and the latter focuses on conserving causality. The first argues to a *First Cause* (back then), and the second argues to a *Necessary Cause* (at present)."[193] The Kalam argument is sufficiently able to explain the existence of the universe at a particular point in time. Many skeptics and atheists attempt to critique this form of the cosmological argument claiming an infinite and eternal world can account for the material world. While we recognize this form of argumentation is fallacious, since several figures have critiqued this failed approach by atheists,[194] it is not the type of argument being offered by Geisler. Geisler's argument is grounded in the present contingency of the universe and the fact if a Necessary Being did not currently exist, then neither would any contingent being(s) currently exist.

Second, while it can be granted that other forms of the cosmological argument or other theistic proofs can tell us certain truths about God's nature, Geisler's Vertical cosmological proof offers us both the *existence* and *attributes* of God. For Geisler, the Thomistic position on the plurality of beings demonstrates that the multiplicity is possible because there are different kinds of being(s). There is a real distinction between existence and essence. Created being is a dynamic and complex composition of essence and existence. It has the principles of potency and act. The central question

---

[192] Owen, *An Elementary Christian Metaphysic*, 1-16; Gilson, *God and Philosophy*, 38-73; Eleonore Stump, *The God of the Bible and the God of the Philosophers* (Marquette: Marquette University Press, 2016).

[193] Norman L. Geisler, *Systematic Theology: Introduction and Bible* (Minneapolis: Bethany House, 2002), 28.

[194] William Lane Craig, *Reasonable Faith: Christian Truth and Apologetics*, 3rd edition (Wheaton: Crossway, 2008), 111-156.

we ask is: what kind of being exists?[195] At one point it was said that most people's view of God is typically nothing more than a glorified Michael the Archangel. People in many respects fail to recognize there that is a difference of kind between the Creator and the creation. God is not in a genus or a species. God is not the most exalted figure at the top of the pyramid. Rather, God is in a category of his own. God is not just the smartest Being. Rather, God's knowledge is unique unto his mode of existence. God is not just a timeless figure who sees the end from the beginning; instead, God is an eternal Being whose nature is incompatible with the nature of time. God is his own existence (i.e., simple Being). God is his own actuality (i.e., Pure Actuality), and he does not derive it from any other being(s) (i.e., Aseity and Necessity). God is that which affects all other beings and whose nature is by no means affected by any other being(s) (i.e., God is immutable and impassible).

In the following chart, Geisler summarizes the different kinds of being and the theological implications for theology proper, angelology, and anthropology. Special attention must be given to the metaphysical classification and distinctions found in each kind of being. The following chart provides the necessary contrast:[196]

|  | God | Angels | Humans |
| --- | --- | --- | --- |
| **Mode of Being** | Uncreated | Created | Created |
| **Limits** | Infinite | Finite | Finite |
| **Nature** | Spirit | Spirit | Spirit-Body |
| **Simplicity** | Absolute simplicity (Pure Act) | Relative simplicity (Act/Pot) | No simplicity (A Complex; Act/Pot) |
| **Duration** | Eternal (uncreated eternity) | Aevieternal (created eternity) | Temporal (created temporality) |

---

[195] Geisler, *Introduction and Bible*, 25.

[196] Norman L. Geisler, *Systematic Theology: God and Creation* (Minneapolis: Bethany House, 2003), 486.

| | | | |
|---|---|---|---|
| Change | None | None in essence, only in will | Changeable in nature and will |
| Relation to Change | Cannot be joined to change | Not changing, but can be joined to change | Can be joined to change by nature |
| Measurability | Only be His own absolute simplicity | By degrees of unity and perfection | By plurality in matter (i.e., in space and time) |
| Space | Time above it and cannot be in it | Above it, but can be in it (relationally) | In it by nature |
| Actuality | Pure Actuality | Completed actuality | Progressively completed actuality |
| Potentiality | None | None uncompleted | Uncompleted potentiality |
| Nature/Will | Neither can change | Only will can change | Both can change |
| Classification | (Species) beyond all classes | Each a class of one | All in one class (a race) |
| Redemption | Source of all redemption | Irredeemable, no change in essence | Redeemable |
| Free Will | Unchangeable before and after the choice | Changeable before but not after choice | Changeable before and after choice |

According to Geisler and the Thomistic tradition, there is an ontological difference of kind between the various types of being(s).

Whenever we compare a large and small triangle, we realize there is an inherent difference of degree between the two figures. The same could be said between a large and small circle. We recognize a difference of degree between the two geometrical figures. However, if we start to add another line onto a triangle in hope of it turning into a circle, we would be traversing a spurious path. The reason is because there is a difference of *kind* between a circle and a triangle. There is a logical chance the triangle may approach a circle. Nevertheless, it is also logically and ontologically impossible for a triangle to actually become a circle.

Similarly, there is a difference of kind between God, angels, and humanity. It is incorrect for someone to claim that a deceased family member becomes an angel after they die. It is no more possible for a human being to become an angel than it is for a triangle to become a circle. They are not essentially related according to their mode of being. There is an inherent ontological difference of kind. Moreover, it is incorrect for someone to claim that they have become God, as is claimed by Mormons and many New Age figures. There is a difference of kind between the nature of humanity and divine Being. God is eternal, infinite, unchangeable, and simple. Humanity is temporal, finite, changeable, and complex. The principles of being do not allow for these two mutually exclusive beings to be similar at the same time and sense. Moreover, one would have to fundamentally change their mode of being in order to become another kind of being; hence, showing a radical discontinuity with their essence, and the principle of identity, which is rationally absurd.

Third, according to Thomistic realism, not only do we demonstrate the existence of God, but we can deduce the attributes of God from our theistic proofs (i.e., 5 Ways). For the sake of argument, it must be noted that God's attribute of Pure Actuality is the most important for both Aquinas and Geisler. The reason for this is because in an *a posteriori* approach, the most well-known difference between God and creatures is the fact that one has potentiality, and the other does not. Since God is an Uncaused and Necessary Being, we see Pure Actuality follows from the premises proven in the Vertical cosmological argument. Moreover, from Pure Actuality all the other metaphysical attributes of God can be deduced: Simplicity follows from Pure Actuality; Aseity follows from Pure Actuality; Immutability follows from Pure Actuality; Necessity follows from Pure Actuality; Eternality (Nontemporality) follows from Pure Actuality; and Infinity follows form Pure Actuality.[197] As Geisler states, "In short, all the basic metaphysical attributes of God follow logically from His pure actuality and His pure actually follows from His being the Uncaused First Cause of

---

[197] Geisler, *God and Creation*, 33-34.

all else that exists."[198] Classical theism is a package deal. If you grant one attribute, you can deduce all the rest. On the other hand, the classical attributes of God stand or fall together. If you deny one, then logically speaking, you can construct an argument to deny the rest of the classical attributes.[199] Several objections have been leveled against classical theism.[200] One can look to Geisler's *Systematic Theology: God and Creation* and his co-authored book with H. Wayne House and Max Herrera, titled, *The Battle for God*, to find his comprehensive response to the objections raised against classical theism.[201]

Fourth, within the Thomistic system, God can be both the object of reason or science and the object of faith. Just like the same truths of physics or mathematics can be believed on the authority of another mind or understood by one's own reason, we too can know God through a variety of ways. The Thomistic system provides a coherent explanation of the relationship between faith and reason. Insofar as faith goes beyond reason, it is not scientifically demonstrable (i.e., the Trinity), even though reason can properly discuss it and refute objections. Reason can properly offer true analogies, arguments, and discuss objections raised against the articles of faith. Just because reason cannot discuss everything about an object does not entail reason cannot offer true statements about an object. One's inability to explain the full complexity of Einstein's theory of general relativity, does not necessarily mean that they cannot explain limited truths about the theory or refute objections raised against it. That said, insofar as human reason can understand and prove the existence and nature of God and some truths about God, it can generate a science of theology, or natural theology.

Fifth, some people claim human reason is too weak to be able to prove the existence and nature of God. They claim what is not proved and known with certainty cannot really be said to be true knowledge. And since God's existence and nature are not known with certainty, we cannot be said to truly have a proper natural theology or philosophical theology. Several things can be said to this type of approach. First, it is simply not

---

[198] Ibid., 34.

[199] More will be said about the current debate over classical realism and theistic personalism in a section below. For now, however, we must see the unity of the classical attributes of God.

[200] I plan to respond to a few objections raised against classical theism by way of illustration later in the chapter. For now, it must be noted that Geisler has offered a significant response to each objection.

[201] Norman L. Geisler, H. Wayne House, and Max Herrera, *The Battle for God: Responding to the Challenge of Neotheism* (Grand Rapids: Kregel, 2001).

true we are unable to prove the existence of God with certainty. If deductive logic brings a certain and undeniable conclusion, and if the terms are clear and the form of the argument is valid, then the conclusion follows necessarily and with certainty. Second, there is a difference between the certainty of an argument and the certainty of the recipient. The subjective factors of an individual do not properly affect the certainty of the argument. No one denies that psychological or sociological factors can affect a person and keep them from accepting an argument for the existence of God. But, even when someone says these factors somehow disprove the certainty of God's existence, they must realize this type of argumentation arises more from an assumed dogma concerning human nature, not a demonstrated conclusion.

Sixth, the task of natural theology and the Thomistic system can account for the noetic effects of sin. First of all, to properly understand the classical system we must recognize the full outline of the *Summa* and Aquinas's other theological works. Aquinas's *Summa* is a long and extended discussion that starts and ends with God. How do we get from God as Creator and back to God as Redeemer? That is the task of the *Summa*. That said, the entire *Summa* is a long and extended treatise on the nature of grace in one's relationship towards God. Second, Frederick Copleston, in his famous multivolume, *A History of Philosophy*, says this about Aquinas:

> Similarly, in the *Summa Theologica*, St. Thomas observes that the truth about God is arrived at by the human reason only by a few men and after a long time and 'with the admixture of errors'. When the Saint says that it is desirable that those truths about God which are rationally demonstrable should be proposed as objects of belief, to be accepted on authority, he emphasizes indeed the practical requirements of many rather than the speculative insufficiency of metaphysics as such, but he does admit that error is frequently mixed with the truth, either because of over-hastiness in jumping to conclusions or because of the influence of passion and emotion or of imagination. Possibly he did not himself apply this idea with perfect consistency in regard to Aristotle and was too ready to interpret Aristotle in the sense which was most compatible with Christian doctrine, but the fact remains that he acknowledges theoretically the weakness of the human intellect in its present condition, though not its radical perversion.[202]

---

[202] Frederick Copleston, *A History of Philosophy: Medieval Philosophy: From Augustine to Duns Scotus*, vol. 2 (New York: Doubleday, 1950), 321.

One must look to the actual outline of the *Summa* as a response to this objection. After Aquinas establishes the existence of God, he spends hundreds of pages explaining what he means by "God" and refuting objections raised against the classical definition. Why would Aquinas do such a thing? It is because people have false views of God and Aquinas knew it was his task to overcome those objections that arose from reason, personal biases, false religions, and sinful idolatry. Aquinas not only responded to them, but he showed the utter and complete impossibility of those false idols in comparison to the true God. In short, those who level this type of objection typically have a very myopic understanding of Aquinas's corpus of literature and are unaware of the secondary literature on the topic.[203]

An example of this type of approach comes from Scott Oliphint and his book on Thomas Aquinas. While it must be granted that Oliphint seems to be well read in many of the secondary resources and much of the original text of Aquinas, there are several places in which he demonstrates a rudimentary knowledge of the Angelic Doctor. Paul Helm responded to one of these types of objections raised by Oliphint. Helm's response proves the point so thoroughly that it is worth quoting him at length. Helm claims:

> Aquinas's discussion of divine simplicity is particularly significant in that it is a notion that is entailed both by his opening remarks on the articles of Christian theology and his proofs of God's existence. Prior to the occurrence of the Five Ways in Question 3 of Part One, Thomas tells us in more than one place that God cannot be known as he is in himself, but by what he brings about, his effects.
>
> He points out in 1a 1.7 that we cannot know what God is but by some effect or effects of nature or grace. For God cannot be defined. He reiterates the point in 1a 2.1, and it is expanded further in 1a 2.3. Shortly after this point, he comes to the Five Ways which are five arguments from effects to their divine cause.
>
> Oliphint ignores almost everything else that Aquinas wrote, both in the ST or elsewhere, and what he reflects on he does not do a very good job.[204]

---

[203] See: Norman L. Geisler, ed. Paul A. Compton, *The Collected Essays of Norman L. Geisler, vol. 3: 1986-1994* (Matthews, Bastion Books, 2019), 218-223.

[204] https://credomag.com/2019/01/who-is-afraid-of-thomas-aquinas-a-reply-to-scott-oliphint-part-1-paul-helm/

Moreover, Helm states:

> Regarding some of these apologetic questions, there is great pressure to think that the proofs of God's existence that Thomas sets forth in ST, 1a 1.2.3 referred to as the Five Ways, are foundational to the existence of the articles of faith, the doctrines of the Christian faith, such that everyone committed to the articles has first to be committed to the proofs. But this is a mistake, as we shall see. This pressure does not come from Aquinas himself, but from the way in which his proofs of the existence of God have become separated from the body of his theology, as rational "proofs" in the Enlightenment and post-Enlightenment sense. Aquinas rarely refers to "foundations" in the modern sense, though they figure prominently in Oliphint's account of him.
>
> Oliphint underscores this, incidentally, by pointing out that several different versions of the proofs are extant in Thomas's writings (56-57). This suggests a philosopher working on arguments that he is not altogether satisfied with, rather than with someone aiming at canonical finality. The reference to Exodus 3:14 in the proofs (1a 2.3) does not detract from their philosophical character in the ST; rather, it shows them to be a philosophical project whose aim is to demonstrate that a conclusion, namely, that God exists, is not only reasonable but is also consistent with the God of revelation.
>
> It is a great pity that the author [Oliphint] has not given to his readers some idea of the sweep of Thomas's philosophical and theological ideas. He has also decided to pay very little attention to the different ways in which he has been influential in the history of theology subsequently, both in Roman Catholicism and in Protestantism. In this review, we shall be following him in his largely unsatisfactory discussion of material in the first articles of Book I of the ST, which he treats in an avowedly ahistorical way (2-3). This extends to the idea of apologetics itself, which Aquinas hardly mentions.[205]

In other words, sometimes the best way to respond to these types of objections raised against Aquinas is to ask the person raising the objection to read more broadly and charitably the original works of Aquinas; and offer a principle of charity that maybe the secondary sources or critics misread Aquinas, therefore, they might be unknowingly buying into that

---

[205] Ibid.

false tradition of interpretation. Geisler is unique amongst Protestant theologians because he allowed Aquinas to speak for himself. Geisler did not immediately fall prey to many of the false claims circulating about Aquinas. In that sense, Geisler was unique amongst present-day Protestant theologians. On the other hand, Geisler's approach towards Aquinas was not unique. He stood upon the shoulders of many Scholastic Reformers, Puritans, and Princetonian theologians, who also read Aquinas with great charity and incorporated many of his views into their systems.[206] Novelty is not found standing on the side of classical theism, rather, it is found aligning oneself with the prevalent neo-theism of present-day evangelicalism.

Seventh, there are several figures within evangelicalism who charge classical theism as being a false Greek synthesis with Christianity. Geisler was uniquely positioned as a trained philosopher and theologian to respond to these types of objections. Geisler claims, "Most major movements in modern philosophy find their source in Greek philosophy, particularly the view from which this objection springs. (Neotheism is a descendant of the process thought of Heraclitus [c. 504/501 B.C.—44/441 B.C.])."[207] He also notes it would be a genetic fallacy to reject a view simply based upon its source. In order to remain consistent with this claim, one would also have to reject the laws of logic, since they are based on supposed Greek thinking.[208] Geisler also insists, "The Christian view of God is not Greek in origin. No Greek ever had a triunity of three persons in one eternal essence. In fact, no Greek philosopher ever identified his ultimate metaphysical principle with his God or gods. This was the unique contribution of theistic thinkers."[209] Copleston goes beyond Geisler in this regard, claiming:

> It would be absurd, of course, to suggest that the Thomist philosophy is simply Aristotelianism, since he makes use of other writers like St. Augustine and the Pseudo-Dionysius, as also of his medieval predecessors and of Jewish (Maimonides in particular) and Arabian philosophers; but none the less the Thomist synthesis is unified by the application of fundamental Aristotelian principles.[210]

---

[206] Manfred Svensson and David VanDrunen, *Aquinas Amongst the Protestants* (Hoboken: John Wiley & Sons, 2018).

[207] Geisler, *God and Creation*, 55.

[208] Ibid., 56.

[209] Ibid.

[210] Copleston, *A History of Philosophy*, 423.

In brief, Aquinas was not slavishly given over to Aristotle. Throughout his writings, Aquinas critiqued Aristotle in favor of Christian principles. Geisler was one figure who was able to do the same. Geisler was committed to the principle: All truth is God's truth. Nonetheless, one must also temper this claim and suggest: *All truth is God's truth, if the matter being adopted is actually true.* No one, Geisler in particular, blindly adopted some vain Greek view of God. Rather, based upon self-evident first principles, Geisler developed a comprehensive argument for the existence and attributes of God.

The following section is going to engage the present-day debate over the nature of God within evangelicalism. Geisler mounted a significant defense of the classical attributes of God over and against mediating models of theism.

## The Significance of Classical Theism

Following the funeral of Norman Geisler, a handful of us who served as his former assistants went out to dinner. That evening we reminisced of the great times we had with Dr. Geisler. Each of us told funny stories or interesting encounters Geisler had with theologians at conferences and various events. That evening, however, new light was shed upon one of Geisler's favorite stories. Dr. Joe Holden, president of Veritas International University, told us about a time Geisler asked Joe to pick him up at the airport in California. Geisler handed Joe the address to the location of his lecture and off they went, weaving in and out of the traffic on their way. As they arrived, Joe noticed it was a large building and Geisler was asked to enter a side door. Upon entering, the building was filled with about two thousand students, including the faculty. The school Geisler was asked to lecture at was BIOLA University. Geisler gave his lecture, went through a Q&A period, and after that, left and moved on to the next event.

Now, we had all heard that story. What we did not know was the fact Joe was his driver and experienced the whole event. The topic of the lecture was Geisler's response to what he labeled as neotheism. The topic centered around the doctrine of God where Geisler offered a defense of classical theism over and against neotheism. Classical theism has a strong commitment to the doctrine of God found in theologians such as Augustine, Anslem, and Aquinas. Classical theism is also the view of God found in the older Protestant confessions such as the Belgic Confession, Thirty-Nine Articles, Westminster Confession of Faith, and the London Baptist Confession of Faith. Classical theism is defined by its clear and unashamed commitment to divine simplicity, aseity, eternality, immutability, and impassibility. There is an explicit allegiance to the belief God is absolutely immutable and Pure Act; hence, God does not derive any of his being from without. God is in no way externally dependent for his existence, knowledge, or essence, upon any outside created being. In contrast to this view is a new approach known as theistic mutualism, or sometimes called theistic personalism. Geisler's lecture at BIOLA was a response to theistic personalism from the vantage point of Thomistic realism.

Whenever you survey the landscape of present-day evangelicalism and theology proper it is clear there is a divide over the nature and attributes of God. James Dolezal has taken up the mantel of defending classical theism over and against theistic personalism. Dolezal defines "mutualism", in his book, *All That is in God*, claiming:

> Mutualism, as I am using the term, denotes a symbiotic relationship in which both parties derive something from each other. In such a relationship, it is requisite that each party be capable of being ontologically moved or acted upon and thus determined by the other. This does not necessarily require parity between the parties involved. Accordingly, a mutualistic relation could obtain even if only one of the parties involved were the architect and ultimate regulator of the relation.[211]

Theistic mutualism has become the predominant view of God amongst evangelical philosophers and theologians, both Reformed and non-Reformed.[212] Prominent philosophers such as Alvin Plantinga, Richard Swinburne, William Lane Craig, Nicholas Wolterstorff, and the late Ronald Nash have each defended in one way or another a form of theistic mutualism. Dolezal lists several evangelical theologians who have also taken up the mantle of defending theistic mutualism, or at least showing sympathy towards the position, including: Clark Pinnock, John Sanders, Richard Rice, William Hasker, David Basinger, Thomas Morris, Bruce Ware, Donald MacLeod, D. A. Carson, John Frame, K. Scott Oliphint, Wayne Grudem, John Feinberg, and Kevin Vanhoozer.[213]

---

[211] James E. Dolezal, *All That is in God: Evangelical Theology and the Challenge of Classical Christian Theism* (Grand Rapids: Reformation Heritage Books, 2017), 1.

[212] The proper citations and justification for listing each of these figures is found in Dolezal's book, *All That is in God*. In his book, Dolezal not only lists these key figures but offers direct quotes and citations from their original writings. It is beyond the scope of this work to list each citation for the listed figures, since Dolezal has already done a fine job of that in his writings.

[213] It ought to be sufficiently noted that there is a world of difference between a figure such as Clark Pinnock, John Sanders, and other open theists verses those who affirm less

From this list of philosophers and theologians, there is a broad range of commitment to mutualism. Clark Pinnock obviously embraces one of the harder forms of the view, whereas Oliphint embraces a softer form. In fact, Dolezal distinguishes between soft and hard forms of mutualism, not only to allow for clarity, but to help distinguish the type of commitment to the view by various philosophers and theologians.[214] Dolezal rightly claims:

> The harder sort regards God as a person who allows other beings to function as first causes or absolute originators of actions, events, or objects and who Himself stands as an onlooker with creation, susceptible to an increase in knowledge. Hard theistic mutualism also tends to regard God as needing the world in some respects; thus, He is compelled to create and sustain it. It is this harder theistic mutualism espoused by open theists and process theists. Soft theistic mutualism, in contrast, tends to hold that God does not create the world by dint of absolute necessity; neither does He need the world in any significant sense. Moreover, many soft theistic mutualists do not believe that God is intellectually open or in process of development. Indeed, many who subscribe to the softer variety of mutualism have stood firmly against intellectual and volitional 'becoming' in God. They maintain that God neither learns nor depends on creation for His knowledge and that His will is not changed by the actions of creatures. Nevertheless, they do allow for a measure of ontological becoming and process in God.[215]

Theistic mutualists approach the doctrine from a variety of angles. For example, figures such as Ronald Nash and Alvin Plantinga claim the concept of the classical theist view of God is incoherent.[216] Belief in the doctrine of simplicity would entail one of God's attributes is identical with another attribute, which they believe is absurd. For others, such as John Frame and Scott Oliphint, classical theism is wrongly based on a Greek view of God and it fails to do justice to the picture of God we find in Scripture.[217] In Scripture, so they claim, we find a picture of God actually responding to our prayers, not a cold and static immutable God. Other figures claim our

---

extreme positions. Nonetheless, each figure to some degree has moved away from the classical theist understanding of God.

[214] Ibid., 3.

[215] Ibid., 3-4.

[216] Ronald H. Nash, *The Concept of God: An Exploration of Contemporary Difficulties with the Attributes of God* (Grand Rapids: Zondervan, 1983); Alvin Plantinga, *Does God Have a Nature?* Milwaukee: Marquette University Press, 1980).

[217] John M. Frame, *The Doctrine of God* (Phillipsburg: P&R, 2002); K. Scott Oliphint, *God With Us: Divine Condescension and the Attributes of God* (Wheaton: Crossway, 2012).

doctrine of the incarnation offers us a different understanding of the nature of God. They contend that Jesus was God, and because Jesus was God and in time; therefore, God is in time. In short, either for reasons related to the logical understanding of the doctrine of God, or the picture of God presented in Scripture, or the religious aspects of how we claim to relate to God, or specific theological reasons; each of these figures reject to some degree the view of God portrayed by classical theism.

Prior to Dolezal and his treatment and defense of classical theism, there was Norman Geisler. Geisler never used the terms "theistic mutualism" or "theistic personalism" to describe the movement. Instead, he used the term "Neotheism." In fact, Geisler wrote a prominent book titled, *The Battle for God: Responding to the Challenge of Neotheism*.[218] In both this book and in his other writings, such as *Systematic Theology: God and Creation*, Geisler defended classical theism over and against neotheist or theistic mutualists views of God. Geisler's lecture at BIOLA was a response to neotheism. Geisler publicly critiqued Clark Pinnock's Open Theism at the Evangelical Theological Society because it undermined the historic definition of God and the classic doctrine of biblical inerrancy.[219] Geisler also grounded his critique in Thomistic realism and its insistence upon the absolute immutability, eternality, simplicity, aseity, and impassibility of God. For Geisler, neotheist views fail to make the proper Creator-creation distinctions because it attributes creaturely characteristics and properties to God. Mutualists tend to reject the idea that God is in a class of his own. Instead, God seems to be the "smartest" or "greatest" being in the genus of beings. It is for that reason, Geisler claimed most evangelical views of God never rise above a gloried Michael the Archangel, because God still maintains creaturely characteristics such as mutability, temporality, and passability.[220] Geisler, House, and Herrera offer this chart as a visual to compare and contrast the theological and practical consequences of neotheism:[221]

---

[218] Geisler, House, Herrera, *The Battle for God*.

[219] Norman L. Geisler, *Preserving Orthodoxy: Maintaining Continuity with the Historic Christian Faith on Scripture* (Charlotte: Bastion Books, 2017), 53-90.

[220] Even in this respect, Geisler did not believe angels held these attributes. For example, Geisler claimed, much like Aquinas, that angels are not eternal or temporal, rather they are aevieternal. Also, that angels can only change in will, not in essence.

[221] Geisler, House, and Herrera, *The Battle for God*, 17.

|  | Theism | Neotheism |
|---|---|---|
| Wisdom and Foreknowledge | God knows all things, past, present, and future. | God knows past and present, but learns future, free events. |
| Emotions | God is impassible: Nothing can hurt or act upon Him. He acts out of His grace and mercy. | God is passible: He can be hurt and acted upon. We can make God feel pain. |
| Transcendence over Time | God is eternal (nontemporal). | God is temporal. |
| Simplicity of Being | God is simple, not composed of parts. He is absolutely and indivisibly one in essence. | God is composite, made of parts. |
| Changeableness | God is immutable: He does not change. He is perfect, and any change would be for the worse. | God is mutable: Change does not necessarily mean imperfection. |
| Authority and Rule | God sovereignly reigns over all things. Not one atom in the universe is outside His control, efficiently or permissively. God allows us to participate in His plan of salvation, but He does not need us. | God is sovereign, but He needs our help to be able to carry out His plan of salvation. God does not control free events. He cannot guarantee in advance how everything will turn out. |
| Power | God is omnipotent: He can do anything that does not contradict His nature. | God is omnipotent: He can do all things that are not contradictory. He |

|  | He gives but does not give away power. His power is infinite. | gives away power. Thus, He is not infinite in power. |
|---|---|---|
| Fallibility | God is infallible: He cannot err in any respect. | God is fallible: He can err, and Scripture states He has erred. |

Upon viewing this chart, one must quickly realize there are degrees in which a theologian or philosopher might agree or disagree with this classification. For example, individuals such as Alvin Plantinga, William Lane Craig, John Frame, and Ronald Nash, even though they disagree over the issue of middle knowledge, would not affirm the proposition, "God knows the past and present, but learns future, free events." Each figure claims God has exhaustive foreknowledge of future events. One could question the consistency of either the middle knowledge position; however, for our sakes, it must be noted that the above chart expresses the harder form of theistic mutualism, not the softer form. The same could be said about God's rule, power, and fallibility.

It has already been stated many more well-known evangelicals whom we consider more orthodox and affirm the softer form, would agree with the notion that God is passible, composite, and mutable. For Geisler, this type of mediating position fares better than the harder forms. Nonetheless, it also seems to unwind the classical view of God by fundamentally blurring the ontological attributes of God and the metaphysical nature of the world by giving God creaturely properties or attributes. Geisler provides the following chart to illustrate his point:[222]

| God | World |
|---|---|
| Not Temporal | Temporal |
| Not Complex | Complex |
| Not Changeable | Changing |
| No Potentiality | Potentiality |

---

[222] Ibid., 214.

According to classical theists, all the classical attributes of God either hang or fall *together*. One of the severe criticisms leveled against theistic mutualism is that it makes God in the image of man (i.e., finite, temporal, changing). In the Five Ways, Aquinas listed several properties of finite or created being. This would include things such as potentiality, movement, complexity of being, and temporality. Aquinas's entire argument entails if any being has any of these properties, then the grounds of their existence must be from another. From that vantage point, and based upon the impossibility of an infinite regress, Aquinas argues that God does not and cannot have any of these creaturely metaphysical characteristics. Hence, based upon that line of reasoning, Aquinas argued that God is altogether immutable and the only immutable Being.[223] In fact, the differences can be charted in the following way, which reveal the central issue:

| Classical Theism | Neotheism | World |
|---|---|---|
| Not Temporal | Temporal | Temporal |
| Not Complex | Complex | Complex |
| Not Changeable | Changing | Changing |
| No Potentiality | Potentiality | Potentiality |

The fundamental concern over both hard and soft forms of theistic mutualism is that the charge of finite godism could be leveled against both positions.[224] Geisler has been upfront and stated, "Though we do not question the sincerity of those evangelicals who advocate neotheism, we do question their understanding of God's nature and the benefits of neotheism to the Christian life."[225] He also claims:

> If God is in time, as they claim He is, He must also be spatial and material, according to Einstein's conception of the universe, which never allows one without the other. It is the space-time-material universe. A temporal God who is material would be subject to the Second Law of Thermodynamics. He would be running out of useable energy. Such a God would not only be finite (since one cannot run out of an infinite amount of energy) but would also be in the process of self-destructing. Such a god is

---

[223] Thomas Aquinas, *Summa Theologica*, Q9.
[224] Geisler, House, and Herrera, *The Battle for God*, 260-262.
[225] Ibid., 14.

not only sub-Christian; it is pagan. At least pagan gods tended to be immortal.[226]

Many practical concerns could be leveled against theistic mutualism too. For example, Geisler also states, "If God is not infinite in His attributes, then many cherished beliefs and expectations of Christians are suspect. The Christian's confidence in God, His Word, our salvation, and our daily dependence on God come into grave doubt."[227] Geisler claims a new understanding of God might affect our worship, as it did the Israelites. He says, "Many worship a god of their own creation, rather than the One who has revealed Himself. To speak of God in ignoble or distorted terms is idolatry."[228] A new concept of God has the potential to affect our view of Scripture, since the way we understand inspiration, inerrancy, prophecy, and many doctrines rests upon the way we understand the nature and actions of God.[229] There could also be serious effects upon our method of interpreting the Bible. Geisler notes, "The neotheist is unwilling to recognize the metaphorical expressions in reference to God changing His mind or repenting or regretting. This leaves biblical interpretation in a hermeneutic quagmire."[230] In other words, not only do the classical attributes of God hang or fall together, so do many other Christian doctrines and practices.

This quick survey indicates that evangelicalism is divided over the very nature of God. We also see the significance of Geisler's lecture before the students and faculty at BIOLA University. If Geisler is correct in his assessment, then neotheism has the potential to completely undermine the internal consistency of our doctrine of God and the entirety of the Christian faith. If the foundation be destroyed, so too goes classic evangelicalism and its commitment to belief in the total truthfulness of Scripture. Moreover, it indicates Geisler and others were correct to oppose the harder forms of theistic mutualism expressed by Clark Pinnock and other Open Theists. The *Evangelical Theological Society* had the opportunity to reject publicly neotheist approaches to God; however, for a variety of reasons, they failed to defend the very definition of God axiomatic to any evangelical expression of the Christian faith.[231]

---

[226] Ibid., 262.
[227] Ibid., 14.
[228] Ibid., 15.
[229] Ibid., 15-16.
[230] Ibid., 16.
[231] Geisler, *Preserving Orthodoxy*, 31-34; 53-90.

# Conclusion

One of the key distinctions of Norman Geisler's approach is his commitment to offering an argument that provides not only rational support for the existence of God, but the classical attributes of God too. Geisler's approach to modernity does not shy away from a full commitment to what Christians have historically meant when they use the term "God." Geisler was wholeheartedly committed to the idea first principles of reality exist and can be known, and that *being* found in the world must have a rational explanation for its existence, which leads to an Unmoved, Uncaused, Necessary Being, also known as the Christian conception of a classical theist view of God. Some may claim classical theism provides us with nothing more than a "God of the philosophers", not the God of the Bible. In response, we can point out that the God of the Bible, if he is any God at all, is nothing less than a Necessary Being, whose attributes of Pure Act, Eternality, Immutability, Simplicity, Aseity, Impassibility, etc., differentiate him from the act/pot, temporal, mutable, complex, and passible creation.

Geisler's understanding of God is not unique unto himself. Classical theism is not a maverick upon the scene of models of Christian theism. Classical theism has rightly been affirmed from the early Church, down through the Reformation, and maintained in our present day. The core insistence upon the belief that we can know God based upon common notions, the light of nature, and from *a posteriori* reasoning finds its roots in Paul's affirmation in Romans 1:18, stating, "For since the creation of the world His invisible attributes, His eternal power, and divine nature, have been clearly seen, being understood through what has been made, so they are without excuse." Classical realism and classical theism both hang and fall together. There is good and necessary reason to affirm the veracity of propositions such as "truth about reality is knowable" and "the God of classical theism exists."

The next chapter will explain Geisler's approach to defending the classic doctrine of biblical inerrancy as expressed in the Chicago Statement on Biblical Inerrancy. Geisler's commitment to the undeniable first principles of reality and a classical theist view of God entail that if God cannot err, and the Bible is the Word of God, then the Bible—which is the Word of God—cannot err. The final chapter will explain the significance of Geisler's approach for present-day evangelical apologists and offer one example from subjectivity and critical theory as a *way* Geisler's method could be used in future generations.

# CHAPTER FOUR

# Defending the Classic Doctrine of Inerrancy

## Introduction

The apologetic situation of our day requires evangelicals to address its two pressing epistemological crises. The first crisis questions whether God *exists*. Modernity presented a barrage of attacks against the existence and knowability of God. If God does not exist, or if we cannot know that he exists, then the Christian belief in God and the Bible as the Word of God is fallacious. The second crisis questions whether God has actually *revealed* himself in meaningful and intelligible propositions. We could also label this as modernity's "crises of revelation." Has God initiated the activity whereby he alone turns his personal privacy into a deliberate and meaningful free communication of his reality, will, and redemption? Has God revealed himself in meaningful words and propositions? In short, now that we know God is *there*, we must ask Schaeffer's second question: *is he silent?*

The crises of revelation produced several mediating evangelical positions concerning an individual's understanding of the authority and integrity of the Bible. The battle lines were clearly drawn between liberals and classic evangelicals. The former denied that the Bible was the Word of God and the latter affirmed the Scriptures to be the inspired, infallible, and inerrant Word of God. For example, Karl Barth was a key mediating figure throughout the twentieth-century. Barth's dialectical position tried to affirm both a belief in the Bible as the Word of God in a qualified sense (i.e., the Bible *becomes* the Word of God), and a commitment to many of the tenets of critical scholarship. Barth's mediating position was viewed by many as a means to rescue liberals from liberalism because it still retained a commitment to a belief in the Bible as the Word of God. Unfortunately, Barth's approach did not rescue liberals out of liberalism but delivered many evangelicals over to dialectical theology and in some cases, full-blown theological liberalism. This tidal wave of scholarship from liberals, neo-orthodox theologians, higher critical scholarship, and various mediating evangelical positions gave way to the twentieth century's Battle for the Bible.

Norman Geisler was one evangelical figure who worked his entire life to demonstrate the fact that God is *there* and he is *not silent*. Geisler considered the inerrancy of Scripture to be both the ontological and epistemological fundamental for every other fundamental of the Christian faith. Geisler based this foundational claim upon the nature of God and the fact that Scripture is God's means of propositional revelation. In the text of Scripture, we have an *assured* disclosure of the mind of God concerning each essential doctrine of the Christian faith. Moreover, for classic evangelical figures, such as Norman Geisler, a commitment to the total truthfulness or inerrancy of the Bible was considered a watershed issue. One's commitment to the classic doctrine of inerrancy was a mark of both evangelical consistency and identity. The following chapter is going to explain the *way* Norman Geisler defended the inerrancy of Scripture and the *significance* of the historic view of the Bible for evangelicals as they address the epistemological crises of revelation. Since previous chapters have already discussed the nature of God, the concept of truth, and the nature of language, we will forego those topics in this chapter.[232] Those discussions, in many ways, were axiomatic and preparatory for any meaningful conversation concerning the doctrine of inerrancy. Therefore, this chapter will briefly explain the *International Council on Biblical Inerrancy* (ICBI) and Geisler's role within the organization, the doctrine of revelation; the concept of inerrancy, truth and inerrancy, and the relationship between hermeneutics and inerrancy. This discussion will prove to be vital for our final chapter as we seek to understand the significance of inerrancy for evangelicals as they address the crisis of revelation in an Age of Unbelief.

## International Council on Biblical Inerrancy

The twentieth-century was marked by an evangelical "Battle for the Bible."[233] This period was shaped by years of eclipse, both internally and externally, for evangelicals concerning the nature of the total truthfulness of the Word of God. Theological liberalism and neo-orthodoxy were in the saddle in many major evangelical denominations and churches and remained the dominant intellectual creed of many places of higher education. The *International Council on Biblical Inerrancy* was formed to address this eclipse, specifically those issues related to the integrity of Sacred Scripture. Methodologically and strategically, the thrust of the battle lines

---

[232] For a greater understanding of our work on the following topic, please see: Norman L. Geisler and William C. Roach, *Defending Inerrancy: Affirming the Accuracy of Scripture for a New Generation* (Grand Rapids: Baker, 2011).

[233] Harold Lindsell, *The Battle for the Bible* (Grand Rapids: Zondervan, 1976).

was clear, and the axiom of inerrancy served as a guideline for evangelical identity and consistent evangelical hermeneutics (i.e., regardless of the genres of Scripture, inerrancy ensures that whenever Scripture speaks, God speaks).

During October 26-28th, 1978, the ICBI held a summit meeting at the Hyatt Regency O'Hare airport in Chicago, Illinois. The result of this summit produced the famous *Chicago Statement on Biblical Inerrancy* (CSBI). The CSBI issued forth nineteen Articles of affirmation and denial, which spoke directly to the authority and integrity of the Bible. By design the ICBI existed for only ten years. They did not want to create a perpetual organization. Rather, they wanted to address with pin-point precision many of the most pressing issues concerning the nature of the Bible. Over the next ten years, two other conferences where held: one on hermeneutics and inerrancy (1984), and one on applying the doctrine of inerrancy to issues of our day (1987). Each conference produced their own statements, with the conferences on inerrancy and hermeneutics producing official commentaries, titled, *Explaining Inerrancy* and *Explaining Hermeneutics*, with R. C. Sproul as author of the former and Norman Geisler the latter. During the same time several scholarly volumes were produced under the watch of ICBI, with the sole purpose of defending the inerrancy of Scripture. These works include *Inerrancy* edited by Norman Geisler;[234] *Hermeneutics, Inerrancy, and the Bible* edited by Earl Radmacher and Robert Preus;[235] *Biblical Errancy: Its Philosophical Roots* edited by Norman Geisler;[236] and *Inerrancy and the Church* edited by John D. Hannah.[237] The Chicago Statement was signed by nearly 300 noted evangelical scholars including James Boice, Norman Geisler, Carl F. H. Henry, Kenneth Kantzer, Harold Lindsell, John Warwick Montgomery, Roger Nicole, J. I. Packer, Robert Preus, Earl Radmacher, Francis Schaeffer, R. C. Sproul, John MacArthur, John Wenham, Greg Bahnsen, Paige Patterson, Russ Bush, Winfried Corduan, and many more.

The draft committee of the CSBI stated in clear terms, "The authority of Scripture is a key issue of the Christian church in this and every age. Those who profess faith in Jesus Christ as Lord and Savior are called to show the reality of their discipleship by humbly and faithfully obeying God's written

---

[234] Norman L. Geisler, *Inerrancy* (Grand Rapids: Zondervan, 1980).

[235] Earl D. Radmacher and Robert D. Preus, *Hermeneutics, Inerrancy, & the Bible: Papers from ICBI Summit II* (Grand Rapids: Zondervan, 1984).

[236] Norman L. Geisler, *Biblical Errancy: An Analysis of its Philosophical Roots* (Eugene: Wipf and Stock, 1981).

[237] John D. Hannah, *Inerrancy and The Church* (Chicago: Moody Press, 1984).

Word."[238] They also warned, "To stray from Scripture in faith or conduct is disloyalty to our Master. Recognition of the total truth and trustworthiness of Holy Scripture is essential to a full grasp and adequate confession of its authority."[239] The framers warned against the denial of the full integrity of the Word of God and the effects that a lapse could have upon individual Christians and the Christian Church at large. The essence of the larger statement has been given in the shorter statement, which states:

1. God, who is Himself Truth and speaks truth only, has inspired Holy Scripture in order thereby to reveal Himself to lost mankind through Jesus Christ as Creator and Lord, Redeemer and Judge. Holy Scripture is God's witness to Himself.

2. Holy Scripture, being God's own Word, written by men prepared and superintended by His Spirit, is of infallible divine authority in all matters upon which it touches: it is to be believed, as God's instruction, in all that it affirms; obeyed, as God's command, in all that it requires; embraced, as God's pledge, in all that it promises.

3. The Holy Spirit, Scripture's divine Author, both authenticates it to us by His inward witness and opens our minds to understand its meaning.

4. Being wholly and verbally God-given, Scripture is without error or fault in all its teaching, no less in what it states about God's acts in creation, about the events of world history, and about its own literary origins under God, than in its witness to God's saving grace in individual lives.

5. The authority of Scripture is inescapably impaired if this total divine inerrancy is in any way limited or disregarded, or made relative to a view of truth contrary to the Bible's own; and such lapses bring serious loss to both the individual and the Church.

While other statements have been produced over the years, including the one at the Lausanne Conference, it has been demonstrated historically that those statements, while decent for their time, fail to address adequately the pressing twists and turns of the Battle for the Bible.[240] Therefore, many organizations such as the *International Society of Christian Apologetics* and the *Evangelical Theological Society*, and institutions such as *Southern Evangelical Seminary* and *Veritas International University*, have decided to

---

[238] R. C. Sproul, *Explaining Inerrancy* (Orlando: Ligonier Ministries, 1996), 59.
[239] Ibid.
[240] See: Francis A. Schaeffer, *The Great Evangelical Disaster* (Wheaton: Crossway, 1984).

use the Chicago Statement as their guide for the precise meaning and definition of inerrancy.

During my graduate level studies at *Southern Evangelical Seminary*, I served as the personal assistant to Norman Geisler. One of the main topics we spoke regularly about was the *International Council on Biblical Inerrancy* and the specific role Geisler played in the organization. In the years following my tenure, I kept in close contact with Dr. Geisler. We spoke regularly about many present-day explicit and subtle attacks upon the classic doctrine of inerrancy. The result of those conversations was the publication of our co-authored book, *Defending Inerrancy: Affirming the Accuracy of Scripture for a New Generation*. In no short order, *Defending Inerrancy* was the first major publication from a leading figure from of the ICBI, and has served as a modern-day version of Lindsell's book, *The Battle for the Bible*. The reception of the book was mixed. One leading figure within the *Evangelical Theological Society* approached me after church one day to rebuke me for it and claimed that I had a "major black eye upon my career for publishing the book with Geisler." Truth be told, the book critiqued several of his colleagues and views. On the other hand, figures such as John MacArthur and J. I. Packer praised the book. Packer wrote the foreword to the book, stating, "Norman Geisler . . . and William Roach interact with evangelical hypotheses that have the effect of confusing that legacy. They are masterly gatekeepers, and I count in an honor to commend this work to the Christian world."[241] First things first, however, we must remember that Packer also said, Geisler "*contributed as much as anyone to ICBI's original legacy.*"[242] In a personal phone call with R. C. Sproul after the publication of our book, we discussed the ICBI and Geisler's role. Sproul was forthright to state that Geisler was one of the charter members and a key figure in the organization, and that without his input the influence of the organization would have had significantly less reach and effect upon the body of Christ. In other words, Geisler was a leading figure within the ICBI and the production of the CSBI, not a secondary figure. In many ways, one of the hallmarks of Geisler's career was his participation and leadership in the ICBI.

One caveat ought to be traversed at this point concerning Norman Geisler and the doctrine of inerrancy: no figure has fought the public battle for the Bible more than Norman Geisler. In a day and age when people are afraid to stand for the integrity of God's Word out of fear of gaining a "black eye upon their career", Geisler realized nothing less than the integrity

---

[241] Geisler and Roach, *Defending Inerrancy*, 11.
[242] Ibid., emphasis added.

of the God Who Speaks was on the line over the doctrine of inerrancy. Geisler spent his career defending Sacred Scripture against figures such as Clark Pinnock, Robert Gundry, Darrell Bock, Michael Licona, Craig Blomberg, and others. It has wrongly been said by Michael Licona in various public venues that Geisler defended his "own view of inerrancy." While it may be true Licona considers himself a historian, it ought to be boldly stated Licona is woefully underread in his knowledge, understanding, and assessment of the history of the Battle for the Bible and the ICBI. Geisler and a host of scholars at the ICBI produced volumes of literature to demonstrate that there is a classic doctrine of inerrancy which has been held by the Church down through the centuries. The CSBI and Norman Geisler represent that historic legacy, and we ought not let any present-day figure, such as Licona, Bock, or Blomberg, confuse or alter that legacy by claiming that it is merely "Geisler's particular view of inerrancy."

Moreover, it must be noted the CSBI is a thorough going Protestant declaration. Time will not permit a full and extended conversation over the significant differences between Roman Catholics and Protestants concerning the issue(s) of *sola Scriptura*. For our sake, however, the central question for Christian discipleship boils down to one of authority. We must ask, "How does Jesus exercise his Lordship over the Church?" It must be noted that the Sacred Scriptures are to be "received" as the Word of God, and that they do not receive their authority from any denomination or tradition. Jesus Christ exercises his authority over his Church through the Scriptures. *How* someone answers the question of biblical authority separates those who view Scripture as merely a source book of information from those who would affirm that the Bible is a book that by its very nature has the authority to impose obligation and bind our conscience. There are many authorities in this world; however, we must recognize Scripture as the *Norma normans et sine normativa*, meaning "the norm of norms and without norm," or the superlative and ultimate standard by which all other authorities are judged. Therefore, Scripture is to be declared the supreme written norm by which God binds the conscience, and that all other creeds, councils, or declarations have far less authority than the Bible.[243]

The following section will proceed to explain the classic doctrine of inerrancy as expressed by the *Chicago Statement on Biblical Inerrancy* and defended by the *International Council on Biblical Inerrancy*, with special emphasis given to the role and influence of Norman Geisler.

---

[243] See: CSBI, Articles 1 and 2.

## The Doctrine of Revelation

Geisler addressed the crises of revelation by arguing that truth exists and can be known, that the existence and nature of God can be demonstrated, and that from these realities we can ensure a revealed Word from God that is totally true, intelligible, and in propositional form. Foundational to Geisler's understanding of the doctrine of revelation is his commitment to first principles and classical theism. For example, if the principle of causality is true, and if God is going to produce a book, then because God must remain consistent with his nature when producing a book, that book must necessarily be true since God, by nature, is true. The only book God produced was the Bible. The Bible is necessarily an effect of God, who served as its Primary Author.[244] Effects do not rise above their causes, and thus if the Cause is perfect and lacks the ability to err, then the effect must necessarily be perfect and without error. In other words, God cannot err, the Bible is the Word of God; therefore, the Bible, which is the Word of God, cannot err. If someone is going to deny the conclusion, they must deny one of the premises. One is left with the pressing question: Do you believe God can err or do you deny that the Bible is the Word of God?

There are a variety of different ways that the concept of revelation has been understood throughout the twentieth and twenty-first centuries. The CSBI Article 3, states, "We affirm that the written Word in its entirety is revelation given by God." The denial states, "We deny that the Bible is merely a witness to revelation, or becomes revelation in encounter, or depends on the responses of men for its validity." The two operant phrases or words in these descriptions are "entirety" and "merely a witness." The so-called dialectical view of revelation affirmed by neo-orthodox theology affirms a dynamic understanding of Scripture, and conversely denies the objective nature of revelation. Revelation must not be understood as an "objective disclosure",[245] but as an existential event requiring some type of inward, subjective human response. R. C. Sproul claims, "Scholars like Emil Bruner, for example, have insisted that the Bible is not itself revelation, but is merely a witness to that revelation which is found in Christ."[246] Also, "It has been fashionable in certain quarters to maintain that special revelation is embodied in Christ and in Christ alone, and that to consider the Bible as

---

[244] More will be said about this point later. However, it must be noted Geisler did not affirm a dictation theory of inspiration or revelation.

[245] See: Norman L. Geisler and William E. Nix, *From God to Us: How We Got Our Bible* (Chicago: Moody Press, 2012), 18.

[246] R. C. Sproul and Norman L. Geisler, *Explaining Biblical Inerrancy: Official Commentary on the ICBI Statements* (Matthews: Bastion Books, 2013), 29.

objective revelation would be to detract from the uniqueness of the person of Jesus Christ who is the Word made flesh."[247] Undergirding this concept of revelation is an understanding of *Wahrheit als Begegnung* or "Truth as Encounter." According to this view of revelation, experience, including experience as contained in the idea of revelation, is necessarily an encounter or existential event. Truth is fundamentally understood as an experience or personal encounter, wherein the individual is bound up in a relationship, not propositions. Revelation is something that occurs in acts or events, but not in words. The Bible is, therefore, a form of revelation, but not a sufficient and objective revelation.

This approach to revelation has been predominant throughout so many denominations and churches in the twentieth-century. In Scripture, are we seeking the *Vox Dei* or the *Verbum Dei*? Are we seeking the voice of God or the Word of God? For those who affirm a neo-orthodox view, even though they are right to deny the liberal belief that Scripture is *not* the Word of God, they err in their view of the Bible as revelation because Scripture is merely the *Vox Dei* or voice of God. Since Scripture is merely a witness to God's revelation, it can and does necessarily include errors, and merely serves as a catalyst for revelation. The Bible is merely a witness to revelation, or it becomes revelation in encounter, and necessarily depends upon the responses of men for its validity.

Geisler, Sproul, and others responded to this aberrant view, claiming, "The spirit of these articles is to oppose a disjunction between the revelation that is given to us in the person of Christ objectively and the revelation that comes to us in equally objective terms in the Word of God inscripturated. Here the Bible is seen not merely as a catalyst for revelation, but as revelation itself."[248] They also state, "If the Bible is God's Word and its content proceeds from Him, then its content is to be seen as revelation. Here revelation is viewed as 'propositional.' It is propositional not because the Bible is written in the style of logical equations or analytical formulas. It is propositional because it communicates a content which may be understood as propositions."[249] Fundamental to this approach to revelation is the idea of an objective reality that can be known and can proceed from God. Geisler's approach to truth is axiomatic for a biblical worldview because one must be able to know truth, and to know it objectively, in order for there to be a revelation from God. Second, God must be able to communicate to humanity in an objective fashion for there to be any *means* or *assurance* of propositional revelation. Third, language must necessarily

---

[247] Ibid.
[248] Ibid.
[249] Ibid.

be the conduit of information, and true information specifically, for there to be any sense of an objectively revealed propositional text of Scripture. In other words, one of the fundamental features of the Bible's notion of revelation is that it entails metaphysical and epistemological realism. Existential approaches to metaphysics and dynamic approaches to language ultimately undermine any assurance of objective revelation, or in a self-defeating way they undercut the very claims of their own view whenever they attempt to communicate their doctrine of revelation, because they expect that *that* very claim (or doctrine) can be objectively placed into meaningful and truthful propositions.

Fundamental to an evangelical view of Scripture is the belief that *all of Scripture* is inspired revelation given by God. Sproul states, "In the affirmation of Article III the words 'in its entirety' are also significant. There are those who have claimed that the Bible contains here and there, in specified places, revelation from God, but that it is the task of the believer individually or the church corporately to separate the parts of Scripture which are revelatory from those which are not."[250] Scripture as a whole is inspired revelation from God. The entirety of its contents, whether it be history, salvation, abstract points, prophecy, and so forth, are all the content of revelation in propositional form. Neo-orthodox and neo-evangelical approaches to Scripture affirm a concept of limited revelation, limited inspiration, and ultimately, limited inerrancy. Whenever someone denies that all of Scripture, or Scripture in its entirety, is true and meaningful revelation, then we are left in the quagmire of trying to figure out what is true revelation given by God and what is not. The difficulty of this process grows exponentially whenever the means of discovering this revelation resides in personal, subjective, and typically ever-changing, personal encounters. All in all, one is left with no sure Word from God, and whatever we deem to be the Word of God, unfortunately, lacks any objective means to remain the Word of God or be justified as the Word of God.

Essential to the crises of revelation is a belief that humanity can have knowledge of God. As was discussed in a previous chapter, Geisler and other classical theists believe we can have knowledge of God through *a posteriori* reasoning and through general and special revelation. The condition of belief for most people following modernity is the assumption we cannot have any true knowledge of God, i.e., agnosticism or various forms of skepticism. As it relates to the text of Scripture, even if God does exist, *how* can we know anything about him? Even more, *how* can we

---

[250] Ibid., 29-30.

know that our language *can* and *does* meaningfully speak about God? If we are finite beings, and *finitum non capax infinitum* (i.e., the finite cannot contain the infinite), then how can we say that the Bible, which is a finite book, using finite human language, gives us any positive knowledge of God? This is another way of stating the fact that modern theology has created a crisis of revelation by declaring human language cannot serve as a means to convey information between God and man. God is considered wholly other—*totaliter aliter*—(i.e., totally different); therefore, we cannot grasp, understand, apprehend, or record any meaningful revelation from or about God. Secondarily, there is a general commitment to the principle of *errare humanum est* (i.e., to err is human) by many neo-orthodox and neo-evangelical scholars. Consequently, even if God could somehow reveal himself, human beings, due to their finitude and fallenness, will fail to rightly record, recognize, or interpret God's revelation.

In response to this approach to revelation and language, the CSBI Article 4, claims, "We affirm that God who made mankind in his image has used language as a means of revelation."[251] Sproul, Geisler, and the CSBI go on to state:

> One of the most significant attacks on biblical inerrancy that has come to light in the twentieth century is that based on the limitations of human language. Since the Bible was not written by God himself, but by human writers, the question has emerged again and again whether such human involvement by virtue of the limitations built in human creatureliness would, of necessity, render the Bible less than infallible. Since men are not infallible in and of themselves, and are prone to error in all that they do, would it not follow logically that anything coming from the pen of man must be errant? To this we reply, erroneousness is not an inevitable concomitant of human nature. Adam, before the fall, may well have been free from proneness to error, and Christ, though fully human, never erred. Since the fall it is a common tendency to err. We deny, however, that it is necessary for men to err always and everywhere in what they say or write, even apart from inspiration.[252]

The first step in any meaningful apologetic is to deny the premise that human beings *always* and by *necessity* err. If we are wholly committed to this premise, then our trust in the all sufficient and perfect active obedience and righteousness of Jesus Christ, who was fully God and fully man, is not

---

[251] Ibid., 30.
[252] Ibid., 30-31.

only eclipsed, but annihilated. Jesus Christ was fully human, and yet without sin (or error). Also, any approach to revelation and language claiming that all knowledge and human language is of necessity errant, has to grab the proverbial bull by the horns and realize that their own thoughts and language are human; hence, they are necessarily erroneous and flawed. In other words, theologically, this approach to language leads to a Christological heresy. Methodologically, the view commits its proponents to too strong of a position. While it may be true that human beings *can* err, they do not *necessarily* err.

The second step to any meaningful apologetic is to deny that there is a difference of *kind* between our knowledge of God and our use of human language to address the nature of God and his revelation. Many people point to Calvin's notion that God lisps to us, implying that God is so wholly different and other that he either does not or cannot use meaningful human language. A few points must be noted. First, there is a difference of kind between the very nature of God and the nature of man. We demonstrated earlier that God is not of the same genus or species as humanity. In fact, because God is a simple Being, he has no genus or species. Second, we also demonstrated the validity of the analogy of being and linguistic analogical predication. This entails that there may be a difference of kind between beings but *being* in and of itself allows for there to be an analogical similarity and a point of contact. Third, as the article states, the image of God creates a likeness between man and God and makes communication possible. Such communication is possible because God fabricated it into his very creation. Fourth, one must distinguish between a grasp or degree of truth and not having truth altogether. God may have a total understanding of truth and humanity a finite understanding of truth. But the proposition "All finite understandings of truth err" is fallacious, for even that every statement is a finite understanding of truth; hence, it would be fallacious. The issue is not an exhaustive understanding of truth, but an adequate understanding of truth. Though our language about God and the acts of God are never comprehensive or exhaustive, it both can and does capture eternal truths and provide adequate truth. Fifth, the nature of accommodation, as stated by Aquinas, Calvin, the Princetonians, and the ICBI, rightly captures the sentiment that God accommodates unto our finitude, not our fallenness. The point of Calvin's analogy is not to say that God accommodates unto human sinfulness. That claim undermines the integrity of the very nature of God and the clear teachings of Scripture. In sum, we can rightly apprehend any truth God has revealed, even if we cannot have a comprehensive knowledge of the truth God has revealed.

From what has been stated, it is evident that Geisler's approach to truth and classical theism is necessarily required for any meaningful doctrine of revelation. Many might reject that thesis and claim they can substantiate a similar doctrine of revelation based upon other approaches to truth and theology proper. They are free to make their case and several theologians have attempted to throughout Church history. The point must not be missed. Geisler's approach, which is the approach of traditional metaphysical realism and classical theism, is rightly and adequately suited to ground an evangelical doctrine of revelation. This can be seen in the following ways.

First of all, Geisler's view allows for *being* to exist and for *being* to be communicated. The sheer fact that we can grant the fundamental principle of being is axiomatic to any commitment to objective revelation. Second, we see the explanatory power that the analogy of being and analogical predication provide evangelicals. Since we have an objective ground for being and a means to substantiate a way to communicate being, the concept of revelation is not irrational. One may still have to demonstrate that revelation has actually occurred, but on the face value, the *de jure* conclusion is that the concept of revelation is not irrational. Third, we see the value of Geisler's method and the effects it has upon our Bibliology. Unlike many approaches, Geisler sees the methodological necessity of prolegomena in his approach. It makes no sense to claim that we have a revelation from God if there is no God. It also makes no sense to claim we have truth from God if truth does not exist, or if reality is not knowable. Methodologically, Geisler's classical realist and classical theist approach can thwart many objections raised against his view of Scripture because he has taken the necessary step of establishing the central philosophical preconditions for revelation. Theology matters and in many respects our theology ought to determine countless aspects of our philosophy. But there are times when philosophy matters, and sometimes our philosophy determines many aspects of our theology. If you are committed to a view that truth cannot be known, communicated, or freed from fallenness, then your concept of revelation and the theology you base upon that doctrine of revelation will be synthesized with that aberrant philosophy. Fourth, from a very practical and historical standpoint it ought to be noted that many present-day approaches to Bibliology seem to be grounded in neo-orthodox understandings of revelation (i.e., where personal truth, or dialectical truth, or subjective truth are the key determinate(s)). Many present-day evangelicals are enamored with Barth's approach. In fact, one could make the case that "flexible" approaches to inerrancy, whether they be grounded in Greco-Roman biography or *Speech Act Theory*, are merely reflecting neo-orthodox concepts of truth and existential approaches to accommodation.[253]

# The Concept of Inerrancy

By its very nature, the concept of inerrancy is rational. As someone considers the very word "inerrancy," we quickly recognize that the term simply means "without error." In other philosophical and theological disciplines, we study the concept of something. For example, much of modern philosophy has been fascinated with the study of the very concept of God. Several atheists and mediating theists have tried to argue that the very concept of God, whether it be the way we understand his attributes or relationship with other beings, is somehow *de jure* irrational. Those scholars do not even proceed to investigate any arguments or evidential support (i.e., *de facto* considerations), because logically they believe that the very concept of God is irrational. Evangelical scholars have responded not only to the charge that "God" is *de jure* irrational, but to the charge that inerrancy is irrational too.

The doctrine of inerrancy has become a shibboleth for evangelicals. Part and parcel of twentieth and twenty-first century battles over the Bible have centered around either the use, abuse, or disregard of the term "inerrancy." During the summit meeting of the ICBI, the leading figures even debated whether they should use the term "inerrancy." Some leaders thought it would be better if they were called the *International Council on Biblical Inspiration* or the *International Council on Biblical Infallibility.* Some prominent figures believed the use of "inspiration" or "infallibility" would better suit their cause and forego many of the hasty generalizations and negative reactions to the term "inerrancy." Fortunately, however, as R. C. Sproul recounts in one of his lectures on inerrancy in the series *Thus Says The Lord: Defending the Inerrancy of Scripture*, J. I. Packer rejected the use of the terms "infallibility" and "inspiration" in favor of the term "inerrancy."[254] Packer, who was a British evangelical, knew many people across the pond rejected the term "inerrancy" as a mark of American fundamentalism. Many influential schools, such as Fuller Theological Seminary, were also removing the term inerrancy in favor of "infallibility" in their doctrinal statements.[255] Nonetheless, Packer noted that the term

---

[253] See: Geisler and Roach, *Defending Inerrancy*, 112-178.

[254] R. C. Sproul, *Thus Says the Lord: Defending the Inerrancy of Scripture* (Orlando: Ligonier Ministries), MP3 audio series.

[255] Lindsell, *The Battle for the Bible*, 106-121.

"inerrancy" was strong enough to keep those who really disagreed with the view from actually using the term. He also went on to state that orthodoxy and heresy have sometimes been distinguished by a proposition, phrase, word, or in one case a single letter in a word (i.e., think of the debates concerning Christology—i.e., *homoousios* vs *homoiousios*). Therefore, not only was the term precise enough to convey the concept and doctrine, but it was strong enough to ward off those who disagreed with the concept of inerrancy.

The Fuller Seminary case has always been viewed as the prime example of quibbling over terms that have dire consequences.[256] Figures such as Dan Fuller, Jack Rogers, and Donald McKim were programmatic in changing the doctrinal statement at Fuller Theological Seminary away from affirming the concept of "inerrancy." Dan Fuller embraced a neo-orthodox understanding of Scripture, whereas Rogers and McKim argued that the doctrine of inerrancy was nothing more than a modernist or rationalist invention, and not the historic doctrine of the Church.[257] Severe criticism came from the ICBI and in particular from John Woodbridge, who penned the book, *Biblical Authority: A Critique of the Rogers/McKim Proposal*.[258] Woodbridge, with painstaking precision and documentation, demonstrated to everyone's satisfaction that the Rogers and McKim proposal that inerrancy was a modernist invention was factually and historically incorrect. The ICBI also responded by asking key figures, such as R. C. Sproul, to travel and discuss the matters with the faculty of Fuller Seminary. The purpose was to bring clarity on the matter and forego any claims to equivocation or misrepresentation. The meetings were found to be fruitful towards fulfilling the goal of clarity, even though no one's mind was changed throughout the course of events. The conclusion derived by Sproul at these meetings was that when Fuller Seminary used the term "infallibility" they really meant "fallibility." And when they used the term "inerrancy" they really meant "errancy." The reason for this conclusion was because they fundamentally redefined the terms and the very concepts of inspiration, infallibility, and inerrancy.

Norman Geisler and the ICBI inerrantists went to painstaking efforts to properly define and explain the terms inspiration, infallibility, and

---

[256] Geisler and Roach, *Defending Inerrancy*, 20-21. See also: George M. Marsden, *Reforming Fundamentalism: Fuller Seminary and the New Evangelicalism* (Grand Rapids: Eerdmans, 1987).

[257] Jack B. Rogers and Donald K. McKim, *The Authority and Interpretation of the Bible: An Historical Approach* (Eugene: Wipf and Stock, 1999).

[258] John D. Woodbridge, *Biblical Authority: A Critique of the Rogers/McKim Proposal* (Grand Rapids: Zondervan, 1982).

inerrancy. The central points of the debate are related to our understanding of reality, the concept of truth, and the nature of revelation. Properly understood, the doctrine of inspiration pertains to the *source* of Scripture, the infallibility of the Bible pertains to the *potentiality* of Scripture, and the inerrancy of Sacred Scripture pertains to the *actuality* of Scripture. More will be said about this later; however, a brief illustration will better make my point. Whenever we speak about the concept of inerrancy, many people wrongly believe that it pertains *only* to the text of Scripture. Fortunately, for the sake of all individuals alive today, that is not the case. There are several inerrant grocery lists, math equations, and term papers. The term "inerrancy" merely refers to the fact that something does not contain an error. On the other hand, we would be incorrect to claim that the term "infallibility" refers to any written text beyond that of Sacred Scripture. Infallibility refers to the potentiality to err. It is one thing to claim that I did not err when I wrote down the grocery list and that I did not err when I picked up the groceries. It is a totally different thing to claim that I *cannot* err whenever I write down the grocery list or pick up the groceries. The reason is because I am clearly and evidently and experientially a fallible being. I have the capacity to err because I am a fallible source. Scripture on the other hand does not have the ability to err (i.e., it is infallible) because the Primary Cause or Ultimate Source of Scripture, who is God, is infallible. God lacks the ability to err, so if something lacks the ability to err, then it necessarily and without question entails that whatever God does or produces is without error. God is not a fumbling husband picking up the groceries. Rather, God is a Perfect, Infallible, Immutable, wholly True Being, who lacks the ability to err in both his nature and activities, including the act of inspiring the very text of Sacred Writ. In sum, a proper explanation of Scripture is rooted and grounded in the proper ordering of the terms inspiration, infallibility, and inerrancy. We ought not change the order. Scripture is sourced in God—inspiration; God lacks the ability to err—infallibility; therefore, the necessarily result is a Bible without error—inerrancy.

Evangelicals are committed to the verbal and plenary inspiration of the Bible. The historic debate concerning Scripture was over viewing Scripture as inspired in a plenary or organic sense. An organic view of inspiration views Scripture as being generally inspired, either in the gist or the intent of Scripture, but not down to the very parts and words. This view of Scripture, also known as limited inspiration, is not committed to the full or total historical accuracy, theological truthfulness, or integrity of Scripture. Plenary inspiration on the other hand, is committed to the belief that the sum or whole of Scripture, and not just the parts, are given by divine inspiration. The whole of Scripture, including historical, redemptive, and theological matters are all equally and validly inspired by God. The notion of *verbal* plenary inspiration entails that the very *words* of Scripture, down to their very choice, case, mood, and tense, are also inspired by God. As will be seen later, this is also coupled with the belief that Scripture is plenarily and equally a fully human book, yet without error. In other words, verbal plenary inspiration properly addresses the extent of inspiration.[259]

God is considered the ultimate Author of Scripture who works through the proximate authorship of specifically chosen Apostles and Prophets. The CSBI Article 7, states, "We affirm that inspiration was the work in which God by His Spirit, through human writers, gave us His Word. The origin of Scripture is divine. The mode of divine inspiration remains largely a mystery to us."[260] The point of Article 7 is that Scripture is inspired because of what it *is*, not because of what it *does*. Scripture contains a special *nature*, which gives rise to specific actions. Many neo-orthodox and neo-evangelical theologians wrongly confuse this principle and argue that inspiration refers to what God *does with Scripture*. Nothing could be further from the truth of the matter. Sproul and Geisler state:

> What the framers of the document have in view here is the primary meaning of the word *theopneustos* in 2 Timothy 3:16, the word translated 'inspired by God.' The word *theopneustos* means literally 'God breathed' and has primary reference to God's breathing out his word rather than breathing in some kind of effect upon human writers. So expiration is a more accurate term than inspiration with respect to the origin of Scripture. But we use the term inspiration to cover the concept of the whole process by which the Word comes to us. Initially it comes from the mouth of God (speaking, of course, metaphorically). From its origin in God it is then transmitted through the agency of human writers under divine supervision and superintendence. The next step in the process of communication is the apprehension of the divine message by human beings. It is explicitly stated in this article that the precise mode by which God accomplishes

---

[259] The ICBI and other proponents of the classic doctrine of inerrancy reject a dictation theory of inspiration. They claim, "The fact that Article VI speaks of divine inspiration down to the very words of the original may conjure up in some people's minds a notion of dictation of the words of Scripture by God. The doctrine of verbal plenary inspiration has often been charged with carrying with it the implication of a dictation theory of inspiration. No such theory is spelled out in this article, nor is it implied. In fact, in Article VII the framers of the statement deny the dictation theory." Sproul and Geisler, *Explaining Inerrancy*, 34.

[260] Ibid., 36.

inspiration remains a mystery. The document makes no attempt to define the 'how' of divine inspiration or even to suggest that the method is known to us.[261]

Paul was conscious of the fact that he was writing Sacred Scripture. Paul did not manufacture a new view of inspiration, rather he rooted and grounded his view in the Old Testament and applied that to the New Testament. Paul's writings were considered Sacred Scripture, just as much as the *graphe* of the Old Testament were considered Sacred Scripture.

Geisler and the ICBI also proceed to explain false views of inspiration. Karl Barth used to charge evangelicals with holding a docetic view of Scripture, whereby they denied the humanity of Sacred Writ. Barth used to claim that the affirmation of the verbal and plenary inspiration of the Bible denied the real human authorship of Scripture. By the notion of denying "real human authorship", Barth really meant that evangelicals were wrong to deny that the Scriptures contain error. Equally wrong were those who affirmed a dictation view of Scripture. The idea that God told the writers of the Bible to spell out a particular word in some type of automatic fashion is a New Age or Occultic notion. This view is most prevalent in the Mormon view of the origin of the Book of Mormon.[262] This robotic or machine-like state is incorrect because it cancels out the personal thought of the human authors. Unfortunately, many Christians affirm both views, and these were two extremes that Geisler and other framers of the CSBI attempted to avoid.

During the time of the Reformation, whenever a Protestant took up the task to debate a Roman Catholic, there was fear and trepidation about debating a Jesuit Priest. The Jesuits served as key figures in the Counter Reformation and the defense of the infallibility of the Roman Catholic Magisterium. Whenever most Protestants first encounter the term "infallibility" it is typically associated with Roman Catholic debates. Today, however, we tend to hear about it negatively. Someone might say, "It's not like I'm infallible." Regardless of the first time we heard the term, each of us has a general understanding of the meaning of the term. Infallibility refers to the ability to err. When applied to the text of Scripture it entails that Scripture has no ability to err. Because God is infallible, God cannot err. Sproul and Geisler state, "Infallibility has to do with the question of ability or potential. That which is infallible is said to be unable to make mistakes

---

[261] Ibid., 36-37.
[262] Walter Martin, *The Kingdom of the Cults* (Minneapolis: Bethany House, 2003), 193-261.

or to err. The distinction here between that definition of infallible and the definition of inerrant is the distinction between potential and actual, the hypothetical and the real."[263] Because God is Pure Act in his very Being, God lacks any potentiality, which in this case would always be a potential towards error, since God is by definition a Perfect Being. Thus, when God infallibly inspired the text of Scripture, he lacked the ability to err, because God does not have the potential to err.

There is a logical and practical relationship between infallibility and inerrancy. While it is true the term "infallibility" has been used more often throughout Church history, that does not mean that the historic use fundamentally redefines or rejects the doctrine of inerrancy. The CSBI Article 11, states, "We deny that it is possible of the Bible to be at the same time infallible and errant in its assertions. Infallibility and inerrancy may be distinguished, but not separated."[264] It makes no logical sense to claim that something lacks the ability to err, and to then assert that it contains errors. This is precisely the erroneous view advocated by Fuller Theological Seminary. The faculty were championing the belief that evangelicals ought to adopt the so-called easier or weaker view of Scripture, because it is more academically respected, or due to greater historical usage, or for a variety of other reasons. However, what is fundamentally at stake is a wrong definition of terms and a *de jure* absurdity. If something is infallible, it by logical and rational necessity *cannot* err. So, while Fuller Seminary thought they were advancing a weaker term they were actually advocating a much stronger term, because whatever lacks the ability to err is greater than a thing that simply has no errors. Hence, we may be able to distinguish between the two terms, much like we can distinguish between a soul and a body. But there is a real and internal metaphysical and logical relationship between infallibility and inerrancy. To be infallible by rational and ontological necessity demands inerrancy. Thus, whenever someone wrongly separates the body and the soul it leads to death. Similarly, whenever someone wrongly separates (not distinguishes) infallibility from inerrancy, it leads to the death of an evangelical view of Scripture.

Figures at Fuller Theological Seminary and other neo-evangelical institutions were championing a view known as limited-inspiration and limited-inerrancy. If they were rationally and theologically consistent, they would also admit that they were forwarding a limited infallibility too. This approach tries to regulate inspiration and inerrancy to salvific matters and deny it concerning historical matters. For that reason, Geisler and the CSBI affirmed the inerrancy of the whole, also known as complete or full

---

[263] Sproul and Geisler, *Explaining Inerrancy*, 43.
[264] Ibid.

inerrancy. This view affirms that inspiration and inerrancy apply to both salvific and historical matters. There can be no historical errors or contradictions within the text of Scripture because God cannot lie, err, or break the first principles of being (i.e., the law of non-contradiction). It has always been recognized that the inspiration and inerrancy of the text of Scripture apply to the original autographs of Scripture, not to the copies. The framers make four key points in Article 10 of the CSBI about the autographic sense of inspiration and inerrancy, claiming:[265]

1. We affirm that inspiration, strictly speaking, applies only to the autographic text of Scripture, which in the providence of God can be ascertained from available manuscripts with great accuracy.

2. We further affirm that copies and translations of Scripture are the Word of God to the extent that they faithfully represent the original.

3. We deny that any essential element of the Christian faith is affected by the absence of the autographs.

4. We further deny that this absence renders the assertion of biblical inerrancy invalid or irrelevant.

Since we do not have the original autographs of Scripture, evangelicals have been committed to the science of lower or textual criticism to reconstruct the original manuscripts. We know that the Bible is not opposed to textual reconstruction. The Bible also shows that copies of the text of Scripture carry equal authority as the originals. The first known case of the need for textual restoration is found in Exodus 32 and 34. The tablets were written by God himself (Exod 32:15-16) but were subsequently destroyed by Moses in his anger (v. 19). In the book, *Inerrancy*, edited by Geisler, Greg Bahnsen states:

> God provided for the rewriting of the words of the original tablets (Exod. 34:1, 27-28), and Scripture makes the point that these second tablets were written 'according to the first writing' (Deut. 10:2, 4). Here is a significant model for all later copying of the biblical autographs; they should reproduce the words that were on the first tablet or page in order to preserve the full divine authority of the message they convey.[266]

---

[265] Ibid., 41.
[266] Geisler, *Inerrancy*, 165.

Paradigmatic therefore, throughout the Bible itself, is the fact that a copy carries the same weight and authority as the original. Present-day evangelicals ought to be committed to the science of textual criticism, since there is such a strong Scriptural warrant for the practice through individuals such as Moses, Jeremiah, Josiah, and other key biblical figures.[267]

Some people try to make the case that if an imperfect copy is sufficient, why can we not have an imperfect original? First, we recognize from the principle of causality that if God creates something, it must bear the perfections of his nature. When God created Adam in the Garden, Adam was upright and sinless. Likewise, with Scripture, God created it upright and inerrant. Moreover, we find in the case of Adam that his posterity erred and that this was perfectly consistent with God creating a perfect Adam. The same is also true of the text of Scripture. The fact that the descendants (i.e., copies) contain errors does not mean that the original contained errors. Second, it is impossible for a perfect God to make a merely adequate but imperfect original. There are many things God cannot do, even by his sovereignty. He cannot change (Mal. 3:6; James 1:13, 17). He cannot deny himself (2 Tim. 2:13). He cannot cease being God (Heb. 1:10-12). He cannot break an unconditional promise (Rom. 11:29). God cannot lie (Heb. 6:17-18). And, as an absolutely perfect God, he cannot produce an imperfect product either in the realm of truth or morals—because it is contrary to the very nature of God to do so.

People also try to claim that inerrancy is irrelevant because God did not preserve perfect copies of the originals. Several responses could be offered to this. First, as we have said, the reason a perfect original is required is because by logical necessity the nature of God requires a perfect original. Second, since God did not breathe out the copies, it is logically possible for them to contain errors. However, we must reject the fundamental claim as such because God has substantially preserved the original in the copies. We have good copies of the manuscripts and there is no good reason to deny that they significantly represent the original copies. Third, there may be further religious reasons for God to not preserve the originals. For example, throughout history there has been a strong propensity by people to worship such artifacts as religious relics. Moreover, if someone had an original copy, and given the propensity of the human heart to distort truth, it would make it much easier to alter the original in a sinful attempt to spite God and his Word.

Many people also try to evade the classic doctrine of inerrancy by charging it with a fallacious deductive approach to reasoning that does not

---

[267] Ibid., 166-167.

consider the inductive aspects of Scripture, and the reality of individual texts. There are several points that can be made against this type of argument. First, if they are going to say "all inductive arguments are fallacious and fail to regard the humanity" of a particular topic, we must see the internal inconsistency of the argument. They are categorically using deductive logic to deny that very claim. 1. All cases of deductive logic are fallacious. 2. The classic formulation of the doctrine of inerrancy is a case of deductive logic. 3. Therefore, classic formulation of the doctrine of inerrancy is fallacious. We merely need to change the second premise to: 2. This very argument is a case of deductive logic; and therefore, it is fallacious. This approach would amount to a denial of the self-evident laws of logic. Second, it is incorrect to claim that we do not perform an inductive search for the doctrine of inerrancy. We fulfill our two deductive premises (1. God cannot err, and 2. The Bible is the Word of God) from an inductive search of the text of Scripture. Third, we arrive at many biblical doctrines such as the Trinity and the Incarnation through a deductive study of the text of Scripture. These truths follow logically and necessarily from deductive premises. Fourth, a deductive reconciliation and approach to theology is the very basis of systematic theology. We base our premises upon the inductive study of Scripture, but we draw several deductive conclusions. Fifth, the Reformed tradition is very clear in the *Westminster Confession of Faith* (chap.1, sect. 6), stating, "the whole counsel of God . . . [is] either expressly set down in Scripture, or by good and necessary consequence may be deduced from Scripture." It must also be noted that those proper deductions carry the same weight as the explicit declarations of Scripture.

    We must also understand that Geisler and the CSBI are committed not only to the inerrancy of the Bible, but also to a correspondence view of truth. Article 13 states, "We deny that it is proper to evaluate Scripture according to standards of truth and error that are alien to its usage or purpose." The framers believe "true-truth" (to steal a phrase from Francis Schaeffer) is the appropriate judge and standard for Scripture. Obviously, God is Truth, and his nature properly defines reality. Sproul and Geisler define what they mean by truth, claiming:

> By biblical standards of truth and error is meant the view used both in the Bible and in everyday life, viz., a correspondence view of truth. This part of the article is directed toward those who would redefine truth to relate merely to redemptive intent, the purely personal or like, rather than to mean that which corresponds with reality. For example, when Jesus affirmed that Jonah was in the 'belly of the great fish' this statement is true, not

simply because of the redemptive significance the story of Jonah has, but also because it is literally and historically true. The same may be said of the New Testament assertions about Adam, Moses, David and the other Old Testament persons as well as about the Old Testament events.[268]

One can find a more thorough explanation and defense of a correspondence view of truth and how it applies to the inerrancy of Scripture in the book, *Defending Inerrancy*. However, for our sake it must be noted that a correspondence view of truth is the one used by philosophers, bankers, scientists, ordinary persons, and the judicial courts. The ICBI was responding to an intentionalist theory of truth. Clark Pinnock, Jack Rogers, and many other figures held to this view of truth.[269] They argued that Scripture is only true insofar as it intends to communicate redemptive matters, not historical matters. We understand the error of this approach. If something is true because someone intends for it to be true, then all sincere statements ever uttered would be true—even those which are explicitly false. But many sincere people can be wrong.

As was already discussed in chapter two, it must be noted that a correspondence view of truth is essential because it entails the objectivity of truth. If truth is what corresponds to reality, then there must be some objective reality to which it can correspond. An objective view of truth entails that truth is not subjective. Truth is the same for everyone, not just some people. The truthfulness is not true for some and not for others. Truth is not sometimes true, and at other times false. When applied to the text of Scripture it means that the Bible is true for everyone, everywhere, all the time, and absolutely. A correspondence view of truth also allows for truth to be communicated in propositional form. Truth can be contained and communicated in language, including truths about God contained in the Bible. Objective reality can be put into propositions. This means that every truth contained in the Bible is a propositional truth, or can be reduced to a propositional truth. In fact, there are no nonpropositional truths in the Bible or anywhere else. For if it is true, then it corresponds to some objective reality, and if it corresponds to objective reality, then it can be put into propositional form.[270]

The following section will discuss the fact that ICBI inerrantists not only believed that inerrancy was a concept taught in the Bible, but that it functions as a proper evangelical hermeneutic. We will consider what the

---

[268] Sproul and Geisler, *Explaining Inerrancy*, 50.
[269] Geisler and Roach, *Defending Inerrancy*, 243-244.
[270] Ibid., 247.

CSBI and the *Chicago Statement on Biblical Hermeneutics* (CSBH) have to say about the best way to interpret objective reality and the Bible.

## The Nature of Hermeneutics and Inerrancy

The ICBI held three conferences. The first and most well-known was the conference that produced the *Chicago Statement on Biblical Inerrancy*. The influence of the CSBI is far reaching and established the precise way to define inerrancy for many organizations. The lesser-known event was the second conference, which produced the *Chicago Statement on Biblical Hermeneutics*. This section will focus on a few issues which indicate that the CSBH defended the historical-grammatical method of biblical interpretation, a qualified understanding of the relationship between epistemology and hermeneutics, and a specific way to approach the method of historical criticism and the use of secondary or outside resources. Before we dive into those matters, we must first address the question: Does inerrancy provide a hermeneutic?

For the ICBI, inerrancy functions as a type of hermeneutic. J. I. Packer states, "The axiom of inerrancy as a guideline for biblical interpretation expresses and safeguards the belief that in all the inspired texts, whatever their literary genre and style, God speaks his mind to us in and through what the human author articulates."[271] Not all present-day biblical scholars would agree with Packer or the ICBI over the notion that inerrancy is a hermeneutic, and claim that inerrancy leads to a wooden or literalistic hermeneutic. For example, David Kelsey does not believe that inspiration or inerrancy produce interpretive agreement among believers.[272] Kevin Vanhoozer states, "While inerrancy is not a fully-orbed hermeneutic, it does give believers confidence that Scripture's teaching is ultimately unified and coherent."[273] Vanhoozer is a well-known critic of the CSBH and what he labels as cognitive-propositionalist theology from literalistic inerrantists.[274]

---

[271] Ibid., 11.

[272] David H. Kelsey, *Proving Doctrine: The Uses of Scripture in Modern Theology* (Harrisburg: Trinity Press International, 1999).

[273] J. Merrick and Stephen M. Garrett, general editors, *Five Views on Biblical Inerrancy* (Grand Rapids: Zondervan, 2013), 202.

[274] William C. Roach, *Hermeneutics as Epistemology: A Critical Assessment of Carl F. H. Henry's Epistemological Approach to Hermeneutics* (Eugene: Wipf and Stock, 2015), 53-57, 251-255; Kevin J. Vanhoozer, *The Drama of Doctrine: A Canonical Linguistic Approach to Christian Theology* (Louisville: Westminster John Knox, 1998); Kevin J. Vanhoozer, *Is There a Meaning in This Text? The Bible, the Reader, and the Morality of Literary Knowledge* (Grand Rapids: Zondervan, 1998).

In his article, *Lost in Interpretation? Truth, Scripture, and Hermeneutics*, Vanhoozer questions the internal coherence of the CSBI and CSBH statements. Quoting Vanhoozer at length will gain the thrust of his critique. He claims:

> In this regard it is interesting to compare the two Chicago Statements. The Statement on Biblical Inerrancy is in my opinion by far the more successful of the two. Interestingly, one looks in vain in that statement for the terms "fact" or "factuality." The Statement speaks instead of the truth of Scripture in "all matters" it addresses (Art. IX, XI). The Statement acknowledges the presence of diverse literary styles (Art. VIII, XVIII) and figures of speech: "So history must be treated as history, poetry as poetry, hyperbole and metaphor as hyperbole and metaphor . . . and so forth." The key claim for our purposes comes in Article XIII: "We deny that it is proper to evaluate Scripture according to standards of truth and error that are alien to its usage or purpose."
>
> In contrast, the second Chicago Statement, on Biblical Hermeneutics, takes back with its left hand what the former offers with its right. On the one hand, Article X affirms "that Scripture communicates God's truth to us verbally through a wide variety of literary forms." And Article XV helpfully adds that "[i]nterpretation according to the literal sense will take account of all figures of speech and literary forms found in the text." These gestures are overwhelmed by other articles, however, where the language of "fact" and "factuality" takes over. Article VI: "We . . . affirm that a statement is true if it represents matters as they actually are but is an error if it misrepresents the facts." Article XIV goes on to affirm that the biblical record of events, "though presented in a variety of appropriate literary forms, corresponds to historical fact." Finally, Article XXII affirms that Genesis 1–11 "is factual, as is the rest of the book." It is difficult to read these affirmations together so as to preserve a healthy tension rather than a contradiction between them. While the second Statement does not actually make shipwreck of biblical interpretation, it does incline the good ship Hermeneutics to list rather dangerously.
>
> Dangerously? Yes, to the extent that it risks imposing extrabiblical categories and standards on biblical narratives. History is not simply a matter of reporting facts, at least not if by "fact" we mean the kind of data that can be verified empirically apart from a fiduciary interpretative framework! That way

positivism lies. Evangelicals must not let a particular theory of truth and factuality determine what the author of Genesis 1–11 is proposing for our consideration. It is the text, not some theory of truth, that ought to determine what kind of a claim is being made. To begin with a theory of truth and argue to a particular interpretation is to put the factual cart before the hermeneutical horse. This was Bultmann's mistake: he assumed that the Bible's truth was existential and then set about demythologizing it. Let us not make a similar mistake and run rough-shod over authorial intent in our haste to historicize.[275]

In this quote, Vanhoozer claims that there is a contradiction between the CSBI and the CSBH view of hermeneutics. His chief charge against the view comes when he questions allowing a correspondence theory of truth to determine our understanding of the biblical text, Genesis in particular.

Geisler and I respond to Vanhoozer's entire approach in our book, *Defending Inerrancy*.[276] We show that the fundamental issue in Vanhoozer's approach is the fact that he denies a correspondence theory of truth. He favors a type of "personal" or "relational" truth. It is quite a philosophical misnomer to believe in "relational" and "personal" truth. There are truths about relationships and truths about persons in Scripture, but truth by itself is not relational. Truth is that which corresponds to a reality about persons and relationships, not some abstract or esoteric idea. Truth is also propositional, that is, it makes a statement that affirms or denies something about reality.[277] All in all, it Vanhoozer's approach to truth is inadequate, hence he desires to expand its definition. Most importantly, Vanhoozer is drawing a false analogy between the CSBH view of truth and Bultmann. Bultmann's approach to truth does not correspond with the standards of everyday life. No one lives according to Bultmann's view of truth, even though they attempt to provide a hermeneutic in accordance with an existentialist approach to reality. Unfortunately, evangelicals, such as Vanhoozer, do the very opposite. They live a particular way, namely, according to a correspondence theory of truth; however, they develop a hermeneutic contrary to the view of truth manifest in reality (which is what the CSBH believes is the definition of truth found in the biblical text). All in all, not only have Geisler and I made the point, but figures such as theologian Gregory Alan Thornbury and

---

[275] Kevin J. Vanhoozer, "Lost In Interpretation? Truth, Scripture, and Hermeneutics." *Journal of the Evangelical Theological Society*, 48 (2005) 98-99.

[276] Geisler and Roach, *Defending Inerrancy*, 132-159.

[277] See: CSBH, Article VI.

philosopher Paul Helm have also demonstrated, that Vanhoozer seems to read classic inerrantists in the worst possible light, and characterizes poorly their position on truth, inerrancy, hermeneutics, and theology.[278]

For the CSBH and the ICBI, inerrancy does function as a particular hermeneutic because not all approaches to understanding and interpreting an object in reality, or regarding a proposition about reality, correspond with a realist metaphysic and epistemology. In other words, the Bible is a thorough going metaphysical realist book, and any approach to metaphysics, epistemology, language, or hermeneutics which undermines those philosophical and theological commitments will fundamentally misunderstand the commonsense approach found in the Bible. We can also understand one's view of Scripture based upon the *way* an individual actually handles the Bible. This can be seen in a variety of other areas of life. If a person views life as something with inherent value, they will necessarily handle or treat a person differently than someone who holds the opposite view. If a person has a low view of Scripture, this will be seen in the way they approach Scripture and the conclusions they make about the Bible. Similarly, one can claim to uphold a high view of Scripture, much like a husband can claim to love his wife; but if a person undermines that claim by the way they handle the Scriptures (or their wife!) it shows a great disconnect between their profession and actions.[279]

Several examples could be offered concerning the nature, role, and function of hermeneutics according to Norman Geisler. He has three primary texts where he explains his approach to hermeneutics both as an epistemology and a method of biblical interpretation. The most precise and thorough understanding can be found in his commentary on the *Chicago Statement on Biblical Hermeneutics*. The second is found in chapter ten of his systematic theology, titled, *Interpretation: The Hermeneutical Precondition*.[280] This chapter outlines Geisler's approach to hermeneutics as an explicit form of interpretation, specifically as it relates to ontology and epistemology.[281] The third approach, which is more of a methodological

---

[278] See: Gregory Alan Thornbury, *Recovering Classic Evangelicalism: Applying the Wisdom and Vision of Carl F. H. Henry* (Wheaton: Crossway, 2013), 105-115; Paul Helm, *Faith, Form, and Fashion: Classical Reformed Theology and Its Postmodern Critics* (Eugene: Cascade Books, 2014).

[279] For an overview of this type of approach with many examples, see my book, *Hermeneutics as Epistemology*, 1-58, 172-230.

[280] Norman L. Geisler, *Systematic Theology: Introduction and Bible* (Minneapolis: Bethany House, 2002), 160-180.

[281] More will be said about this topic in the final chapter as it relates to applying the method of Norman Geisler in an age of unbelief.

chapter, is found in his co-authored book, *When Critics Ask*.[282] The purpose of the book is to tackle difficult Bible challenges raised by skeptics and critics of the Bible. For our sake, however, we must consider how Norman Geisler approached the issues of hermeneutics as epistemology and hermeneutics as methodology. Specifically, Geisler's (and the ICBI's) approach to preunderstanding, meaning, human understanding, and specific guidelines for biblical interpretation.[283]

*Preunderstanding, Meaning, and Human Understanding*

Prevalent throughout evangelical scholarship is the notion of "horizons" of biblical interpretation, whereby we "fuse" the text and an interpreter in a particular way, whereby this ontological act ultimately controls the meaning of the text.[284] This approach is also known as the hermeneutical spiral or hermeneutical circle.[285] CSBI signer and past president of the *Evangelical Theological Society*, Robert Thomas, warned about this approach to hermeneutics. He claims in his book, *Evangelical Hermeneutics*, that this whole approach is grounded in Kantian subjectivity and various forms of idealistic and phenomenological approaches to metaphysics and epistemology.[286] Thomas provides the following chart, titled, "The Origin of Preunderstanding: From Explanation to Obfuscation", as a way to understand the two different approaches:

---

[282] Norman Geisler and Thomas Howe, *When Critics Ask: A Popular Handbook on Bible Difficulties* (Grand Rapids: Baker, 1992), 11-27.

[283] Geisler interacted with many issues affecting hermeneutics and inerrancy. Cases could also include Robert Gundry, Michael Licona, Clark Pinnock, Darrell Bock, and Murray Harris. Several of these are explained in Geisler's book: *Preserving Orthodoxy: Maintaining Continuity with the Historic Christian Faith on Scripture* (Matthews: Bastion Books, 2017). Each of these figures approached the text using some form of higher biblical criticism. Since Geisler spent ample and sufficient time dealing with each of these cases, we will forego those examples in favor of two lesser known cases.

[284] See: Anthony C. Thiselton, *New Horizons in Hermeneutics: The Theory and Practice of Transforming Biblical Texts* (Grand Rapids: Zondervan, 1992); Grant R. Osborne, *The Hermeneutical Spiral: A Comprehensive Introduction to Biblical Interpretation* (Downers Grove: IVP, 2006); Jeannine K. Brown, *Scripture as Communication: Introducing Biblical Hermeneutics* (Grand Rapids: Baker Academic, 2007).

[285] Roach, *Hermeneutics as Epistemology*, 14-25, 48-53.

[286] Robert L. Thomas, *Evangelical Hermeneutics: The New Versus the Old* (Grand Rapids: Kregel, 2002), 41-62.

| Period | Starting Point | Associated Considerations |
|---|---|---|
| Post-1970s | Importance of Preunderstanding | Post-Kantian emphasis on subjectivity |
| | | Tentativeness of interpretive conclusions |
| | | Definitions of preunderstanding (depending on the source consulted): |
| | | • Prejudice and commitment to traditional view of inspiration **or** |
| | | • Hermeneutical self-awareness **or** |
| | | • One's views regarding life and ultimate realities and about the nature of the text being studied **or** |
| | | • A body of assumptions and attitudes that a person brings to the perception and interpretation of reality or any aspect of it **or** |
| | | • The literal, the grammatical, the historical, the textual design, and the theological **or** |
| | | • As a supernatural book, the Bible is authoritative and |

|  |  | trustworthy; as a natural book, it uses human communication **or** |
|  |  | • The colored lenses through which the reader views the text |
| Pre-1970s | Quest for Objectivity | Exclusion of personal biases |
|  |  | Certainty of propositional truths |
|  |  | Centers attention: |
|  |  | • God's ability to communicate instead of man's inability to receive communication |
|  |  | • God's purpose to communicate instead of man's cultural limitations |
|  |  | • Holy Spirit's illumination in achieving objectivity |
|  |  | • Neutral objectivity achieved throughout church history. |

The central difference between the two approaches is seen in that the post-1970s approach, unlike the pre-1970s approach, denies that truth about reality is knowable. This special emphasis upon the interpreter is ultimately the result of the Kantian emphasis on subjective knowledge as distinct from objective knowledge. Thomas goes on to discuss the effects of the post-1970s approach, claiming:

Uncertainty among hermeneutical theoreticians is widespread, resulting in multiple 'preunderstandings' of *preunderstanding.* They agree only regarding its influences on the outcome of the interpretive endeavor. In line with this acknowledged subjectivism, most advocate that one must view personal interpretive conclusions as tentative. This relativism leads easily to divesting the Scripture of any value in stating propositional truth, though one writer would limit the uncertainty to ambiguous areas such as sovereignty and responsibility, the millennial issue, and church government. Others pass of this uncertainty as tolerance of fellow believers for the sake of unity—i.e., "I don't agree with your conclusions . . . , but I concede your interpretation." If allowed to progress to its logical end, however, this outlook may lead to a realization that what we have considered to be cardinal dogmas—such as the deity of Christ, His second coming, and His substitutionary atonement—are merely the myopic conclusions of Western, white, middle-class males. Such a hermeneutical approach would spell the end of meaningful Christian doctrine.[287]

The CSBH warned about this new hermeneutical approach and attempted to evade its embrace by many evangelical scholars. Unfortunately, many evangelicals did not heed their warning and the horizons approach is the predominant view amongst professing evangelical scholars.

The CSBH, Article 9, titled: Hermeneutics and Meaning, states:

> We Affirm that the term hermeneutics, which historically signified the rules of exegesis, may properly be extended to cover all that is involved in the process of perceiving what the biblical revelation means and how it bears on our lives.
>
> We Deny that the message of Scripture derives from, or is dictated by, the interpreter's understanding. Thus we deny that the 'horizon' of the biblical writer and the interpreter may rightly 'fuse' in such a way that what the text communicates to the interpreter is not ultimately controlled by the expressed meaning of Scripture.[288]

To evade what has been understand as "hermeneutical nihilism", the CSBH rejected the notion of preunderstanding as an approach compatible with inerrancy. Geisler explains:

---

[287] Ibid., 45-46.
[288] Sproul and Geisler, *Explaining Inerrancy,* 70.

The Denial notes that the meaning of a passage is not derived from or dictated by the interpreter. Rather, meaning comes from the author who wrote it. Thus the reader's understanding has no hermeneutically definitive role. Readers must listen to the meaning of a text and not attempt to legislate it. Of course, the meaning listened to should be applied to the reader's life. But the need or desire for specific application should not color the interpretation of a passage.[289]

The CSBH in Article 19, titled: Dangers in Preunderstanding, states:

> We Affirm that any preunderstanding which the interpreter brings to Scripture should be in harmony with scriptural teaching and subject to correction by it.
>
> We Deny that Scripture should be required to fit alien preunderstandings, inconsistent with itself, such as naturalism, evolutionism, scientism, secular humanism, and relativism.[290]

Geisler explains this article, claiming:

> The question of preunderstanding is a crucial one in contemporary hermeneutics. The careful wording of the Affirmation does not discuss whether one should approach Scripture with a particular understanding, but simply which kinds of preunderstanding one has are legitimate. The question is affirming that only those preunderstandings which are compatible with the teaching of Scripture are legitimate. In fact, the statement goes further and demands that all preunderstanding be subject to "correction" by the teaching of Scripture. The point of this article is to avoid interpreting Scripture through an alien grid or filter which obscures or negates its true message. For it acknowledges that one's preunderstanding will affect his understanding of a text. Hence, to avoid misinterpreting Scripture one must be careful to examine his own presuppositions in the light of Scripture.[291]

The central point to note from this last article is that the CSBH and ICBI do not deny the functional roles that presuppositions and preunderstanding may serve within interpretation. The major distinction centers around the fact that one is not ontologically trapped or determined by these modes of

---

[289] Ibid., 70-71.
[290] Ibid., 80.
[291] Ibid.

preunderstanding. Many evangelicals would claim to agree with this article and to being committed to not interpreting the Bible according to alien categories; however, many of the dominant modes of philosophy pervasive throughout their books and articles on hermeneutics indicate that, *methodologically*, they are unable to reconcile their philosophy (which mandates this approach to metaphysics and epistemology) with their verbal profession.

What is unique about Geisler's approach to hermeneutics is his commitment to metaphysical realism. Pervasive throughout the evangelical world is a commitment to the dominant German forms of metaphysics and epistemology. There seems to be a commitment to Heidegger, Gadamer, and Wittgenstein as it pertains to existentialism and phenomenology, historical conditioning and situatedness, and a conventionalist theory of meaning. It was demonstrated earlier that Geisler's commitment to the Platonic tradition and its affirmation that "truth about reality is knowable" distinguishes his approach from many present-day evangelicals. This approach to philosophy necessarily undergirds his understanding of reality, including the reality of the biblical text and the proper method for interpreting the biblical text (since the Bible is an object in reality, which requires a proper method of interpretation). Geisler's approach allows for an objective interpretation of reality, whereas present-day philosophical and evangelical views not only reject objectivity, but necessarily cannot account for the metaphysical and epistemological preconditions of objectivity. Geisler responded to these dominant forms of subjectivist hermeneutics throughout his career.[292]

For our purposes, it is worth noting not only the *fact* of Geisler's criticism, but the *method* of his criticism. Whether subjectivist evangelicals are willing to admit it or not, their view is grounded in the context of Enlightenment and/or Postmodern metaphysics and epistemology. If someone does not want to reap the negative results of subjectivity, they must not allow for modernity to set the axioms and control the necessary preconditions of their philosophy. Geisler was unique amongst evangelicals because he rejected the dominant philosophies of the Enlightenment in favor of pre-modern philosophical realism. Note how Geisler responds to Heideggerian approaches, as these quotes illustrate our point:

- Heidegger's subjective existential hermeneutic involves the unfounded assumption that Being is unintelligible in itself. But how could Heidegger know this about Being unless Being were intelligible?

---

[292] Geisler, *Introduction and Bible*, 164-165.

- It is self-defeating to attempt to express the inexpressible. If Being is beyond description, how is it that Heidegger succeeds in describing it for us.

- Language does not establish being but expresses it. It does not found Being but reveals it to us, that is, if it is truly descriptive of it.

- Heidegger's assertion against a correspondence view of truth is self-destructive, for he assumes that his denial of a correspondence view of truth corresponds with reality. But correspondence with reality is precisely what is meant by a correspondence view of truth.

- He [Heidegger] purports an openness to Being but rejects God, who *is* Being—Pure Actuality. Every contingent being (which Heidegger admits man is) needs a Necessary Being to ground its existence.

- Heidegger neglects the analogical ability of language to speak meaningfully of God, and he rejects the descriptive ability of language for its evocative dimension.

- Heidegger asks the right question but rules out an adequate answer. He responds to "Why something, not nothing?" by saying it can be asked about God too. But it cannot— at least not meaningfully. God is an Uncaused Being, and of such a Being it is not meaningful to ask what caused the Uncaused. One may as well ask, "Who is the bachelor's wife?"

- Heidegger expects all readers of his books to use the standard hermeneutic of searching for the author's meaning. But this is directly contrary to the subjective hermeneutic he taught to be used on other writings.

- Heidegger's hermeneutic reduces to an unverifiable mysticism. How does he know that the "mittances" of light obtained through the "pathological" poets are not from the angel of light (2 Cor. 11:14)?[293]

In sum, it ought to be recognized that Geisler and the CSBH reject existential and phenomenological approaches. They reject the premise that

---

[293] Ibid.

we are by ontological necessity locked into a particular metaphysical state of being, which is necessarily conditioned historically and linguistically. Instead, Geisler grounded his approach in the realist tradition as explained in chapter one. In the forthcoming chapter, we will discuss the significance Geisler's approach has for addressing existential and phenomenological approaches, specifically as it applies to hermeneutics, race, and critical theory.

*Guidelines for Biblical Interpretation*

The second aspect we must address is hermeneutics as *methodology*, or the actual way a person approaches the biblical text. Geisler has two different cases of methodology. The first affects the broader method of doing theology. The second offers specific guidelines for biblical interpretation. In his *Systematic Theology*, Geisler offers these guidelines about method, claiming:

Two things should be apparent from the foregoing discussions:

(1) The method should fit its object.

(2) The method should not be contrary to the results it is supposed to produce.

A third can be added:

(3) No one method can suffice for the many steps involved in developing an evangelical theology.[294]

For Geisler, there is not one overarching method for all disciplines. As he says, there are steps and each method must be developed according to its object. Unlike modern scientific approaches to reality, which mainly rely upon the scientific method as the one method to secure knowledge in all areas, Classical Realists recognize that each object has a different nature; hence, a different method may be required for each approach. Geisler offers his readers the following nine steps for an evangelical method:[295]

1. An Inductive Basis in Scripture.
2. A Deduction of Truths from Scripture.
3. The Use of Analogies.
4. The Use of General Revelation.

---

[294] Ibid., 218.
[295] Ibid., 218-224.

5. The Retroductive Method.

6. Systematic Correlation (of all information into a fully orbed doctrine through use of the laws of logic that insist all truth must be noncontradictory).

7. Each Doctrine is Correlated with All Other Doctrines.

8. Each Doctrine is Expressed in View of the Orthodox Teaching of the Church Fathers.

9. Livability is the Final Test for Systematic Theology.

Geisler explains the first five steps of his method by using inerrancy as his example. Steps six through nine are self-explanatory and Geisler's point is clear. Geisler offers this breakdown to explain the first five steps:[296]

1. The Inductive Basis:

    a. God cannot err.

    b. The Bible is God's Word.

2. The Deductive Conclusion:

    a. The Bible cannot err.

3. The Use of Analogies:

    a. Just as Christ was divine and human and yet without sin, even so the Bible is divine and human yet without error.

    b. Just as nature (God's general revelation) presents difficulties with possessing errors, so does the Bible (God's special revelation).

4. The Use of General Revelation:

    a. The earth is not square.

    b. The sun does not move around the earth.

5. The Retroductive Method:

    a. The biblical teaching is fleshed out in view of facts known from general revelation and the data (phenomena) of Scripture.

---

[296] Ibid., 222-223.

b. There are errors in the manuscript copies.

c. The Bible uses figures of speech and other literary devices, round numbers, everyday (nontechnical) language, paraphrases, etc.

d. The deductive conclusion (point 2a) is understood in the light of the retroductive enhancement. For example:

   i. The Bible is without error only in the original text, not in all the copies.

   ii. Round numbers, observational language, figures of speech, and paraphrased citations are not errors.

For Geisler, an orthodox methodology is crucial to an evangelical theology. There are orthodox and unorthodox methods. Evangelicals ought to study method *per se* to forego the false conclusions and unnecessary errors of aberrant methods.

Geisler also discusses several mistakes people make when they interpret the Bible. For evangelicals, the Bible is the Word of God and, as such, it cannot have any errors. Obviously, the Bible contains interpretive difficulties. Geisler was known for quoting St. Augustine, who said, "If we are perplexed by any apparent contradiction in Scripture, it is not allowable to say, the author of the book is mistaken; but either the manuscript is faulty, or the translation is wrong, or you have not understood."[297] The mistakes are not in the revelation of God, but in the method of interpretation used by the person interpreting the Bible. Geisler claims their mistakes fall into one of these main categories:[298]

1. Assuming the Unexplained is not Explainable.

2. Presuming the Bible Guilty Until Proven Innocent.

3. Confusing Our Fallible Interpretation with God's Infallible Revelation.

4. Failing to Understand the Context of the Passage.

5. Neglecting to Interpret Difficult Passages in Light of Clear Ones.

---

[297] St. Augustine, *Reply to Faustus the Manichean* 11.5 in Philip Schaff, *A Select Library of the Nicene and Ante-Nicene Fathers of the Christian Church* (Grand Rapids: Eerdmans, 1956), vol. 4).

[298] Geisler and Howe, *When Critics Ask*, 15-26.

6. Basing a Teaching on an Obscure Passage.

7. Forgetting that the Bible is a Human Book with Human Characteristics.

8. Assuming that a Partial Report is a False Report.

9. Demanding that NT Citations of the OT Always Be Exact Quotations.

10. Assuming that Divergent Accounts Are False Ones.

11. Presuming that the Bible Approves of All it Records.

12. Forgetting the Bible Uses Non-technical, Everyday Language.

13. Assuming that Round Numbers Are False.

14. Neglecting to Note that the Bible Uses Different Literary Devices.

15. Forgetting that Only the Original Text, Not Every Copy of Scripture, Is Without Error.

16. Confusing General Statements with Universal Ones.

17. Forgetting that Latter Revelation Supersedes Previous Revelation.

For Geisler, mediating positions of evangelical hermeneutics and approaches to inerrancy are typically grounded in a faulty method or illegitimate mistakes concerning one's approach to the Bible. Mediating evangelical positions come from dramatic approaches, narrative theology, post-critical hermeneutics, genre criticism, historical criticism, and many other places. They try to emphasize the authority of Scripture to some degree; however, they undermine an evangelical view of Scripture as God's inerrant Word by the *way* they approach and interpret Holy Writ.

## Conclusion

Norman Geisler was one of Evangelicalism's greatest defenders of the inerrancy of Scripture. Page for page, probably no one evangelical figure penned more in defense of the total truthfulness of God's Word than Norman Geisler. Geisler's approach to Scripture differs significantly from many present-day evangelical apologists. Geisler does not want to argue for the general reliability of the Bible, or for some view of Scripture that contains errors and contradictions. Geisler and other classic evangelicals were committed to the highest view of Scripture, and that determined both their theology and goals in apologetics.

Foundational to the classic doctrine of inerrancy is a wholehearted commitment to classical realism and classical theism. If truth exists and truth about reality can be known, then there are self-evident first principles about reality. If God exists and possesses the classical attributes of God, then any revelation of God must possess those perfections (based upon the principle of causality). God provides the ontological and providential grounds to ensure that we possess an inspired, infallible, and inerrant revelation contained in Sacred Scripture. In many ways, just as classical realism and classical theism hang together, so does a realist view of God's creation and the total truthfulness of the Word of God.

The final chapter will explain the issues of modernity faced by evangelical apologists, specifically modernity understood as a turning away from the Platonic tradition. The chapter will also discuss certain aspects of Geisler's use of Aquinas and will conclude by offering one example of the application of Thomism to the contemporary issues of subjectivity and critical theory. Finally, it will offer advice from Geisler concerning the *mood* evangelicals ought to maintain in their defense of truth in our age.

# CHAPTER FIVE

# Defending Classic Evangelicalism

## Introduction

Modernity presents Christianity with an apologetic crisis. There used to be a tide of individuals who came into our churches affiliated with Christianity only as Easter and Christmas Christians. They would attend on these historic Christian holidays to satisfy some sense within, whether that be from family tradition, to ease their consciences, or fulfill a personal religious ideal. Since that time, however, it seems like the Christmas and Easter Christians gave birth to "no religious affiliation—'None's'", who deem themselves as secular and not in need of religion altogether.[299]

Many evangelical commentators have embraced the paradigm that Christianity is on the decline and atheism is in the saddle. Many evangelicals champion the notion that secularism has such a binding effect upon society, and we will lose both the Church and our children, lest we engage the present-day apologetic situation. Numerous explanations have been offered by secular and religious commentators for the cause(s) of this decline of Christianity in the public sphere. The predominant explanation, which seems to be found ubiquitously throughout much of the apologetic literature, is that education and secular reason provided the explanations and elements required to erode Christian belief in the West. They join John Lennon, who in his 1966 interview with the *Telegraph*, claimed, "Christianity will go. It will vanish and shrink. I needn't argue about that; I'm right and will be proved right."[300] In other words, a secular age is about to come upon us. We merely need to sit-back, relax, and let reason do its work.

There is no doubt that modernity has caused a crisis of epistemology within evangelicalism. We are downstream from Schaeffer's line of despair

---

[299] J. P. Moreland, *Scaling the Secular City: A Defense of Christianity* (Grand Rapids: Baker Academic, 1987); J. P. Moreland, *Love Your God With All Your Mind: The Role Reason in The Life of The Soul* (Colorado Springs: Navpress, 1997).

[300] Maureen Cleave, "The John Lennon I Knew," *Telegraph*, September 8, 2005, www.telegraph.co.uk/culture/music/rockandjazzmusic/3646983/The-John-Lennon-I-knew.html.

and we must be willing to address the psychological, rational, and cultural conditions of belief. As we have argued throughout this book, Norman Geisler attempted to jettison this intellectual trajectory by secularists, atheists, and liberal theologians. No doubt, Geisler fought many other battles against world religions, cults, issues in ethics, and much more. We should not downplay or disregard the role these other issues have towards capturing a proper understanding of the scope and nature of Geisler as an apologist. Nevertheless, many of those topics are secondary to the primary issues of truth, God, and the Bible. After we establish the objective nature of truth, the existence of God as understood by classical Christian theism, and the Bible as the inerrant Word of God, much of the task that is left can be relegated unto exegesis, counter cult ministry, or polemics.[301]

This final chapter will demonstrate the significance of Geisler's unique synthesis of theology and apologetics. First, by offering a more robust understanding of the role modernity plays within the West; second, by discussing in very specific ways that Geisler's method is significant for present-day issues and conditions of belief in an Age of Unbelief; and third, by offering important practical advice that Geisler gave the evangelical church over the years to maintain both a consistent evangelical scholarship and academy.

## Isn't Religion Going Away?

In his groundbreaking work, *Making Sense of God*, Timothy Keller engages skeptics, believers, and the concept of modernity. Keller raises the question: *Isn't Religion Going Away?*[302] Keller answers that question by highlighting several significant aspects of the modern-day intellectual climate. First, Keller suggests that there are three ways to understand the term "secular." He claims, "One applies the term to the social and political structure. A *secular society* is one in which there is a separation of religion and the state. No religious faith is privileged by the government and the most powerful institutions."[303] Keller and many other Christians throughout history support this definition of "secular" because it concedes the premise that the religious institutions or government ought not control the local church. Religious freedom from hierarchical ecclesiastical or political control

---

[301] For example, consult the book: Norman L. Geisler and Ron Rhodes, *When Cultist Ask: A Popular Handbook on Cultic Misinterpretations* (Grand Rapids: Baker, 1997); Norman L. Geisler and Abdul Saleeb, *Answering Islam: The Crescent in Light of the Cross* (Grand Rapids: Baker, 2002).

[302] Timothy Keller, *Making Sense of God: An Invitation to the Skeptical* (New York: Viking, 2016), 9-28.

[303] Ibid., 2.

seems to be a throughgoing mark or a central tenet for many in the West.[304] Keller then goes on to claim:

> 'Secular' may also be used to describe individuals. A *secular person* is one who does not know if there is a God or any supernatural realm beyond the natural world. Everything, in this view, has a scientific explanation. Finally, the term may describe a particular kind of culture with its themes and narratives. A "*secular age*" is one in which all the emphasis is on the *saeculum*, on the here-and-now, without any concept of the eternal. Meaning in life, guidance, and happiness are understood and sought in present-time economic prosperity, material comfort, and emotional fulfillment.[305]

For Keller and other commentators, it is helpful to distinguish each of these aspects of the term "secular", because they are not identical.[306] Keller notes that a society could have a secular state even if there were very few secular people within that society.

Keller also applies the reality of each type of secular with special emphasis upon individuals in society. He writes:

> Individuals could profess to not be secular people, to have religious faith. Yet, at the practical level, the existence of God may have no noticeable impact on their life decisions and conduct. This is because in a secular age even religious people tend to choose lovers and spouses, careers and friendships, and financial options with no higher goal than their own present-time personal happiness. Sacrificing personal peace and affluence for transcendent causes becomes rare, even for people who say they believe in absolute values and eternity. Even if you are not a secular person, the secular age can "thin out" (secularize) faith until it is seen as simply one more choice in life—along with job, recreation, hobbies, politics—rather than as the comprehensive framework that determines all life choices.[307]

Keller is clear with his warning: secularism comes in a variety of ways, even affecting those who claim to be religious. Unfortunately, we are all aware of these types of "secular-religious" folk. These are the type of people who

---

[304] Ibid., 3.
[305] Ibid.
[306] Ibid.
[307] Ibid.

attend and take leadership roles in large churches, claim to run so-called Christian businesses, go on service mission trips, and put on the external marks of being very religions. Nevertheless, the entire time none of their business decisions are marked by their Christian commitments. They will undermine the reputation of a person to remove them from their business, fire a widow months after her husband dies leaving her without insurance and no means of providing for herself, take secret bonuses at the expense of neglecting the general welfare of their staff, and slander their business partners before clients and referring offices. A person can profess religious ideals with their mouth, while denying them in their actions. One can claim Christianity while functioning as a secularist. Jesus once said, "Rightly did Isaiah prophesy about you: This people honors me with their lips, but their heart is far from me. In vain do they worship me, teaching as doctrines the precepts of men" (Mt. 15:8-9). In short, scripturally speaking, this form of secularism ought to be recognized as a form of false conversion.

The second key aspect Keller notes is the notion of "Impossible to Believe" plays more of a psychological, rather than a rational, role in modern society. Whenever someone surveys the vast amount of literature from secular atheists, they claim that unbelief is a rational function of modern society, and that religion is still present due to underlying psychological effects from a distant age. Keller questions the secular thesis and argues that religion, especially confessional and orthodox Christianity, is not going away. Keller points to several newspapers and sociologists to make his point, claiming:

> After a major new study by the Pew Research Center, the *Washington Post* ran an article titled "The World Is Expected to Become More Religions—Not Less." While acknowledging that in the United State and Europe the percentage of people without religious affiliation will be rising for the time being, the article distilled research findings, namely, that in the world overall religion is growing steadily and strongly. Christians and Muslims will make up an increasing percentage of the world's population, while the proportion that is secular will shrink. Jack Goldstone, a professor of public policy at George Mason University is quoted: "'Sociologists jumped the gun when they said the growth of modernization would bring a growth of secularization and unbelief. . . . That is not what we're seeing,' he said. 'People . . . need religion.'"[308]

---

[308] Ibid., 9-10.

As evangelicals, obviously we recognize that these numbers may not be as high as sociologists claim. We do not believe a conversion to generic theism or Islam ought to count as a true conversion to Christianity. In fact, we would say the exact opposite, because anything less than faith in the God of Trinitarian Theism as found in the final work of Jesus Christ is not saving faith. The point being, however, many people are finding aspects of secularism anemic as it pertains to answering life's major questions. People are looking beyond materialistic explanations for transcendent questions. Sociologists of religion are noticing that people believe in God not merely because of some emotional or psychological need or crutch, rather because it rationally and holistically makes sense of the world and experience.[309]

Keller further explains his findings to demonstrate that secularism, milder forms of religion, and theological liberalism will not win the long game battle. Keller points to figures such as the birthrates of conservative religious people, the decline of inherited vs the incline of converted religious faith, and the inadequacy of secular preconditions to explain the *way* society functions as justification for claiming, alongside Kaufmann, a Canadian academic and secularist, that the "religious shall inherit the earth."[310] Namely, Keller notes:

> Sociologists Peter Berger and Grace Davie report that "most sociologists of religion now agree" that the secularization thesis—that religion declines as a society becomes modern—"has been empirically shown to be false." Countries such as China are becoming more religions (and Christian) even as they modernize. Other sociological studies, such as the pathbreaking work by Georgetown professor José Casanova, have fond no simple downward trend for religion as societies become modern.[311]

In other words, secularism has not created a necessary and fatalistic rope around the necks of modern-day people. The empirical data demonstrates that the notion of "Impossible to Believe" provides more of a psychological, rather than logical, explanation for the present-day condition of society. We should not downplay the significant role of unbelief. The unbelief is real, but people can be freed from their unbelief. Humanists' ideals are not necessarily valid "reasons" for unbelief, but are actual beliefs about unsubstantiated "beliefs." They do not necessarily

---

[309] Ibid., 23.
[310] Ibid., 25-27.
[311] Ibid., 24.

present a rational case against Christianity since secular beliefs fail to explain the data of the world and the complexities of human experience.

Furthermore, evangelical apologists have worked tirelessly to address the actual arguments presented by modernity. They have shown how the arguments no longer rationally bind a person or keep them from embracing Christianity. The true picture indicates that Christian belief can withstand the rational objections raised by secularists. Therefore, evangelicals should highlight the fact that it is actually *possible* for modern man to believe in the Christian faith.[312]

While Keller is correct when he states that modernity has led to a variety of different conditions of belief, we must ask: Is there another way to understand modernity? Has evangelicalism bought into modernity in different *ways*?

## Rejection of the Platonic Tradition[313]

The rise of modern philosophy seemed to eclipse the Platonic tradition found in the philosophies of Plato, Aristotle, Plotinus, Augustine, Anselm, and Aquinas. The so-called Enlightenment seemed to eclipse the dominant metaphysical and epistemological account prevalent throughout Western society. In his book, *Interpreting Scripture with the Great Tradition*, Craig Carter calls for the "recovering of the genius of premodern exegesis."[314] Throughout his book, Carter calls for not only an embrace of Christian Platonism (which is his way of discussing the "Great Tradition" or the Platonic tradition) as a dominant metaphysical theme, but an exegetical theme as well. He asks, "What is modernity?"[315] Carter answers:

> Modernity is a cultural pathology caused by the breakdown of the Great Tradition and the rise of neopaganism in Western civilization. It is particularly a reversion to ancient paganism, but it properly should be called "neopaganism" because the new paganism incorporates certain ideas derived from Christianity (preeminently the idea of history as linear and progressive). Thus,

---

[312] Clearly, due consideration must be understood by this claim. We are not saying humanity has the ability for self-regeneration. Rather, it is a mere statement of fact that the intellectual defeaters against Christianity are not insurmountable. Nor are the psychological effects of secularism so binding that one cannot overcome the great gulf of unbelief.

[313] See: Peter Kreeft, *The Platonic Tradition* (South Bend: St. Augustine's Press, 2018); Peter Kreeft, *Summa Philosophica* (South Bend: St. Augustine's Press, 2012).

[314] Craig A. Carter, *Interpreting Scripture with the Great Tradition: Recovering the Genius of PreModern Exegesis* (Grand Rapids: Baker, 2018).

[315] Ibid., 85.

from one angle the current cultural malaise is a form of neopaganism, but from another it could equally be defined as a Christian heresy. We will consider this ambiguity in what follows. There are three phases to modernity: early modernity (1300—1650), high modernity (1650-1800), and late modernity (1800—present).[316]

Carter defines the Great Tradition as the metaphysics of Christian Platonism. For Carter and others, this tradition is the realist metaphysical system dominant throughout the first thirteen centuries of the Church. Carter explains what he means by early modernity, claiming, "The breakdown of the medieval synthesis and the creation of the modern, mechanistic worldview in the context of the rise of modern, technological science."[317] He also says, "The metaphysical realism of the medieval synthesis was replaced by the rise of voluntarism and nominalism, and the doctrine of God underwent a fundamental change."[318] Carter explains that high modernity or the Enlightenment was characterized by materialism and that reason was viewed as an alternative to a supernatural worldview.[319] From this time period, Enlightenment thought continued to "exercise a stranglehold on the Western conception of nature" because it maintained a strong commitment to nominalism, materialism, and mechanism.[320] For Carter, the skepticism and agnosticism of Hume and Kant morphed and broke down into epistemological and ethical relativism as postmodernism questioned not just the Enlightenment, but ethics and scientific laws as well.[321] Carter concludes his point, stating, "We need to understand that Christian Platonism and *resourcement* constitute a rival tradition to modern metaphysics and the liberal project. Christianity and modernity cannot be reconciled and cannot coexist permanently; they must inevitably clash in the struggle for cultural supremacy."[322] In sum, there are irreconcilable metaphysical and epistemological differences between modernity and the Great Tradition.

According to the Platonic tradition, especially for Christians following the Platonic tradition, we must recognize that there are certain facts about God and the world that can be known and demonstrated to be true. Much

---

[316] Ibid., 85-86.
[317] Ibid., 86.
[318] Ibid.
[319] Ibid., 88.
[320] Ibid.
[321] Ibid., 89.
[322] Ibid., 90-91.

like the modern world believes they can demonstrate certain truths about the nature of the physical universe, many premodern theologians and apologists believed that they could demonstrate certain truths about metaphysics, including the nature of God and reality, too. Some of the differences can be understood in this way:[323]

| Platonic Tradition | Modernity |
|---|---|
| Realist View of Metaphysics | Idealist View of Metaphysics |
| God Has a Nature | God Does Not Have a Nature |
| Hylomorphic View of Humanity | Materialist View of Humanity |
| Theistic View of the Universe | Materialist View of the Universe |
| Truths of Metaphysics Can Be Demonstrated | Truths of Metaphysics Cannot Be Demonstrated |
| Universals Exist (Realism) | Universals Do Not Exist (Nominalism) |
| Objectivity is Possible | Objectivity is Impossible |
| Certainty is Possible | Certainty is Impossible |
| Cognitive-Propositionalism | Modified or Non-Cognitive Propositionalism |
| Classical Realist Method | Transcendental Method |

These differences indicate that modernity departs significantly from the Platonic tradition in almost every respect. It would be incorrect and inaccurate to claim that all of modernity bears each of these marks and characteristics. It would be accurate to claim that most modern philosophers are marked by some or most of these characteristics. For example, if we take Kantianism as a hallmark of modern philosophy that synthesized with modern theology, we recognize a drastic shift in our understanding of the nature of God, reality, and the concept of revelation. We are left with a worldview in which religion is relegated within the bounds of mere reason. There is no known divine revelation, no special revelation, no natural theology, and ultimately, no true foundation for the Christian faith. In the wake of Kant's philosophical conclusions, religion fundamentally changed. One could look to figures such as Schleiermacher, Hegel, and Feuerbach to understand how modern theology was affected

---

[323] Several of these points can be found in Carter's book, *Interpreting the Great Tradition*, 79-81. I chose to add a few more points and make it into a chart.

by Kantian philosophy. Post-Kantian theologians attempted to "redeem" Kant's concept of the *synthetic a priori* which resulted is a non-cognitive, non-propositional religion based upon a sense of absolute dependence, and not upon any concept of divine revelation. Kant's idealism resulted in the fabrications of Lessing's ditch, Hegel's appropriation of dialectical theology, Schleiermacher's universal process of human beings reaching their religious consciousness, Ritschl's denial of the traditional doctrines about Jesus, Von Harnack's historical biblical criticism, Kierkegaard's existentialism, and Barth's neo-orthodoxy. In short, anyone who attempted to "redeem" Kant's philosophical paradigm ended up eroding the essence of the Christian faith.[324]

Someone might claim that these examples are "extreme" applications or examples of the effects of modernity upon Christian theology. That may be correct. Someone might respond by noting that these are the consistent applications of modernity upon the Christian faith. Nevertheless, one must grant the fact that some figures did buy into many of the beliefs presented to us by modernity without embracing the logical or consistent conclusions and applications of modernity. In fact, for those who embrace a classical realist and classical theist understanding of reality, God, and the Bible, they would claim that any embrace of nominalism, theistic personalism, biblical errancy, and the like, is to embrace some mediating form of modernism. They may not be consistent modernists; however, to some degree they are modernist nonetheless, because they have embraced the dominant metaphysic, epistemology, and method of modern philosophy.[325]

As we apply the definitions and forms of modernism explained by Keller, we must admit that several evangelical theologians and institutions have been able to resist the dominant forms of modernity. Nonetheless, if we accept a broader understanding of modernity offered to us by Carter, namely, one that encapsulates the denial of the Platonic tradition and an embrace of the new forms of metaphysics, epistemology, and language over and against the Great Tradition, then we must admit that much of present-day evangelicalism is whole-heartedly committed to mediating forms of modernity, hence creating mediating forms of evangelicalism. A rose by any other name is still a rose, and any embrace of nominalism,

---

[324] John M. Frame, *A History of Western Philosophy and Theology* (Phillipsburg: R&R Publishing, 2015), 251-291.

[325] See: Diogenes Allen and Eric O. Springsted, *Philosophy for Understanding Theology*, 2nd ed (Louisville: Westminster John Knox, 2007); Etienne Gilson, *The Unity of Philosophical Experience* (San Francisco: Ignatius Press, 1964); Etienne Gilson, *Methodical Realism* (Front Royal: Christendom Press, 1990).

voluntarism, epistemological relativism and subjectivity, hermeneutics of suspicion, linguistic conventionalism, and so forth, are all ideas grounded and rooted in the dominant philosophies of modernity. One of the hallmarks of classical realism and classical apologetics, as defined by figures such as Norman Geisler, R. C. Sproul, and John Gerstner, is a marked commitment to rejecting each of the philosophical tenets that define or characterize anti-Platonic and secular forms of modernity.[326]

In other words, the way forward for classic evangelical apologetics is to not play modernity's game according to modernity's metaphysic, or modernity's epistemology, or modernity's approach to language. The modern turn in philosophy has proven itself to be unfruitful. Therefore, to understand the methodology of Norman Geisler and the way he approached apologetics is to recognize with him: *the only way to address the conditions of belief raised by modernity is to reject the philosophical paradigm of modernity.*

## The Significance of Norman Geisler's Approach

The nature of apologetics is to offer a defense. In ancient Greece, to offer an *apologia* was to offer a defense before a court of law in answer to an accusation. Socrates was accused of atheism and corrupting the youth. He was eventually convicted and sentenced to die. The dialogue by Plato in which we read Socrates' defense is titled *The Apology*—not indicating that he was apologizing for his actions, but rather that he defended both his integrity and actions.

Christians throughout the ancient world knew what it was like to face accusations from the world around them for their religious convictions. They were thought to be drunkards and liars and were mocked and persecuted for their beliefs. Stephen was accused of opposing previous revelation given by God (Acts 6:11-14). Paul was accused of introducing new gods (Acts 17:18-20). The Church was accused of political insurrection and societal chaos (Acts 17:6-7). Experts and individuals opposed the views of Christians (Acts 13:45; 14:2). The Christian message was viewed as a stumbling block to Jews and foolishness to the Greeks (1Cor.1:23). Their views were even synthesized with other religious groups such as the

---

[326] J. V. Fesko, *Reforming Apologetics: Retrieving the Classic Reformed Approach to Defending the Faith* (Grand Rapids: Baker, 2019); R. C. Sproul, John Gerstner, and Arthur Lindsay, *Classical Apologetics: A Rational Defense of the Christian Faith and a Critique of Presuppositional Apologetics* (Grand Rapids: Zondervan, 1984); Norman L. Geisler, *Is Man the Measure? An Evaluation of Contemporary Humanism* (Eugene: Wipf & Stock, 2005); Norman L. Geisler, *Christian Apologetics* 2nd ed (Grand Rapids: Baker, 2013).

Judaizers, so the early Church had to face both internal and external threats to the gospel. Twenty-first century believers can sympathize with these kinds of threats and accusations towards the early Church. The primary difference being that we are living in a secular age marked by modern expressions of unbelief.

What kind of response do we find the early Church making to these types of apologetic challenges? Scripture presents a clear case that the early Christians were not relativists, subjectivists, or eclectics. They never responded to claims raised against their views by suggesting that nobody can know anything about reality (supernatural reality included), or that there is no absolute truth. Religious disagreements were not the mere product of different cultures, standpoint epistemologies, or perspective. We do not read anything in the Bible like, "That view may be true for you, but not for me" or "We need to undo our ethnicity (i.e., typically whiteness) to interpret the Bible." Nor do we find any willingness to accommodate to new views of God or alternative views of the Bible. Nowhere in Scripture do we see people fundamentally changing the attributes of God or altering the total truthfulness of Scripture unto pagan ideas or culturally accepted Greco-Roman academic standards. Instead, what we find is an answer to the ridicule and false ideas—an *apologia*, or an apologetic.

First-century Christians, as well as Christians throughout the centuries, were able to defend the truth of Christianity. After all, if truth about reality is knowable, then conversely, we must admit the truth is not truly taught unless whatever contradicts it is also refuted. The defense of Christianity is not only an academic enterprise. It also reflects our obedience unto the Lordship of Jesus Christ and our commitment to the purity of the Bride of Christ. The New Testament qualifications for church leadership included the ability to exhort in sound doctrine and refute those who contradict it (Titus 1:9). We cannot avoid the conclusion, therefore, that apologetics has a strong justification and warrant in the New Testament, both by example and direct command.

### *Geisler's Apologetic Method and Ministry*

One of the key distinctives of the life and ministry of Norman Geisler was his commitment to defending the entirety of the gospel of Jesus Christ. During an age when many Christians were willing to accommodate relativism, neotheism, and the errancy of the Bible, Geisler stood as a strong voice for the total truthfulness of Christianity. Not only did Geisler offer a positive defense of the Christian faith, but he was also willing to endure the ridicule and hardship that one faces when they refute those ideas which contradict the gospel or any tenet of Christianity. Geisler knew how to balance that defense with an appropriate pastoral application. Many apologists tend to merely "stand for truth"; however, Geisler went beyond that and demonstrated charity towards his hearers, some of whom were skeptics inside the Church, who needed both the intellectual acumen of a noted theologian and the pastoral care of a minister of the gospel.

Christians still face public opposition and hostility to the gospel of Jesus Christ. During the twentieth-century, many of the attacks raised against Christianity came from aberrant philosophical views and the hard sciences. Much of the debate centered around naturalism, evolution, and atheistic expressions from those ideologies. Many of the books had to respond by offering scientific evidence for the truthfulness of Christianity. During the twenty-first century, many of the former debates are still front and center. We still face criticism from the New Atheists offering scientific and naturalistic charges against Christianity. However, there appears to be an ever-growing shift during our time where Christianity is now facing more opposition from the social sciences than the hard sciences. There seem to be new psychological and sociological attacks against Christianity as being narrow minded, ethically-bigoted, racist, misogynistic, oppressive, and so forth. People no longer disregard the Bible just because it might have errors. Rather, they no longer believe in the Bible as God's Word because they believe many of the stories are true, and if the stories (like the slaughter of the Canaanites) are true, then God is a moral monster.[327] People also reject Christianity's marked approach to God because we can use other means, such as the Enneagram, as appropriate psychological and religious ways to know ourselves and rightly connect with God.[328] In other words, the defense of the faith never rests because the attacks against the faith never sleep. We must be ready to defend the gospel against the issues of our day, most of which we never get the pleasure to choose.

*Geisler's Use of Thomas Aquinas*

One of the key aspects people need to remember when following the approach or methodology of any figure, whether it be an apologetic methodology or any other academic discipline, is the key figures representing that method addressed the issues of *their* day. In order to not become an irrelevant catalog of facts about past issues in a bygone era, we must realize there are certain principles we can extract from any approach

---

[327] Paul Copan, *Is God a Moral Monster? Making Sense of the Old Testament* (Grand Rapids: Baker, 2011).

[328] Don and Joy Venoit and Marcia Montenegro, *Richard Rohr and the Enneagram Secret* (Wonder Lake: MCOI Publishing, 2020).

to help us address both the past issues and the task(s) at hand. Norman Geisler serves as an example of a good *way* to take the best of a theologian or philosopher's thought and method and apply it to the present-day issues. Geisler was a committed Thomist and an evangelical theologian. There are several things we can learn from Geisler in this regard both as a warning and a commendation.

First, Geisler was a committed Thomist who found in Aquinas principles useful for evangelical apologetics. Geisler encouraged evangelicals to not forget Aquinas's teaching about the nature of God, Scripture, faith, reason, and other key issues in apologetics. In that sense, Geisler offered a positive explanation and application of Thomistic principles in the modern context. One of the central facets of Geisler's ministry was the updating of Aquinas into the present-day conversations in philosophy and theology. If the Aristotelian-Thomistic method is truly the perennial philosophy it claims to be with its commitment to timeless and objective truths, then it must have a rightful place in the current dialogues with modern and postmodern philosophy. Truth, especially perennial truth, does not merely dissolve or fade away into a forgotten era. Rather, truth is that which endures, and the truths found in the Thomistic philosophical and apologetic method are essential to defending the catholicity of the Christian faith, and the central tenets of realism in our modern age.

Second, Geisler was Thomistic with Thomas's Thomism. Much like it is a false characterization to claim Aquinas is nothing more than a baptized Aristotelian, it would be incorrect to claim that the good evangelical doctor was nothing more than a "Roman Geisler." Geisler was not blindly committed to everything Aquinas taught, especially many things Aquinas taught and believed about Roman Catholicism. Just like Aquinas differed with Aristotle when his views contradicted the clear teachings of Scripture, Geisler attempted to differ and critique Aquinas when he believed Aquinas's views differed with Scripture. Several theologians, especially Scott Oliphint, believe Geisler was inconsistent and utterly compromised in this regard.[329] Many of Oliphint's criticisms arose because a handful of Geisler's students converted to Roman Catholicism. Oliphint believed these conversions occurred because Geisler was committed to a compromised method. Several things could be said about the matter, much of which is not beneficial here. However, Geisler responded to this line of thinking in an

---

[329] See: https://www.youtube.com/watch?v=cpSwqV2RnaY

article titled, *Does Thomism Lead to Catholicism?*[330] Geisler argued that people convert to Roman Catholicism for a variety of reasons, not just because of a commitment to Thomism. Geisler argued that one can follow the method of Aquinas without converting because Aquinas rightly distinguished between faith and reason. For Geisler, this allows him to suggest that people can follow the *philosophy* of Aquinas because it is true, without being committed to the Roman Catholic *theological* entailments Aquinas drew from his broader works. Geisler also claims Aquinas was less Catholic than contemporary Catholicism. Geisler writes:

> Aquinas was a pre-Trentian Catholic, part of what may be called the "Old Catholic Church" with which Episcopalians would be happy on most counts. As such, Aquinas was not committed to the immaculate conception of Mary, the bodily assumption of Mary, the infallibility of the Pope and a number of other Roman Catholic idiosyncrasies. Further, Aquinas was committed to sola Scriptura, exposition of Scripture, and other characteristic doctrine of Protestantism. His basic Bibliology (minus the Apocrypha), Prolegomena, Apologetics, Theology Proper, and Christology are compatible with evangelicalism.[331]

Geisler continues by drawing this analogy with C. S. Lewis, claiming:

> So, my attraction to Thomism is somewhat like my attraction to C. S. Lewis. There are many things I like about Lewis's views (e.g., his apologetics, his belief in absolute truth and morals, his classical theism, his defense of New Testament miracles, his affirmation of the Virgin Birth, the Incarnation of Christ, his belief in the resurrection of Christ, eternal punishment [Hell]). However, there are also some of Lewis's beliefs that I do not accept (e.g., his denial of some Old Testament miracles, his belief that the OT contains myths and errors, and his belief in evolution and in Purgatory). But none of these hinder my acceptance of the many positive values I find in Lewis. But in spite of my acceptance of all these positive features in Lewis, I have never been tempted to become an Anglican (as he was).[332]

One can disagree on whether or not Geisler accomplished his goal of incorporating the best of Aquinas and disregarding what he believed to contradict Scripture. One could also raise the same question about

---

[330] Norman L. Geisler, ed. Paul A. Compton, *The Collected Essays of Norman L. Geisler, vol. 5: 2006-2018* (Matthews: Bastion Books, 2019), 428-436.

[331] Ibid., 433.

[332] Ibid., 434.

Aquinas's use of Aristotle. Nevertheless, those same individuals must concede the point that Geisler attempted to make this distinction in his theology and apologetic methodology.

Third, Geisler was also a man committed to truth and if he found something true in a method or principle outside of Thomism, Geisler readily accepted it. For example, Geisler was a committed Copernican; he believed the earth revolved around the sun. Geisler embraced many truths taught in modern science and medicine. Geisler was committed to the belief there is something true in almost every philosophy espoused or people would not believe it. He offered a unique approach to evaluating views. First, he would discuss what he believed was true in the view. Second, he would offer a critique of each view. One specific caveat is required at this point to help use ward off erroneous syntheses. One must affirm the notion, "All truth is God's truth." That statement must be balanced by adding, "All truth is God's truth *if* the truth claim is *actually* true." Unfortunately, many people cover a multitude of intellectual errors and embrace a variety of heresies under the guise of "All truth is God's truth." The false use of that truism has created numerous accommodations unto serious error. The notion of general revelation does entail that there are truths outside of the scope of Sacred Scripture. But we must be balanced and discerning to realize that there are also significant errors in the predominant philosophies and ideologies of our day.[333]

Since Geisler has spent so much time defending the way his approach might respond to issues in postmodernism, theology proper, and the inerrancy of the Bible, we will forego those immediate applications and illustrations. If someone is interested in seeing the *way* Geisler responded to Open Theism, Molinism, Higher Criticism, Clark Pinnock, Mike Licona, or any other movement or figure, there are several resources available.[334] This section will illustrate one significant *way* in which Geisler's method is relevant for today, much like Geisler illustrated various *ways* Aquinas's method was still relevant during his day. Moreover, it will provide a

---

[333] For example, many Southern Baptists are currently enamored with Critical Race Theory and Intersectionality. They are attempting to use these ideas as neutral analytical tools. They justify the whole approach by claiming, "All Truth is God's Truth." The problem with such an approach is that CRT and Intersectionality are blatantly false ideologies contrary to the gospel of Jesus Christ. See: Helen Pluckrose and James Lindsay, *Cynical Theories: How Activist Scholarship Made Everything about Race, Gender, and Identity—and Why This Harms Everyone* (Durham: Pitchstone Publishing, 2020).

[334] See: Norman L. Geisler, *Baker Encyclopedia of Christian Apologetics* (Grand Rapids: Baker, 1999); Norman L. Geisler, *Preserving Orthodoxy: Maintaining Continuity with the Historic Christian Faith on Scripture* (Matthews: Bastion Books, 2017).

paradigm for a *way* someone could use Geisler's method to engage apologetically other conditions of belief prevalent in today.

## Hermeneutics, Subjectivity and Critical Theory

Modernity seems to be an ever-changing system. The significant issues affecting evangelicals today rest upon each of the core disciplines in philosophy: metaphysics, epistemology, and ethics. As we discussed in chapter two, Geisler was an ardent defender of objectivity. Geisler's Aristotelian-Thomistic philosophy served as an ontological and epistemological foundation to ground the notion and concept of objectivity. There are several people who raise objections to this type of approach.

For example, Tim Keller seems right in his understanding of modernity, even though he opposes the concept of objectivity. Keller writes, "We have seen, then, that people neither adopt nor discard faith in God through pure, objective reasoning, because no such thing is possible."[335] Keller is not alone in his analysis. Several evangelicals gave up on the quest for objectivity.[336] No figure charts this decline away from objectivity and towards subjectivity better than Geisler's student, Thomas Howe. Howe maps out how figures such as Grant Osborne, Moises Silva, Craig Blomberg, and several other standard evangelical books in hermeneutics jettison objectivity. In one way or another, Howe claims the subjectivist argument boils down to this:[337]

1. Everyone comes to the world with his own framework of understanding.

2. No particular framework of understanding is universally valid.

3. But universal validity is precisely what is implied in the notion of objectivity.

4. Therefore, no interpreter can be objective in interpretation.

5. But, if no interpreter can be objective, then no interpretation is universally valid.

6. But, if no interpretation is universally valid, then the concept of a *correct* interpretation is at best relative or at worst empty.

---

[335] Keller, *Making Sense of God*, 50.
[336] Thomas Howe, *Objectivity in Biblical Interpretation* (Altamonte Springs: Advantage Books, 2004).
[337] Ibid., 84-85.

7. Since there is no such thing as a correct interpretation, there is no means of adjudicating between interpretations.
8. In fact, the very idea of adjudicating between interpretations is at best relative and at worst empty.

Howe goes on to make this essential point:

> Additionally, it would seem that the adamant rejection of classical foundationalism, as we considered in chapter 3, has simply been replaced by a fixed and immutable phenomenological foundationalism. This foundationalism is composed of the notion that presuppositions, or preunderstandings, or prejudices, or horizons of expectation, or historical situatedness, or theory ladenness, or linguistic determinism, or whatever other term may be used, are the necessary and inevitable foundation of interpretation. However, this precondition for interpretation is no less a foundation than the classical foundation which virtually all modern theorists reject. Additionally, it is presented as being just as universally and absolutely true as the classical foundations were supposed to have been. Although these preconditions are subject to change, alteration, and even elimination, the fact of a preconditionedness, and particularly a preconditionedness that is decidedly rational, or mental, or phenomenological is beyond question, self-evident, and undeniable. There can be no preconditionlessness in interpretation, no presupositionless interpretation. This view is no less a foundation for interpretation in biblical hermeneutics than in philosophical hermeneutics. This foundation has almost all the earmarks of classical foundationalism. The one thing it does not seem to have is a grounding in anything outside the mind of the interpreter.[338]

From the two quotes by Howe, we can see that the key issue is premise 2. Many non-evangelical and evangelical scholars reject the notion of universal validity because they believe it affirms some type of neutrality, which they believe is incompatible with premise 1. They believe that philosophy has demonstrated that there are no universally valid points of view or perspectives to adjudicate frameworks. Hence, there is no objective interpretation of any aspect of reality, the Bible included.

One of the lasting and essential hallmarks of Geisler's method has been his commitment to objectivity. Thomas Howe was a student of Geisler and

---
[338] Ibid., 239-240.

wrote a thorough defense of objectivity. I (Bill Roach) am also committed to the defense of objectivity in interpretation, biblical interpretation included. In my personal experience, the *sine qua non* that Geisler contributed to evangelicalism was his robust defense of classical realism. The evangelical landscape is dominated by idealistic metaphysics, phenomenology, and critical philosophy. In previous generations, evangelical students were taught that ontological situatedness (i.e., Heidegger) or historical situatedness (i.e., Gadamer) or linguistic situatedness (i.e., Wittgenstein) were fundamental and necessary to embrace to have a humble and realistic understanding of hermeneutics. Perhaps as a means of remaining humble in our scholarship, evangelicals either knowingly or unknowingly bought into modern and postmodern philosophy. Geisler stood against these approaches to scholarship. In fact, one of the highlights of Geisler's career was his presidential address before the *Evangelical Theological Society* in 1998 titled, *Beware of Philosophy: A Warning to Biblical Scholars*.[339] In that lecture, Geisler offered thirteen different philosophies biblical scholars should know and beware of. Geisler started to pinpoint many of the central issues affecting evangelical scholarship. One issue was the influence of modern and postmodern philosophy. Geisler warned ETS about the inroads of subjectivism and the effects it would have upon evangelical theology.

That lecture was given in 1998, and today, more than 22 years after Geisler's warning, it is safe to state: Evangelicals did not heed Geisler's warning. Evangelicals have unfortunately embraced several tenets of subjectivism, even radical Marxist forms of subjectivism. Today the evangelical landscape is marked by an ironic commitment to a view of epistemology and ethics known as *Critical Theory*.[340] Helen Pluckrose and James Lindsey in their book, *Cynical Theories*, claim, "A critical theory is chiefly concerned with revealing hidden biases and underexamined assumptions, usually by pointing out what have been termed 'problematics,' which are ways in which society and the systems that it operates upon are going wrong."[341] They also claim:

> From its original conception, a Critical Theory was to be set aside from a traditional theory, which seeks to understand and explain phenomena in terms of what it is and how it works, including social phenomena. A critical theory, by contrast, must satisfy all

---

[339] Norman L. Geisler, *Beware of Philosophy: A Warning to Biblical Scholars*, JETS 42/1 (March 1999) 3–19.

[340] Richard Delgado and Jean Stefancic, *Critical Race Theory: An Introduction* 3rd ed., (New York: New York University Press, 2017).

[341] Pluckrose and Lindsey, *Cynical Theories*, 13–14.

of three criteria. First, it must arise from a "normative" vision, which is to say a set of moral views about how society ought to be, and this moral vision should both inform the theory and serve as a goal for a new society. Second, it must explain what is wrong with society or its current systems, usually in terms of "problematics," which are shortcomings in the system or ways in which it fails to accord with or generative the normative moral view of the theory. Third, it must be actionable by social activists who wish to use it to change society.[342]

Pluckrose and Lindsey further explain:

> The postmodern Theorists adopted the critical method, or at least the critical *mood*, of the Frankfurt School and adapted it into the structuralist context, particular its view of power. The "critical" goal remained the same, however: to make the problems inherent in "the system" more visible to the people allegedly oppressed by it—however happily they might be living their lives within it—until they come to detest it and seek a revolution against it. The Frankfurt School developed the Critical Theoretic approach specifically to expand beyond critiques of capitalism, as Marxists had been doing, and to target the assumptions of Western civilization as a whole, particularly liberalism as a sociopolitical philosophy and Enlightenment thought in general. It was this approach to critique that the postmodernists turned upon the entire social order and its institutions, insisting that hegemonic power structures (a concept adopted by Antonio Gramsci) exist across all facets of difference and require exposing and eventually overturning.[343]

Critical Theory in many ways is a synthesized form of postmodernism and Marxism applied to groups throughout society. Critical Theory attempts to understand how varying groups have specially allocated forms of knowledge and how power structures function throughout society. This approach has been applied to areas of race, gender, sexuality, and fat studies.[344]

In the online video series, titled, *The Trojan Horse*, Michael O'Fallon, James Lindsey, and Peter Boghossian discuss the real effects of Critical

---

[342] Ibid., 272.
[343] Ibid.
[344] Ibid., 89-180.

Theory upon society.[345] Lindsey helped explain much of the academic talk about Critical Theory through the use of a grayscale analogy. According to Critical Theory (whether it be critical race, critical queer, or critical feminist), Lindsey claims that it suggests that knowledge is relative unto particular groups and levels of oppression. So, for example, if you are a white male living in Western society, everything may appear gray to you. If you are a white female everything may appear in shades of gray and pink. The white man does not see the pink, only the female does, and it is her responsibility to make the white male aware of different ways he is suppressing her knowledge-power in society, since she is able to see it, not him. As this process continues, one could say a black woman sees other colors a white man and white woman cannot see. As one continues to add greater levels of oppression, what one must recognize is the more oppressed you are, whether it be from race, gender, sexuality, or religion, the greater insights into reality you have.

This form of social justice scholarship attempts to make levels of oppression known; hence, that is what they mean by "critical." The goal is to enact some kind of social revolution to undo these levels of oppression. At its fundamental core, however, this approach to knowledge has tried to bifurcate what might be understood as Eurocentric verses Afrocentric approaches to truth (one could change Afrocentric for any other race, gender, sexuality, or religion). They view Eurocentric approaches to knowledge as predominantly white, male, and Christian. Whitecentric knowledge would include things such as logic, mathematics, science, or any other predominant academic power in Western society. Therefore, critical scholars, such as Derek Bell and Kimberly Crenshaw, attempt to deconstruct or decolonize society to undo what they view as various forms of oppression.[346]

Unfortunately, in a variety of ways and different degrees, evangelicals have bought into forms of Critical Theory and Intersectionality—Critical Race Theory in particular. For example, in 2019 the Southern Baptist Convention passed Resolution 9, which was a resolution on race relations in America. Even though the statement tried to ground the resolution in Scripture and make many qualifications to maintain a strong evangelical theology, they seemed to undermine it in this statement: *RESOLVED, That critical race theory and intersectionality should only be employed as analytical tools subordinate to Scripture—not as transcendent ideological*

---

[345] See: https://www.youtube.com/watch?v=YDFL3xwEEG8&list=PLZJe-MWy0cYfcPwUzLnGqqLCFoSo05JeK

[346] Pluckrose and Lindsey, *Cynical Theories*, 181-236.

*frameworks*[347]. They undermine it first, because there is a difference between a fundamental principle of reality (i.e., law of identity, law of non-contradiction, law of excluded middle) and theories that are not fundamental principles of reality. The only things that could come close to being "neutral" in that sense are principles of being, not the so-called tools of CRT and Intersectionality. Second, one must only look at the history of any other institution or organization that has employed these "tools" to see that they have been nothing but destructive. Third, the very theories that birthed these "tools" are totalitarian by nature, hence, they demand absolute obedience, not some third-way approach whereby we merely use them as a way to understand society. They never function as neutral analytical tools, but as tools of segregation and destruction.

The broader evangelical world has also bought into this dominant philosophy. You have books published by Eric Mason titled, *Woke Church* or *The Color of Compromise* by Jemar Tisby that clearly advocate for CRT and Intersectionality as dominant epistemologies and means to understand society.[348] Evangelicals are starting to grow obsessed with diversity points of view concerning theology, Scripture, hermeneutics, and philosophy. Each discipline seems to offer another type of feminist, African American, Asian, or Hispanic interpretation of the Bible. For example, *Southeastern Baptist Theological Seminary* hosted a panel with Danny Carroll and three of their professors: Walter Strickland, Miguel Echevarria, and Ronjour Locke, titled, *Cultural Diversity and Hermeneutics*.[349] Throughout the panel each person reflects on Carroll's previous lecture titled, *Reading the Bible Latinamente*.[350] One interesting point made during the panel was the unanimous agreement that no one could have an objective interpretation of the Bible. We are so influenced by our culture and those dominant modes of thought, that it would be incorrect to claim there is *one* interpretation of the Bible.

The issue seems to be very clear: *The dominant philosophies of our day are grounded in post-Kantian philosophy or idealism, which is a fundamental denial of metaphysical and epistemological realism.* These

---

[347] https://www.sbc.net/resource-library/resolutions/on-critical-race-theory-and-intersectionality/

[348] Eric Mason, *Woke Church: An Urgent Call for Christians in America to Confront Racism and Injustice* (Chicago: Moody Press, 2018); Jemar Tisby, *The Color of Compromise: The Truth About the American Church's Complicity in Racism* (Grand Rapids: Zondervan, 2020).

[349] https://www.youtube.com/watch?v=mA8b1yE8VVM

[350] https://www.youtube.com/watch?v=cSfRr2mNDJc

paradigm shifts, preunderstandings, historical conditions, racial perspectives, and gender perspectives are encapsulated in premises one and two of Thomas Howe's summary of the subjectivist's argument:

1. Everyone comes to the world with his own framework of understanding.
2. No particular framework of understanding is universally valid.

These figures would not be able to offer their subjective approaches if they believed in universally valid frameworks of understanding (which Geisler taught was provided by Thomistic realism). CRT and Intersectionality were selected for discussion because they appear to illustrate the issue(s) so well, not because they just happen to be trending. After the Kantian turn, philosophers of both the evangelical and non-evangelical type jettisoned objectivity for subjectivity. They have each adopted the belief that truth about reality is not knowable. Instead, "truth" is something manufactured or created by the subjective individual. One of the significant errors of this entire approach by CRT and other subjectivists is a false causal or deministic understanding of the way in which certain factors (whether they be race, gender, sexuality, etc.) affect our knowledge of reality. It is false to say that accidental features such as skin color determine or somehow "create" or "cause" our perceptions of reality, not just record them. There is a significant difference between believing that certain features *can* influence our view of reality versus believing that certain factors *must necessarily* determine our understanding of reality. If it merely can influence our view, then it can be corrected. If they must necessarily determine our view, then they cannot be corrected, nor can they be properly communicated; since, one person cannot properly grasp another person's framework of understanding due to significant historical, cultural, or linguistic differences. In short, this approach could reduce unto a form of epistemic ethnic or cultural-ethnic solipsism because we can only know what our culture and/or ethnicity determine for us to know about reality.

There are many other significant things to consider as we approach the topic of subjectivity and various hermeneutics of suspicion. Advocates of these approaches ask us to set aside our power and establishmentarianism to recognize that "truth" is something relative to race, class, gender, and sexual orientation. The main problem with these approaches is that they are not consistent because they never apply that standard to their own theories. For if they did, not only would it disqualify their own theories, but it would also disqualify themselves from debate as merely advocating different powerplays. Unfortunately, powerplays and word games are not arguments; they are mere games. Truth cannot be reduced unto power any more than light can be reduced unto heat; these are mere arbitrary and unjustified category mistakes. Moreover, to say that truth is somehow relative unto race, class, gender, or sexual orientation is in many ways claiming that "truth is relative to accidental, not essential categories." If applied consistently, why could we not also apply truth to other accidental categories such as height, location, or relative temperature, and so forth? Would any of these individuals really want to be consistent and offer a "Hermeneutics of Short Guys Who Stand Left of the Flagpole"? This type of argumentation is pure silliness and lacks any seriousness or honesty. It truly reduces unto absurdity if applied consistently.[351]

These approaches to knowledge also seem to fundamentally misunderstand that individual people have knowledge, not groups. Let me illustrate the incoherence of their claim. According to this view if there are one hundred people in a room and fifty are black and fifty are white, each of those groups will represent a particular sociology of knowledge. The black people will think one way and the white people will think another. Each group can think according to their own sociology of knowledge. However, according to this view it really seems like there are not one hundred people in the room, but one hundred two people in the room; the two-extra thinking "things" would be the "white group" and the "black group." Moreover, the two extra "individuals" seem to hold the most power over the individual member, not only mandating but dictating what each participant can and must think. This view seems to be fallacious for a few reasons. First, thinking is a property of a person or an individual, not a group. Groups do not have minds, individual people do. Hence, they lack the ontological features required to think or function as a rational being. Second, there are clear examples throughout history where people are mavericks to their group. Not all black or white people think the same way. We are all capable of individual thought contrary to whatever identity group we represent, or sociology of knowledge placed upon us. Third, it would be overtly racist to dictate that a white or black person must necessarily think a particular way *just because* they are one race. Fourth, each of these approaches decry oppressive powers forcing certain races to behave, think, or act in a particular way. But, by definition, the larger group forces the individual member of the race to think, behave, and act in a particular way. These groups control all the power over every individual. In short, by decrying oppressive groups and power over individuals they have created a theory which offers the most powerful and oppressive group

---

[351] See: Peter Kreeft, *A Refutation of Moral Relativism: Interviews With An Absolutist* (San Francisco: Ignatius Press, 1999).

over an individual—namely, it completely obliterates the very concept of there being a person with individual thoughts, actions, or motives.

Advocates of these types of approaches openly deny objectivity. There are several interesting factors about their arguments in this regard, most of which all reduce unto self-defeating philosophies. First, they offer very elaborate and detailed theories and reasons for why people should disregard objectivity. They write books, give speeches, translate those speeches into different languages, and argue for them in a variety of venues. The message they are trying to communicate is clear: Objectivity is impossible. However, if they are correct about their approach, then what about the very theories and claims that "objectivity is impossible" which *they* are trying to communicate? If objectivity is impossible, then how can I know that very theory against objectivity? It would seem these individuals are selective in their approach. On the one hand, they deny objectivity and the ability to know reality in-and-of-itself. On the other hand, they expect you can objectively know their theories about reality, communicate them objectively to others, objectively translate them into different languages, and make them objectively known in other cultures. If they were to remain consistent with their own theories, these types of tasks would be impossible for *all* public forms of knowledge, literature, or communication. It seems like these guys are in one sense arguing: Everyone's view and interpretation cannot be objective, except mine, or my books, or my lectures, in which I offer an objective interpretation to objectively communicate that objective interpretations and communication are impossible. These mediating evangelical views are self-defeating.

One of the significant features of Geisler's approach for the present cultural and evangelical climate is his commitment to the Platonic tradition. As was discussed in the previous chapters, Geisler affirmed that truth about reality is knowable. The realist tradition does not deny that subjective factors exist and can affect people. However, these subjective factors do not and specifically cannot undercut or deny the principles of being. For any of these views to exist, communicate their theories, distinguish their theories from contrary views (i.e., Eurocentric vs Afrocentric, Gay Interpretation vs. Straight interpretation), or account for causal factors in the world (i.e., that man's whiteness caused this or his European Colonial views caused that), they must use the very first principles of reality—the law of identity, law of non-contradiction, law of excluded middle, and law of causality. If they are using the laws of logic and being, they are using formal, rational, known, communicated, transcultural, transracial frameworks for understanding. In the very act of communicating their subjectivist views they are presupposing metaphysical realism, all while denying metaphysical realism. The issue over objectivity verses subjectivity is not that objectivity can be proven in every instance, but that it is unavoidable. It is a fundamental feature of reality. It is how we live and function in the world. To deny these principles, we must fundamentally use the principles of reality. One of the ironic situations in social justice scholarship is their commitment to doing away with logic as some type of Western, Colonial, Male authoritarian powerplay upon people. But, again, to communicate that very view, they must use the Master's Tools (logic, grammar, mathematics) to deny the Master's Tools. Maybe these advocates should realize these Master's Tools are not the constructs of white men, but something created into humanity by the very Lord and Master of all created being—the Lord Jesus Christ himself!

Geisler's view is superior in answering issues raised by subjectivists over and against many other competing evangelical epistemologies. First of all, the commitment to common notions and metaphysical realism is philosophically necessary in our age. Approaches to philosophy committed to varying forms of perspectivalism or presuppositionalism seem to be in a difficult situation. There is no other way to put it: Perspectivalism, even so-called redeemed, God-honoring, born again perspectivalism, is still perspectivalism. The view can even claim to have objective, existential, and situational forms of perspectivalism; however, the view still cannot account for any universally valid frameworks because they are mere *perspectives*.[352] Second, transcendental approaches to reality offered by Christians may be able to offer a coherent explanation of phenomena. They also may be able to demonstrate the impossibility of contrary positions. However, those views still maintain the notion that truth about reality is not directly knowable. Transcendental reasoning by its very nature affirms a Kantian approach to reality; hence, it is still a form of subjectivity.[353] Also, even though you can prove that contrary views are impossible, that still is not an actual argument for *your* view. One of the strengths of presuppositional approaches is its ability to dissect and critique opposing views. One of the severe weaknesses of presuppositional approaches is its inability to start with an argument from the "impossibility to the contrary" and arrive at the positive case that any position (or in their case, the totality of the Christian faith) is true. They would have to have another argument to offer a positive case for the truthfulness of any position, Christianity included.

---

[352] See: John M. Frame, *The Doctrine of the Knowledge of God* (Phillipsburg: R&R Publishing, 1987).

[353] Greg L. Bahnsen, *Presuppositional Apologetics: Stated and Defended* (Powder Springs: 2011).

Geisler's view seems to offer an elaborate and coherent explanation to these dominant modes or conditions of belief. In previous generations, we discussed the central issues affecting Christianity which came from the hard sciences. Today, the central issues we face will come both from the hard sciences and the social sciences. Geisler's view seems to address many of the dominant forms of modernity expressed in Critical Theory because: First, it provides a proper metaphysic to distinguish between a substance, accident, essence, and modes of existence. At its very core, critical theories wrongly believe that accidental properties are modes of knowledge. Classical realism teaches that a person knows things through their accidents (i.e., John <a person> knows a book <a thing> through its size, color, location, and so forth <accidents>). Substances/forms are the object of knowledge (i.e., objects in reality), not accidents abstracted from objects. Second, it provides a realist understanding to allow for universally valid frameworks. Aristotelian-Thomistic realism offers both an ontological and epistemological foundationalism (not a Cartesian form of foundationalism) to ground thought in *reality*, not our subjective appropriations about reality or our mental representations about reality. Third, if truth about reality can be known, it can also be communicated. Geisler's approach offers a way to objectively know and communicate reality. Fourth, Geisler's approach allows for there to be a means to offer a positive defense of the Christian faith. We are not left with a mere perspective or impossibility to the contrary. We can have genuine and true *reasons* for believing in an objective gospel of Jesus Christ.

What is essential to Geisler's approach to addressing the conditions of belief is that it offers a true response to nominalism, skepticism, agnosticism, and the necessarily consequences that follow from each dominant idea throughout modern philosophy. There are obvious subjective or psychological reasons people do not come to Christ. There are also many issues related to the nature of justification and the work of God required in justification for why people do not believe in Christ. None of these factors can be downplayed. Nevertheless, the dominant intellectual reason people reject Christianity is because of vain and false philosophies that raise themselves up against the knowledge of Christ. There are many positive features to modern thought, science, and technology. I do not know a single person who is protesting electricity, indoor plumbing, or modern medicine. But modernity is like a multicolored cloak. Some of those features are beautiful and manifest the truthfulness of Christianity. Others are antithetical and opposed to the truthfulness of Christianity. Geisler's approach is unique because it provides a relevant understanding of reality that can forego skepticism and agnosticism; hence, it provides a way to overcome the idea that Christianity is "impossible to believe." If truth about reality can be known, then it is the task of the Christian apologist to demonstrate that Christianity is true and represents reality.

One of the interesting features of so many apologetic methodologies today is a universal agreement that modernity presents Christianity with a host of defeaters. If modernity is true, we are left with a deistic or atheistic view of our origins, no grounds for morality, no true sense of revealed religion, and ultimately no hope for the afterlife. If naturalism is true, then we are to be pitied above all men, for then the resurrection is not only false, but impossible. That said, even knowing the effects of modernity, it is ironic how many present-day apologists use mediating apologetic methodologies which synthesize significant aspects of modern thought into their approaches. In that sense, Christianity might offer a better argument than modernity and modernity's conditions of belief; but it seems to only be better by degree, not kind. Geisler's Aristotelian-Thomistic approach seems to offer a difference of *kind* to modernity's arguments, because it does not grant modernity's premises, presuppositions, and dominant philosophies. In other words, the way forward is to present a view of metaphysics and epistemology not based upon the assumptions of nominalism, idealism, Kantianism, existentialism, phenomenology, conventionalism, or analytic philosophy. Rather, we need to base our metaphysic and epistemology in the perennial philosophy of the Platonic tradition expressed in the thought of Aristotle and Aquinas. Moreover, we do not need to retreat to the Middle Ages for us to see real progress as defenders of classical realism. Rather, just like Aquinas used Aristotle to address the issues of his day, and Geisler used Aquinas to address the issues evangelicalism was facing during his lifetime, we who are followers of this tradition need to learn from our intellectual forefathers and apply the truths of philosophical realism to the dominant philosophies that raise themselves up against reality in our age. In other words, Geisler's approach offers a solution to the conditions of belief faced by modernity by not starting in modernity's philosophy, but in reality.

Geisler's approach to apologetics also calls for us to go beyond a defense of mere theism or generic theism. Classical theism is not a generic theism. Rather it is a robust understanding of a unique eternal, immutable, infinite, God whose existence is his essence. This view of God is unique to the Judeo-Christian concept of God. Classical theists are also Trinitarian in their approach. If you read the original writings of Augustine, Anselm, and Aquinas (plus the Reformed Scholastics and evangelical figures such as Geisler, Gerstner, and Sproul) they offered a full defense of the Trinity, the deity of Christ, and the deity of the Holy Spirit; not just some mere generic deistic concept of God. This view of God brings with it a specific understanding of divine providence, human freewill and foreknowledge, the problem of evil and suffering, and the nature of the afterlife.[354]

Finally, Geisler's approach calls for us to defend the totality of God's revelation contained in the Scripture. Geisler's approach would commend each of us to be committed to not only believing but defending the full, verbal, plenary, inspiration, infallibility, and inerrancy of the Bible. Not only was inerrancy the view held by the Church down through the ages, it is also the view held by classic evangelicals. Inerrancy is not just a mark of evangelical consistency but evangelical identity. Christians are called to *have* the same view of Scripture that Christ affirmed and taught, which was the classic doctrine of inerrancy. Moreover, Christians are called to *defend* the same view of Scripture Christ defended, which was the classic doctrine of inerrancy.[355]

# Conclusion

The questions facing evangelicals are: *How will we engage the apologetic situation of our day?* And *will our apologetic method consistently defend classic evangelicalism?* This book has argued that Norman Geisler was a titan in the defense of truth and that evangelicalism would not be as evangelical as it is if it were not for Dr. Geisler. To defend evangelicalism, one must be cognizant of modernity and the effects it has played upon Western society. We must not allow the present conditions of belief cause us to defend a dwarfed view of truth, God, or the Bible. Geisler serves as an example to present-day apologists that we can defend *true truth*, classical theism, and the notion of the Bible as God's inerrant Word in an Age of Unbelief.

If Geisler were still alive today, he would also warn us that orthodoxy can be lost both intellectually and practically. In many places, Geisler cautioned people to never place fraternity over orthodoxy, or uniformity over orthodoxy, naiveite over knowledge, scholarship over Lordship, contemporaneity over antiquity, or anxiety over orthodoxy.[356] Geisler used to tell me: *There are two fears in life: fear of God and fear of man. Never let your fear of man trump your fear of God.* How do we let our fear of man trump our fear of God? As evangelicals, we do it by an overcommitment to fraternity, uniformity, vain academic scholarship,

---

[354] See: Paul Helm, *Eternal God: A Study of God Without Time* 2nd ed (Oxford: Oxford University Press, 2010); Paul Helm, *The Providence of God* (Downers Grove: IVP, 1993); Carter, *Interpreting Scripture With the Great Tradition*, 55-58.

[355] John Wenham, *Christ and the Bible* 3rd ed (Eugene: Wipf and Stock, 2009); J. I. Packer, *"Fundamentalism" and the Word of God* (Grand Rapids: Eerdmans, 1972).

[356] Geisler, *Preserving Orthodoxy*, 135-143.

contemporary ideas as the locus of truth, and a fear of being viewed as divisive for our defense of truth.

During the twentieth and early twenty-first centuries, borrowing from the great author, it "was the best of times and the worst of times, it was an age of foolishness, it was the epic of belief, it was the epoch of incredulity, it was a season of Light, it was a season of Darkness, it was a spring of hope, it was a winter of despair . . . ." But, standing there was Norman Geisler and a host over other evangelical witnesses willing to defend the truth of the gospel once for all delivered unto the saints. Let us learn from their example. Let us sanctify Christ as Lord, always being ready to make a defense to everyone who asks us to give an account for the hope that is within, with gentleness and reverence, keeping a good conscience so that we will not be put to shame by those who slander us or the Lord whom we defend.

# APPENDIX A

# Norman Geisler: Professional Ministry

## Education

- Emmaus Bible School, 1950 (diploma)
- William Tyndale College, 1950-55 (diploma)
- University of Detroit, 1956-57
- Wheaton College, 1958 (B.A. in philosophy)
- Wheaton Graduate School, 1960 (M.A. in theology)
- William Tyndale College, 1964 (Th.B.)
- Wayne State University Graduate School, 1964 (work in philosophy)
- University of Detroit Graduate School, 1965-66 (work on M.A. in philosophy)
- Northwestern University, Evanston, 1968 (work in philosophy)
- Loyola University, Chicago, 1967-70 (Ph.D. in philosophy)

## Professional Experience

- Graduate Assistant in Bible-Philosophy Department, Wheaton College, 1959
- Part-time Instructor in Bible at Detroit Bible College, 1959-1962
- Full-time Assistant Professor of Bible and Apologetics at Detroit Bible College, 1963-1966
- Full-time Associate Professor of Philosophy at Trinity College, 1970-1971
- Visiting Professor of Philosophy of Religion, Trinity Evangelical Divinity School, 1969-1970

- Chairman of Philosophy of Religion, Trinity Evangelical Divinity School, 1970-79
- Professor of Systematic Theology, Dallas Theological Seminary, 1979-1988
- General Editor and Director of Publications for the International Council on Biblical Inerrancy (ICBI), 1977-1987
- Member of the Drafting Committee for the International Council on Biblical Inerrancy (ICBI), 1977-1987
- Dean of Liberty Center for Research and Scholarship, Liberty University, Lynchburg, VA, 1989-1991
- Co-founder of Southern Evangelical Seminary, 1992
- Dean of Southern Evangelical Seminary, 1992-1999
- President of the Evangelical Theological Society, 1998
- President of Southern Evangelical Seminary, 1999-2006
- Dean of Southern Evangelical Seminary, 2006-2007
- Distinguished Senior Professor of Theology and Apologetics, Southern Evangelical Seminary, 2014-2019
- Co-founder of the International Society of Christian Apologetics, 2006
- President of the International Society of Christian Apologetics, 2006-2008
- Co-founder of Veritas Evangelical Seminary (later Veritas International University), 2007
- Chancellor of Veritas International University, 2007-2019
- Distinguished Professor of Apologetics at Veritas International University, 2007-2019
- General Editor of Defending Inerrancy, 2014-2019
- Retired from teaching and writing in May 2019
- Passed from this world into the presence of Christ on July 1st, 2019

# Pastoral/Pulpit Ministries

- Director of Northeast Suburban Youth for Christ, near Detroit, 1952-54

- Pastor of Dayton Center Church, Silverwood, Michigan, 1955-57 (ordained here 1956)
- Assistant Pastor of River Grove Bible Church, River Grove, Illinois, 1958-59
- Pastor of Memorial Baptist Church, Warren, Michigan, 1960-63
- President of Alumni of Detroit Bible College, 1961-62
- Several interim pastorates in Michigan, Illinois, and Texas, 1965+
- "Quest for Truth," radio ministry 1981-1991
- Senior Pastor of Southern Evangelical Church, Charlotte, NC, 2003-2007
- Internationally known speaker at churches, retreats, pastor's conferences, universities, radio, and television from 1960 to 2018.

## Honors and Recognitions

- Graduated with honor from Wheaton College (1958)
- Chosen as an "Outstanding Educator of America" (1975)
- *Philosophy of Religion* chosen as a "Choice Evangelical Book of the Year" by Christianity Today (1975)
- First president of Evangelical Philosophical Society (1976)
- Elected to the Wheaton Scholastic Honor Society (1977)
- Invited to become a founding member of the International Council on Biblical Inerrancy (1977)
- Listed in Who's Who in Religion, Writers Who's Who, and Men of Achievement
- Honored as Alumnus of the Year – William Tyndale College (1982)
- Quoted in Time magazine (Jan. 1982, Sept. 1985)
- *General Introduction to the Bible* won the Cornerstone Magazine book of the year award in its category (1986)
- *When Skeptics Ask* was nominated for the Medallion Award of the year in the category of Missions/Evangelism (1991)
- President of Evangelical Theological Society (1998)
- Gold Medallion Award for *Legislating Morality* (1999)

- Silver Medallion Award for *Baker Encyclopedia of Christian Apologetics* (2000)

- Founder and first President of the *International Society of Christian* Apologetics (2006)

- Outreach Magazine recognized *If God, Why Evil?* as the 2012 Outreach Resource in Apologetics

- *I Am Put Here for the Defense of the Gospel: Dr. Norman L. Geisler: A Festschrift in His Honor* by Terry L. Miethe (Editor) (Pickwick Publications, 2016)

- Veritas International University added the Norman L. Geisler School of Apologetics in the Fall of 2018.

- Southern Evangelical Seminary renamed their "Veritas Graduate School" to the "Norman L. Geisler Graduate School of Apologetics" in May 2019

- "Unqualified" A Documentary Honoring the Life or Norman Geisler by NGIM.org, projected for 2021

William C. Roach

# APPENDIX B

# Norman Geisler: Publications

Below is the list of all the *books* authored, co-authored, or edited by Dr. Geisler. This list also includes a * to indicate books that have been reprinted through another publisher or at a different date. Some of them include the new publisher with Bastion Books without the *.

For historical purposes, it ought to be noted Bastion Books was a publishing company founded by Norman L. Geisler. Many of his out-of-print books were updated and reprinted through Bastion Books later in his life as a means to keep Geisler's publications in circulation.

For a complete list of Geisler's articles, both in order and in print, see: Norman L. Geisler and Paul A. Compton, *The Collected Essays of Norman L. Geisler*, 5 vols (Matthews: Bastion Books, 2020)

A special thanks to Christopher Haun and www.normangeisler.com for the complete list of Norman Geisler's book publications.

## Books Authored, Co-Authored, and/or Edited by Dr. Geisler

1. *A General Introduction to the Bible* (Moody, 1968)

2. *Christ the Theme of the Bible* (Moody, 1968 | Bastion Books, 2012)

3. *Ethics: Alternatives and Issues* (Zondervan, 1971)

4. *The Christian Ethic of Love* (Zondervan, 1973)

5. *Philosophy of Religion* (Zondervan, 1974)

6. *From God to Us* (Moody, 1974)

7. * *To Understand the Bible Look for Jesus* (1975, reprint and retitle of *Christ: The Theme of the Bible*)

8. *Christian Apologetics* (Baker, 1976)

9. *A Popular Survey of the Old Testament* (Baker, 1977)

10. *The Roots of Evil* (Zondervan, 1978) (Second edition, Zondervan, 1981)

11. *Inerrancy* (Zondervan, 1979)
12. *Introduction to Philosophy: A Christian Perspective* (Baker, 1980)
13. *Options in Contemporary Christian Ethics* (Baker, 1981)
14. *Biblical Errancy: Its Philosophical Roots* (Zondervan, 1981 | Bastion Books, 2013)
15. *Decide for Yourself: How History Views the Bible* (Zondervan, 1982)
16. *The Creator in the Courtroom "Scopes II"*: The 1981 Arkansas Creation-Evolution Trial (Baker, 1982)
17. *What Augustine Says* (Baker, 1982 | Bastion Books, 2013)
18. *Is Man the Measure? An Evaluation of Contemporary Humanism* (Baker, 1983)
19. *Cosmos: Carl Sagan's Religion for the Scientific Mind* (Quest, 1983)
20. *Religion of the Force* (Quest, 1983)
21. *To Drink or Not to Drink: A Sober Look at the Problem* (Quest, 1984)
22. *Perspectives: Understanding and Evaluating Today's World Views* (Here's Life, 1984)
23. *Christianity Under Attack* (Quest, 1985)
24. *False Gods of Our Time: A Defense of the Christian Faith* (Harvest House, 1985)
25. *A General Introduction to the Bible*, Second Edition, Revised and Expanded (Moody, 1986)
26. *Reincarnation Sensation* (Tyndale, 1986)
27. *Origin Science* (Baker, 1987)
28. *Philosophy of Religion* (Expansion and Revision of #5. Wipf and Stock, 1988)
29. *Signs and Wonders* (Tyndale, 1988 | Bastion Books, 2019)
30. * *Worlds Apart: A Handbook on World Views* (Baker. Reprint and retitle of #22)
31. *Knowing the Truth About Creation* (Servant, 1989 | Bastion Books, 2013)

32. *The Infiltration of the New Age* (Tyndale, 1989)
33. *The Battle for the Resurrection* (Thomas Nelson, 1989 | Bastion Books, 2013)
34. *Apologetics in the New Age* (Baker, 1990)
35. *Come Let Us Reason: An Introduction to Logical Thinking* (Baker, 1990)
36. *When Skeptics Ask: A Handbook on Christian Evidences* (Baker, 1990, 2013)
37. *Gambling: A Bad Bet* (Fleming H. Revel, 1990 | Bastion Books, 2013)
38. *The Life and Death Debate* (Greenwood, 1990)
39. *In Defense of the Resurrection* (Quest, 1991 | Bastion Books, 2015)
40. *Thomas Aquinas: An Evangelical Appraisal* (Baker, 1991)
41. *Matters of Life and Death: Calm Answers to Tough Questions* (Baker, 1991)
42. *Miracles and the Modern Mind: A Defense of Biblical Miracles* (Baker, 1992 | Bastion Books, 2012)
43. *When Critics Ask: A Handbook on Bible Difficulties* (Victor, 1992)
44. *Answering Islam* (Baker, 1993)
45. *Roman Catholics and Evangelicals: Agreements and Differences* (Baker, 1995)
46. *Love is Always Right* (Word, 1996)
47. *Creating God in the Image of Man?* (Bethany, 1997)
48. *When Cultists Ask* (Baker, 1997)
49. *The Counterfeit Gospel of Mormonism* (Harvest House, 1998)
50. *Legislating Morality* (Bethany, 1998)
51. *Baker's Encyclopedia of Christian Apologetics* (Baker, 1999)
52. *Chosen But Free: A Balanced view of God's Sovereignty and Free Will* (Bethany, 1999)
53. *Unshakable Foundations* (Bethany, 2001)
54. *Why I Am a Christian: Leading Thinkers Explain Why They Believe* (Baker, 2001)

55. *The Battle for God: Responding to the Challenge of Neotheism* (Kregel, 2001)
56. *Living Loud: Defending Your Faith* (Broadman & Holman, 2002)
57. *Answering Islam*, Updated and Revised (Bethany, 2002)
58. *Who Made God?* (Zondervan, 2003)
59. *Is Your Church Ready? Motivating Leaders to Live an Apologetic Life* (Zondervan, 2003)
60. *I Don't Have Enough Faith to Be an Atheist* (Crossway, 2004)
61. *Systematic Theology, Vol. 1* (Bethany, 2002)
62. *Systematic Theology, Vol. 2* (Bethany, 2003)
63. *Systematic Theology, Vol. 3* (Bethany, 2004)
64. *Systematic Theology, Vol. 4* (Bethany, 2005)
65. *Bringing Your Faith to Work: Answers for Break-Room Skeptics* (Baker, 2005)
66. *Correcting the Cults: Expert Responses to Their Scripture Twisting* (Baker, 2005)
67. \* *Why I Am a Christian: Leading Thinkers Explain why They Believe* (revised for Baker, 2006)
68. *Integrity at Work: Finding Your Ethical Compass in a Post-Enron World* (Baker, 2007)
69. *Creation and the Courts: Eighty Years of Conflict in the Classroom and the Courtroom* (Crossway, 2007)
70. *A Popular Survey of the New Testament* (Baker, 2007)
71. *Love Your Neighbor: Thinking Wisely about Right and Wrong* (Crossway, 2007)
72. *Reasons for Faith: Making a Case for the Christian Faith* (Crossway, 2007)
73. *Conviction Without Compromise: Standing Strong in the Core Beliefs of the Christian Faith* (Harvest House, 2008 | Bastion Books 2020)
74. *The Apologetics of Jesus: A Caring Approach to Dealing with Doubters* (Baker, 2008)

75. *Conversational Evangelism* (Harvest House, 2008)
76. *Is Rome the True Church?* (Crossway, 2008)
77. * *The Big Book of Bible Difficulties* (Baker 2008, reprint of #43)
78. * *Making Sense of Bible Difficulties* (Baker, 2009, abridgement of #43)
79. *Chosen But Free: A Balanced View of God's Sovereignty and Free Will* (third edition, revised and expanded, Bethany, 2010)
80. *Christian Ethics*, Second Edition (Baker, 2010)
81. *If God, Why Evil?* (Bethany, 2011)
82. *Systematic Theology in One Volume* (Bethany, 2011)
83. *Defending Inerrancy: Affirming the Accuracy of Scriptures for a New Generation* (Baker, 2012)
84. *Reasons for Belief: Easy-to-Understand Answers to 10 Essential Questions* (Bethany, 2012)
85. *Reasons for Belief Study Guide* (Bastion Books, 2014)
86. *A Popular Handbook of Biblical Archaeology: Discoveries that Confirm the Reliability of Scripture* (Bethany, 2012)
87. *The Big Book of Christian Apologetics* (Baker, 2012) (Minor revision of *The Baker Encyclopedia of Christian Apologetics*)
88. * *Christian Apologetics* (revised, Baker, 2012)
89. *Twelve Points that Show Christianity is True* (NGIM, 2012)
90. *Explaining Biblical Inerrancy: Official Commentary on the ICBI Statements* (Bastion Books, 2011)
91. * *The Christian Ethic of Love* (2012, a minor revision of #4)
92. *From God to Us* (Moody, 2012 | Bastion Books, 2013) (a major revision and update of #6 with some additions from #25.)
93. *Is the Pope Infallible: A Look at the Evidence* (Bastion Books, 2012)
94. * *The Roots of Evil* , Third Edition (Bastion Books, 2013. A Minor revision of #4)
95. *Should Believers Make Ashes of Themselves? Cremation, the Burning Question* (Bastion, 2013)

96. \* *Should Old Aquinas Be Forgotten?* (Bastion Books, 2013. Revision and expansion of #37)

97. *The Atheist's Fatal Flaw* (Baker, 2014)

98. *The Jesus Quest: The Danger from Within* (Xulon, 2014)

99. *The Bible's Answer to 100 of Life's Biggest Questions* (Baker, 2015)

100. *The Shack: Helpful or Hurtful?* (Bastion Books, 2011)

101. *Teacher's Guide to Twelve Points That Show Christianity is True* (NGIM, 2012).

102. *Beware of Philosophy* (Bastion Books, 2012)

103. *A History of Western Philosophy: Vol 1: Ancient and Medieval* (Bastion Books, 2012)

104. *A History of Western Philosophy: Vol 2: Modern and Contemporary* (Bastion Books, 2012)

105. \* *A Handbook on World Views: A Catalogue for Worldview Shoppers* (Bastion Books, 2013) (A minor revision of *Worlds Apart*)

106. \* *Biblical Inerrancy: The Historical Evidence* (Bastion Books, 2013)(A minor Revision of #15)

107. \* *What in Cremation is Going On?* (Bastion Books, 2014) (Abridgement of # 86)

108. *The Official Study Guide to I Don't Have Enough Faith to be an Atheist* (Xulon Press, 2014)

109. *The Religion of the Force* (Bastion Books, 2015) (Update and expansion of #19)

110. *God: A Philosophical Argument* (Bastion Books, 2015)

111. *Evidence of an Early New Testament Canon* (Bastion Books, 2015)

112. *Romans in Logical Form* (Bastion Books, 2015)

113. *Vital Issues in the Inerrancy Debate* (Wipf & Stock, 2016) (review)

114. *How to Know God* (Bastion Books, 2016)(In English and Spanish)

115. *A Prolegomena to Evangelical Theology* (Bastion Books, 2016)

116. *A Popular Survey of Bible Doctrine* (Bastion Books, 2015)

117. *A Prolegomena to Evangelical Theology* (Bastion Books, 2016)

118. *The Bible: Its Origin, Nature and Collection: NGIM Guide to Bible Doctrine, Book 1* (NGIM.org, 2015)

119. *The Doctrine of God: NGIM Guide to Bible Doctrine, Book 2* (NGIM.org, 2015)

120. *The Doctrine of Christ: NGIM Guide to Bible Doctrine, Book 3* (NGIM.org, 2016)

121. *The Doctrine of Creation: NGIM Guide to Bible Doctrine, Book 4* (NGIM.org, 2016)

122. *The Doctrine of Angels & Demons: NGIM Guide to Bible Doctrine, Book 5* (NGIM.org, 2016)

123. *Preserving Orthodoxy: Maintaining Continuity with the Historic Christian Faith on Scripture* (Bastion Books, 2017)

124. *Somewhere Under the Rainbow: A Christian look at Same-Sex "Marriage"* (Bastion Books, 2017)

125. *Having Fun Under the Sun: A Study of Ecclesiastes* (Bastion Books, 2018)

126. *The Collected Work of Norm Geisler*, Volumes 1-5 (Bastion Books, 2019).

127. *\*The Essentials of the Christian Faith* (NGIM.org, 2021? – Forthcoming) (An abridgement of #73)

128. *Is Man the Measure? An Evaluation of Contemporary Humanism and Transhumanism* (Bastion Books, 2021? – Forthcoming)(A major update to and expansion of #18)

## Book Contributions

- *The Harvest Handbook of Christian Apologetics* (Harvest, 2018)
- *Four Views on Eternal Security* (Zondervan, 2002)
- "Colossians" in *The Bible Knowledge Commentary on the New Testament*
- *Predestination and Free Will: Four Views of Divine Sovereignty and Human Freedom* (IVP, 1986)
- *Mission Shift: Global Mission Issues in the Third Millennium* (B&H, 2010)

- *Evangelicals Engaging Emergent: A Discussion of the Emergent Church Movement* (B&H, 2009)
- *The Apologetics Study Bible* (2007)
- *The Portable Seminary: A Master's Level Overview in One Volume* (Bethany House, 2006)
- *Passionate Conviction: Contemporary Discourses on Christian Apologetics* (B&H, 2007)
- *The New Evidence that Demands a Verdict* (1999. A "managing editor.")
- *The Cult of the Virgin: Catholic Mariology and the Apparitions of Mary* (1992)
- "Biblical Studies" in *Opening of the American Mind: The Integration of Biblical Truth in the Curriculum of the University* (Baker, 1991)
- "God, Evil, and Dispensations" in *Walvoord: A Tribute* (Moody, 1982)
- "What is Apologetics and Why do we Need It?" in *The Harvest Handbook of Christian Apologetics* (Harvest Publishers, 2018)
- *Why I'm Still A Christian: Leading Thinkers Explain Why They Believe* (Baker, 2001)

# APPENDIX C

# Norman Geisler: Debates

To the best of our ability given the audio debates we have, and the information found through other publications, below is a list of the known debates by Dr. Norman Geisler. If there is a debate not on this list and you can verify it occurred, please contact Dr. William C. Roach at roawil@gmail.com

- "Can the Existence of God Be Proven?" with Professor Milton Rosenberg at College of Lake County (1973)
- "Sexual Morality: Relative or Absolute?" with Professor Kenneth Simonson at College of Lake County (1973)
- "Is Christianity Credible?" with Dr. Michael Scriven, University of Calgary (1974)
- "Is Humanistic Ethics Superior to Biblical Christianity?" with Dr. Joseph E. Barnhart at North Texas State University (January 24, 1974)
- "Can the Existence of God Be Proven?" with Dr. Jonathan Saville (Spring 1976) at University of California, San Diego
- "The Existence of God," with Dr Michael Quinn, Southern Methodist University (March 30,1977)
- "Is Christianity Credible?" with John Riteris at IUPU, Indianapolis (November 2, 1977)
- Christianity vs Utilitarianism with Dr. Paul Beattie
- "The Reasonableness of God's Existence" with Dr. William Wisdom, Temple University (November 8, 1979)
- "Does God Exist?" with Dr. Wisdom, Temple University (February, 1980)
- "Christianity vs. Humanism" with Dr. K. Kolenda, Rice University (March 14, 1980)
- "Inerrancy of Scripture" with Dr. Norman Beck (January, 1981)

- "Does God Exist?" with Dr. William De Vries, Mount Holyoke College, Massachusetts (April 8, 1981)
- "The Inerrancy of Scripture" with Dr. Thor Hall, University of Tennessee, Chattanooga
- "Creation/Evolution" with Dr. Claud Rupert (January 10, 1982, NBC-TV)
- "Creation/Evolution" with Dr Charles Wood of Perkins School of Theology (Oct 12, 1982)
- "Is the Bible Inerrant?" with Berthold and Hyde (April 1983)
- "Operation Rescue: Biblical or Unbiblical?" with Joseph Foreman
- "Creation vs. Evolution" with Dr. Paul Edwards (May 1983)
- "Should Creationism be Taught (as science) in the Public School? with Fred Edwards and Steve Schafersman (May 6, 1983)
- "Does God Exist?" with Harry Benswanger (April 9, 1984)
- "Why do Bad Things Happen to Good People?" a TV debate with Rabbi Kushner (1984)
- "Should Creation be Taught in Public Schools?" with Philip Kitcher (November 8, 1985)
- "Should Roe vs. Wade (Abortion) Decision Be Reversed?" with Charlotte Taft (January 17, 1986)
- "Creation vs. Evolution" with Dr. Miles Richardson, Louisiana State University (1986)
- "Christianity vs. Secular Humanism" with Dr. Paul Kurtz (1986)
- "Is Christianity Rational?" with Harvey Siegel (1987)
- "Christianity vs. Humanism" with Delos McKown, Auburn University (1987)
- "Separation of Church and State" with Dr. James Buchanan, University of Virginia (1987)
- "Are the Tactics of Operation Rescue Biblical?" with Randall Terry
- "Unity vs Christianity" with Unity Ministers
- "Process Theism vs. Classical Theism" with John Cobb, Claremont School of Theology (April 1988)

- "Should Creation be Taught in the Public Schools" with ACLU attorney Crawford (March 5, 1991)
- "Did Jesus Rise from the Dead" with Farrel Til (March 1994)

# APPENDIX D

# Tribute to Norman Geisler

### 7/1/2019

"I am put here for the defense of the gospel"—The Legacy of Dr. Norman L. Geisler

The death of Dr. Norman L. Geisler is yet a reminder of what the noted Reformer Martin Luther saw when he wrote: "Let goods and kindred go, this mortal life also; The body they may kill: God's truth abideth still, His kingdom is forever." Dr. Geisler died today in Charlotte, NC surrounded by family and loved ones. He had recently retired from public ministry in early May due to health concerns.

For me, the story of Dr. Norman Geisler begins on the streets of Cabrini Green in Chicago, Illinois. As a nineteen-year-old struggling to serve a church in downtown Chicago I was confronted by false teachings and objections to the Christian faith. Those objections came from secularists, college students, members of the church, and close friends. I was surrounded by a culture of increasing philosophical relativism and confusion due to the wave of what became known as postmodernism in a post-Christian age. I knew Jesus Christ was my Lord and Savior and I needed to preach the gospel and defend the historic Christian faith. But where could I go to find answers?

One Friday night after failing to answer the questions and objections from a close friend, I went on a walk of lament down Chicago Avenue until I made my way to Michigan Avenue. As I walked the streets and spent several hours people watching, I kept asking myself if I could ever engage individuals in our culture with the gospel of Jesus Christ. While walking back to the church I stopped at *Moody Bible Institute's* bookstore. On the shelf was Lee Strobel's *The Case for Faith*, so I bought the book hoping to find answers to the various objections raised against Christianity. Strobel interviewed a collection of scholars on various objections to the Christian faith, one of whom was Dr. Norman Geisler. I read that book in one weekend and it lit a fire in my bones to defend the historic Christian faith and study under this man named Norman Geisler.

Fast forward one more year. I signed up for a theology class in college and I was required to purchase *The Baker Encyclopedia of Christian Apologetics* by Dr. Geisler. The professor of the class, Herb Flinkman, was a DMin student at *Southern Evangelical Seminary* and he required all his theology students to read Geisler's encyclopedia. At the time, Herb was one of my heroes. One of the things that intrigued me the most, however, was the fact that he personally knew Dr. Geisler. I remember thinking to myself, "I hope I get to meet Norman Geisler someday."

During the summer break following my sophomore year of college, I signed up to take Introduction to Apologetics as a distance student at *Southern Evangelical Seminary* under Dr. Geisler. One day, while studying for the course, my phone rang and I heard this voice say, "Hello, I am Norman Geisler. I was given your contact information by Herb Flinkman. He told me you would be interested in attending *Southern Evangelical Seminary*." My jaw dropped and I thought it was a prank phone call. Could this really be THE Norman Geisler calling *me*? To my surprise, not only was Dr. Geisler on the line, but by the end of the conversation he had invited me to tour *Southern Evangelical Seminary* and stay at his house during my visit.

That day, I drained my bank account and bought a plane ticket for Charlotte, NC. I landed in Charlotte on a hot summer day, traveled on the Billy Graham Parkway, drove down Tilley Morris Road, and arrived at *SES*. I remember waiting in the library and the door flew open and a short man walked up to me and said, "I am Norman Geisler, and you must be Bill Roach." After a few moments of small talk, we quickly walked to his car (i.e., there is a reason they call him "Stormin Norman.") and drove to his house. I remember meeting his lovely wife Barbara and several of his family members. We all went out to eat at an Asian restaurant near their home. I recall the waitress asking, "Do you want a table *or* a booth" and Dr. Geisler replied, "Yes." I thought to myself, "Wow, this guy even logically analyzes the claims of hostesses!" (This example makes sense to all who learned disjunctive logic under Dr. Geisler).

During that trip God changed the trajectory of my life. I discovered that Dr. Geisler and I had very similar backgrounds; in fact, we used to joke about it quite often. Both of us were raised in non-Christian homes, our mother's would not allow us to play football as kids, we both had alcoholic parents, struggled significantly in school, and most importantly—after our conversion to Christ we both had to face objections to the Christian faith. Dr. Geisler used to say he got into apologetics because he was stumped by a drunk on the streets of Detroit who claimed to be a graduate of "Moody Instita Bibiltute." Dr. Geisler knew that he either had to find answers to people's objections or he must stop sharing his faith. Since the latter is not an option, Dr. Geisler dedicated his life to defending the historic Christian faith. I knew this was the man I wanted to study under. Therefore, I packed my bags and moved halfway across the country to Charlotte, NC.

In the years to come I came to know Dr. Geisler as more than a professor. In fact, he became my best friend and a father figure. Throughout Bible College and Seminary, Dr. Geisler and his wife would invite me to their home for holidays, meals, and special events (like the time we went to see the Carolina Panthers and Dallas Cowboys and met the players because he was the chaplain). Upon graduation from Bible College, Dr. Geisler asked me to serve as his research assistant. This role allowed me to sit at the feet and learn from one of the world's leading apologists. Dr. Geisler taught me how to research, write, lecture, and defend the historic Christian faith. I was privileged to have an office in his home and an open door to discuss any pressing question that happened to be on my mind that day.

Dr. Geisler did more for me than just teach me how to defend the Christian faith. He also taught me to live the Christian faith. I feel like I was able to see a side of Dr. Geisler outside of the classroom very few were privileged to witness. I remember watching him love his wife Barbara and serve her daily, sing goofy Johnny Cash songs with his grandchildren, pray with those who were struggling, advise and tutor students at his home whenever they asked, financially support those in need, give up a room in his home to someone in dire straits, lend a car to someone when theirs broke down, and so much more. Dr. Geisler was much more than a scholar. He was truly a man who lived that which he believed and sacrificed for those whom he loved.

My indebtedness to Dr. Geisler is very personal. I was a young man who had serious questions about Christianity and needed a role model and a father figure in the faith. God used Dr. Geisler to provide for those great needs. He was full of knowledge and unafraid to defend the Christian faith against all opponents. He was full of love and willing to disciple me during a pivotal point in my life. In no small way my own calling as a theologian and an apologist can be traced back to Dr. Norman Geisler's influence. I was inspired by Dr. Geisler's intellectual engagement and deeply motivated by his vision to defend the historic Christian faith.

My indebtedness extends to the fact that Dr. Geisler seemed to be there at every significant event in my adult life. Dr. Geisler was there the day I graduated from college and seminary, he was the first one to call and congratulate me when I finished my PhD and consoled me in the weeks following my father's death. He officiated my wedding and offered some of the best marriage advice minutes leading up to the ceremony and was numbered among the elders who laid hands on me at my ordination. Lastly, Dr. Geisler was influential in helping me become an author, speaker, professor, and president of the *International Society of Christian Apologetics*. Truly, the stamp of Dr. Norman Geisler is over so much of my adult life and for that, I am eternally thankful.

As we reflect upon the life of Dr. Norman Geisler, I am reminded of Luther's hymn *A Mighty Fortress is Our God*. The famous line: "Let goods and kindred go, this mortal life also; The body they may kill: God's truth abideth still, His kingdom is forever" captures best the final chapter of Dr. Geisler's earthly life. Dr. Geisler has now let goods and kindred go, this mortal life also, but God's truth abideth still. In an era of church history when theology is in chaos, and the church is being shaken at its very core, and reality seems to be tossed to-and-fro with every wave of the sea, we are grateful for the example of Dr. Geisler who stood as a beacon of truth shining forth in the midst of a dark world.

Those of us who have benefitted significantly from the life and ministry of Dr. Geisler ought to remember that Christ's kingdom is forever. It does not rest solely upon the life of any one individual. The mark of a great leader is found in their ability to live beyond the grave and pass the baton to the next generation. Dr. Geisler has now joined the great host of witnesses that have gone before us and he has passed the baton onto each of us. Therefore, it is now our responsibility to say during this time in history: I am put here for the defense of the gospel.

In closing, I once said, "I hope I get to meet Norman Geisler someday." Not only was I able to meet him, but God used Dr. Geisler to change my life. Not only was I able to meet him, but one day because of the resurrection of Jesus Christ, Norm and I will meet again.

William C. Roach, PhD

President, *International Society of Christian Apologetics*.

# Bibliography

Adler, Mortimer. *Ten Philosophical Mistakes*. New York: Simon & Schuster, 1985.

Allen, Diogenes and Eric O. Springsted, *Philosophy for Understanding Theology*, 2nd ed. Louisville: Westminster John Knox Press, 2007.

St. Augustine, *Reply to Faustus the Manichean* 11.5 in Philip Schaff, *A Select Library of the Nicene and Ante-Nicene Fathers of the Christian Church*. Grand Rapids: Eerdmans, 1956.

Aquinas, Thomas. *Summa Theologica*.

Bahnsen, Greg L. *Presuppositional Apologetics: Stated and Defended*. Nacogdoches: Covenant Media Press, 2011.

Beisner, Frederick. *German Idealism: The Struggle Against Subjectivism 1781-1801*. Cambridge: Harvard University Press, 2002.

Bennett, William. *The Index of Leading Cultural Indicators*. Colorado Springs: Waterbrook Press, 1999.

Brown, Jeannine K. *Scripture as Communication: Introducing Biblical Hermeneutics*. Grand Rapids: Baker Academic, 2007.

Carter, Craig A. *Interpreting Scripture with the Great Tradition: Recovering the Genius of PreModern Exegesis*. Grand Rapids: Baker, 2018.

Caygill, Howard. *A Kant Dictionary*. Cambridge: Blackwell Publishers, 1995.

Chesterton, G. K. *Orthodoxy*. San Francisco: Ignatius, 1908.

Christian, C. W. *Friedrich Schleiermacher: Makers of the Modern Theological Mind*. Peabody: Hendrickson Publishers, 1979.

Clark, Gordon H. *Religion, Reason, and Revelation*. Nutley: Craig, 1961.

Copan, Paul. *Is God a Moral Monster? Making Sense of the Old Testament*. Grand Rapids: Baker, 2011.

Copleston, Frederick. *A History of Philosophy*. 9 vols. New York: Doubleday, 1994.

Craig, William Lane. *Reasonable Faith: Christian Truth and Apologetics*, 3rd ed. Wheaton: Crossway, 2008.

D'Elia, John A. *A Place at the Table: George Eldon Ladd and the Rehabilitation of Evangelical Scholarship in America.* New York: Oxford University Press, 2008.

Delgado, Richard and Jean Stefancic, *Critical Race Theory: An Introduction* 3rd ed. New York: New York University Press, 2017.

Dolezal, James E. *All That is in God: Evangelical Theology and the Challenge of Classical Christian Theism.* Grand Rapids: Reformation Heritage Books, 2017.

Frame, John M. *Apologetics: A Justification of Christian Belief.* Phillipsburg: R&R Publishing, 2015.

_____. *A History of Western Philosophy.* Phillipsburg: R&R Publishing, 2015.

_____. *Cornelius Van Til: An Analysis of His Thought.* Phillipsburg: R&R Publishing, 1995.

_____. *The Doctrine of God.* Phillipsburg: P&R, 2002.

_____. *The Doctrine of the Knowledge of God.* Phillipsburg: R&R Publishing, 1987.

Fesko, J. V. *Reforming Apologetics: Reviving the Classic Reformed Approach to Defending the Faith.* Grand Rapids: Baker, 2019.

Geisler, Norman L. *Baker Encyclopedia of Christian Apologetics.* Grand Rapids: Baker, 1999.

_____. *Beware of Philosophy: A Warning to Biblical Scholars*, JETS 42/1 (March 1999) 3–19.

_____. *Biblical Errancy: An Analysis of its Philosophical Roots.* Eugene: Wipf and Stock, 1981.

_____. *Christian Apologetics* 2nd ed. Grand Rapids: Baker, 2013.

_____. *Inerrancy.* Grand Rapids: Zondervan, 1980

_____. *Is Man the Measure? An Evaluation of Contemporary Humanism.* Eugene: Wipf and Stock, 1983.

_____. *Miracles and the Modern Mind: A Defense of Biblical Miracles.* Eugene: Wipf and Stock, 1992.

_____. *Preserving Orthodoxy: Maintaining Continuity with the Historic Christian Faith on Scripture.* Charlotte: Bastion Books, 2017.

_____. *Systematic Theology: God and Creation.* Minneapolis: Bethany House, 2003.

_____. *Systematic Theology: Introduction and Bible.* Minneapolis: Bethany House, 2002.

_____. *Thomas Aquinas: An Evangelical Appraisal.* Eugene: Wipf and Stock, 1991.

Geisler, Norman L. Paul A. Compton, ed. *The Collected Essays of Norman L. Geisler.* 5 vols. Matthews, Bastion Books, 2019.

Geisler, Norman and Winfried Corduan, *Philosophy of Religion.* Eugene: Wipf and Stock, 1988.

Geisler, Norman L., H. Wayne House, and Max Herrera, *The Battle for God: Responding to the Challenge of Neotheism.* Grand Rapids: Kregel, 2001.

Geisler, Norman L. and Thomas Howe. *When Critics Ask: A Popular Handbook on Bible Difficulties.* Grand Rapids: Baker, 1992.

Geisler Norman L and William E. Nix. *From God to Us: How We Got Our Bible.* Chicago: Moody Press, 2012.

Geisler Norman L. and Ron Rhodes, *When Cultist Ask: A Popular Handbook on Cultic Misinterpretations.* Grand Rapids: Baker, 1997.

Geisler, Norman L. and William C. Roach, *Defending Inerrancy: Affirming the Accuracy of Scripture for a New Generation.* Grand Rapids: Baker, 2011.

Geisler, Norman L. and Abdul Saleeb, *Answering Islam: The Crescent in Light of the Cross.* Grand Rapids: Baker, 2002.

Geisler, Norman L. and Frank Turek, *I Don't Have Enough Faith to Be an Atheist.* Wheaton: Crossway, 2004.

Gilson, Etienne. *Being and Some Philosophers.* Toronto: Pontifical Institute of Mediaeval Studies, 1949.

Gilson, Etienne. *God and Philosophy*, 2nd ed. New Haven: Yale University Press, 1941.

Gilson, Etienne. *Methodological Realism.* Front Royal: Christendom Press, 1990.

Gilson, Etienne. *The Christian Philosophy of St. Thomas Aquinas.* New York: Random House, 1956.

Gilson, Etienne. *The Unity of Philosophical Experience.* San Francisco: Ignatius Press, 1964.

Grenz, Stanley J. *A Primer on Postmodernism.* Grand Rapids: Eerdmans, 1996.

Hannah, John D. ed. *Inerrancy and The Church.* Chicago: Moody Press, 1984.

Helm, Paul. *Eternal God: A Study of God Without Time* 2nd ed. Oxford: Oxford University Press, 2010.

_____. *Faith, Form, and Fashion: Classical Reformed Theology and Its Postmodern Critics.* Eugene: Cascade Books, 2014.

_____. *The Providence of God.* Downers Grove: IVP, 1993.

Henry, Carl F. H. *God, Revelation and Authority.* 6. vols. Waco: Word Books.

_____. *Toward A Recover of Christian Belief.* Wheaton: Crossway Books, 1990.

Hitler, Adolf. *Mein Kampf.* London: Hurst and Blackett Ltd., Publishers, 4th printing, 1939.

Holloway, Maurice R. S.J., *An Introduction to Natural Theology.* New York: Appleton-Century, 1959.

Howe, Thomas. *Objectivity in Biblical Interpretation.* Altamonte Springs: Advantage Books, 2004.

Hume, David. *An Inquiry Concerning Human Understandings*, ed. C. W. Hendel. 1748; repr., New York: Bobbs-Merrill, 1955.

Kant, Immanuel. *Critique of Pure Reason.* New York: Cambridge University Press, 1998.

_____. *Prolegomena to Any Future Metaphysics*, trans. Paul Carus, revised by James W. Ellington. Indianapolis: Hackett, 1977,

_____. *Religion within the Boundaries of Mere Reason*, edited by Allen Wood and George di Giovanni. Cambridge: Cambridge University Press, 1998.

Keller, Timothy. *Making Sense of God: An Invitation to the Skeptical.* New York: Viking, 2016.

_____. *Preaching: Communicating Faith in an Age of Skepticism.* New York: Penguin Random House, 2015.

Kelsey, David H. *Proving Doctrine: The Uses of Scripture in Modern Theology.* Harrisburg: Trinity Press International, 1999.

Kreeft, Peter. *A Refutation of Moral Relativism: Interviews With An Absolutist.* San Francisco: Ignatius Press, 1999.

_____. *Back to Virtue.* San Francisco: Ignatius, 1986.

_____. *Socratic Logic: A Logic Text Using Socratic Method, Platonic Questions, and Aristotelian Principles.* South Bend: St. Augustine's Press, 2014.

_____. *Socrates Meets Kant: The Father of Philosophy Meets His Most Influential Child.* San Francisco: Ignatius Press, 2009.

_____. *Summa Philosophica.* South Bend: St Augustine's Press, 2012.

_____. *Summa of the Summa.* San Francisco: Ignatius Press, 1990.

_____. *The Platonic Tradition.* South Bend: St. Augustine's Press, 2018.

Korner, S. *Kant.* London: Penguin Books, 1990.

LaGrange, Garrigou. *God, His Existence and Nature: A Thomistic Solution to Certain Agnostic Antinomies.* New York: Herder Books, 1934.

Lawhead, William F. *The Voyage of Discovery*, 2nd ed. Belmont: Wadsworth, 2002.

Lewis, C. S. *The Abolition of Man.* San Francisco: Harper One, 1974.

Lindsell, Harold. *The Battle for the Bible.* Grand Rapids: Zondervan, 1976.

Machen, J. Gresham *Christianity & Liberalism*, New Edition. Grand Rapids: Eerdmans, 2009.

Martin, Walter. *The Kingdom of the Cults.* Minneapolis: Bethany House, 2003.

Marsden, George M. *Reforming Fundamentalism: Fuller Seminary And The New Evangelicalism.* Grand Rapids: Eerdmans, 1987.

_____. *Understanding Fundamentalism and Evangelicalism.* Grand Rapids: Eerdmans, 1991.

Marx, Karl. *Marx and Engels on Religion.* New York: Schoken Books, Inc., 1964.

Mason, Eric. *Woke Church: An Urgent Call for Christians in America to Confront Racism and Injustice.* Chicago: Moody Press, 2018.

Merrick, J., and Stephen M. Garrett, general editors. *Five Views on Biblical Inerrancy.* Grand Rapids: Zondervan, 2013.

Moreland, J. P. *Love Your God With All Your Mind: The Role Reason in The Life of The Soul.* Colorado Springs: Navpress, 1997.

———. *Scaling the Secular City: A Defense of Christianity.* Grand Rapids: Baker Academic, 1987.

Nasalli, Andrew David and Collin Hansen, *Four Views on The Spectrums of Evangelicalism.* Grand Rapids: Zondervan, 2011.

Nash, Ronald H. *Faith and Reason: Searching for a Rational Faith.* Grand Rapids: Zondervan, 1988.

———. *The Concept of God: An Exploration of Contemporary Difficulties with the Attributes of God.* Grand Rapids: Zondervan, 1983.

Nietzsche, Friedrich. *Gay Science,* in Walter Kaufmann, *The Portable Nietzsche.* New York: The Viking Press, 1968.

O'Callaghan, John P. *Thomist Realism and the Linguistic Turn: Toward a More Perfect Form of Existence.* Notre Dame: University of Notre Dame Press, 2003.

Oliphint, K. Scott. *Aquinas (Great Thinkers).* Philipsburg: R&R Publishing, 2017.

———. *God With Us: Divine Condescension and the Attributes of God.* Wheaton: Crossway, 2012.

Orr, James. *The Christian View of God and the World as Centering in the Incarnation.* Edinburg: Andrew Elliot, 1907.

Osborne, Grant R. *The Hermeneutical Spiral: A Comprehensive Introduction to Biblical Interpretation.* Downers Grove: IVP, 2006.

Owens, Joseph. *An Elementary Christian Metaphysic.* Notre Dame: University of Notre Dame Press, 1963.

———. *An Interpretation of Existence.* Houston: Center for Thomistic Studies, 1968.

———. "A Note on the Approach to Thomistic Metaphysics," *New Scholasticism,* 28 (1954), 454-476.

———. "A Note on the Intelligibility of Being," *Gregorianum,* 36 (1955), 169-193.

———. *Cognition.* Houston: Center For Thomistic Studies, 1992.

Packer, J. I. *"Fundamentalism" and the Word of God.* Grand Rapids: Eerdmans, 1972.

Plantinga, Alvin. *Does God Have a Nature?* Milwaukee: Marquette University Press, 1980.

_____. *Warranted Christian Belief.* New York: Oxford University Press, 2000.

Pluckrose, Helen and James Lindsay. *Cynical Theories: How Activist Scholarship Made Everything about Race, Gender, and Identity—and Why This Harms Everyone.* Durham: Pitchstone Publishing, 2020.

Radmacher Earl D and Robert D. Preus. *Hermeneutics, Inerrancy, & the Bible: Papers from ICBI Summit II.* Grand Rapids: Zondervan, 1984.

Roach, William C. *Hermeneutics as Epistemology: A Critical Assessment of Carl F. H. Henry's Epistemological Approach to Hermeneutics.* Eugene: Wipf and Stock, 2015.

Rogers Jack B and Donald K. McKim. *The Authority and Interpretation of the Bible: An Historical Approach.* Eugene: Wipf and Stock, 1999.

Schaeffer, Francis. *The Complete Works of Francis Schaeffer.* Wheaton: Crossway, 1982.

_____. *The Great Evangelical Disaster.* Wheaton: Crossway, 1984.

Schleiermacher, Friedrich. *Christian Faith: A New Translation and Critical Edition.* Louisville: Westminster John Knox Press, 2016.

_____. *On Religion: Speeches to its Cultured Despisers*, edited by Richard Crouter. Cambridge: Cambridge University Press, 1996.

_____. *On Religion: Addresses in Response to Its Cultured Critics.* Richmond: John Knox Press, 1969.

Sire, James W. *Apologetics Beyond Reason: Why Seeing Reality is Believing.* Westmont: Intervarsity Press, 2014.

Smith, James K. A. *How (Not) To Be Secular: Reading Charles Taylor.* Grand Rapids: Eerdmans, 2014.

Sproul, R. C. *Explaining Inerrancy.* Orlando: Ligonier Ministries, 1996.

_____. *Thus Says the Lord: Defending the Inerrancy of Scripture.* Orlando: Ligonier Ministries, 2005.

Sproul R. C. and Norman L. Geisler, *Explaining Biblical Inerrancy: Official Commentary on the ICBI Statements.* Matthews: Bastion Books, 2013.

Sproul, R. C., John Gerstner, and Arthur Lindsley, *Classical Apologetics: A Rational Defense of the Christian Faith and a Critique of Presuppositional Apologetics.* Grand Rapids: Zondervan, 1984.

Stump, Eleonore. *The God of the Bible and the God of the Philosophers.* Marquette: Marquette University Press, 2016.

Svensson, Manfred and David VanDrunen. *Aquinas Amongst the Protestants.* Hoboken: John Wiley & Sons, 2018.

Taylor, Charles. *A Secular Age.* Cambridge: Harvard University Press, 2007.

Thiselton, Anthony C. *New Horizons in Hermeneutics: The Theory and Practice of Transforming Biblical Texts.* Grand Rapids: Zondervan, 1992.

Thomas, Robert L. *Evangelical Hermeneutics: The New Versus the Old.* Grand Rapids: Kregel, 2002.

Thornbury, Gregory Alan. *Recovering Classic Evangelicalism: Applying the Wisdom and vision of Carl F. H. Henry.* Wheaton: Crossway, 2013.

Tisby, Jemar. *The Color of Compromise: The Truth About the American Church's Complicity in Racism.* Grand Rapids: Zondervan, 2020.

Vanhoozer, Kevin J. "Lost In Interpretation? Truth, Scripture, and Hermeneutics." *Journal of the Evangelical Theological Society*, 48 (2005) 98-99.

_____. *Is There a Meaning in This Text? The Bible, the Reader, and the Morality of Literary Knowledge.* Grand Rapids: Zondervan, 1998.

_____. *The Drama of Doctrine: A Canonical Linguistic Approach to Christian Theology.* Louisville: Westminster John Knox, 1998.

Veatch, Henry B. *Two Logics: The Conflict Between Classical and Neo-Analytic Philosophy.* Editones Scolasticae, 2019.

Venoit, Don and Joy, and Marcia Montenegro. *Richard Rohr and the Enneagram Secret.* Wonder Lake: MCOI Publishing, 2020.

Weaver, Richard M. *Ideas Have Consequences: Expanded Edition.* Chicago: University of Chicago Press, 2013.

Webber, Robert E. *The Younger Evangelicals: Facing the Challenges of the New World.* Grand Rapids: Baker, 2002.

Wells, David F. *The Courage to Be Protestant: Truth-lovers, Marketers, and Emergents in the Postmodern World.* Grand Rapids: Eerdmans, 2008.

Wenham, John. *Christ and the Bible* 3rd ed. Eugene: Wipf and Stock, 2009.

Woodbridge, John D. *Biblical Authority: A Critique of the Rogers/McKim Proposal.* Grand Rapids: Zondervan, 1982.

Zacharias, Ravi. *The Real Face of Atheism.* Grand Rapids: Baker Books, 2004.